Contesting the Repressive State

Contesting the Repressive State

Why Ordinary Egyptians Protested During the Arab Spring

KIRA D. JUMET

Oxford University Press is a department of the University of Oxford. It furthers
the University's objective of excellence in research, scholarship, and education
by publishing worldwide. Oxford is a registered trade mark of Oxford University
Press in the UK and certain other countries.

Published in the United States of America by Oxford University Press
198 Madison Avenue, New York, NY 10016, United States of America.

© Oxford University Press 2018

All rights reserved. No part of this publication may be reproduced, stored in
a retrieval system, or transmitted, in any form or by any means, without the
prior permission in writing of Oxford University Press, or as expressly permitted
by law, by license, or under terms agreed with the appropriate reproduction
rights organization. Inquiries concerning reproduction outside the scope of the
above should be sent to the Rights Department, Oxford University Press, at the
address above.

You must not circulate this work in any other form
and you must impose this same condition on any acquirer.

CIP data is on file at the Library of Congress
ISBN 978-0-19-068846-2 (pbk.); 978-0-19-068845-5 (hbk.)

9 8 7 6 5 4 3 2 1

Paperback printed by WebCom, Inc., Canada
Hardback printed by Bridgeport National Bindery, Inc., United States of America

CONTENTS

PREFACE VII
ACKNOWLEDGMENTS XV

1. Introduction 1

PART I. **The Downfall of Mubarak**

2. Grievances against the Mubarak Regime 23

3. Political Participation Online: From Facebook to the Streets 51

4. The January 25th Uprising: Government Violence and Moral Shock 85

PART II. **The Transition and Downfall of Morsi**

5. Protest Dynamics under the Supreme Council of the Armed Forces Transitional Government 121

6. Grievances against the Morsi Government 151

7. The June 30th Coup 171

8. Conclusion 215

NOTES 229
BIBLIOGRAPHY 231
INDEX 257

PREFACE

As my taxi made its way from the airport into downtown Cairo, I stared out the window in awe and bewilderment. Posters with the faces of presidential candidates were plastered on overpasses, and the sides of residential and public buildings were covered in political graffiti. This was not the Egypt I remembered from my days living in Cairo between 2004 and 2008, when the only politician's face to grace a billboard was that of Hosni Mubarak, and dissenting graffiti in public spaces was inconceivable. It was 2012, the first democratic elections were approaching, and I was in a whole new Egypt. In fact, it was a whole new Middle East.

The wave of protests that began in Tunisia at the end of 2010 and spread to Egypt, Libya, Bahrain, Yemen, and Syria took the world by surprise. For years, scholars had produced works on why and how authoritarian regimes persisted in the Middle East, but few were prepared to explain the toppling of the leaders presiding over these repressive states. That is not to say that researchers believed that citizens of these countries were content. Scholars such as Lisa Wedeen (1999) have demonstrated the subtle ways in which people contested authoritarian rule. However, images of the masses taking to the streets to publicly express their dissatisfaction and demand change presented uncharted territory.

Like everyone else who studied the Middle East, I spent the end of 2010 and all of 2011 glued to my television screen watching Al Jazeera reports of protests and government violence. As someone who had spent many years living in Cairo, I had heard jokes and disparaging remarks about Mubarak in the privacy of people's homes, but I never imagined that people would take action on their discontent. I was even more shocked by the sustained resistance of Syrians and Libyans, who were confronting even harsher repressive states than were Egyptians and whose leaders showed little concern for the opinion of the international community as they slaughtered peaceful protesters.

As protests around the Middle East continued to unfold, one clear question remained in my mind: Why do people protest under a repressive regime? In countries such as the United States and France, protest is a normalized practice for contesting the state; it is accepted as part of the political process and sometimes even lauded as a sign of a healthy democracy. In many countries in the Middle East where authoritarianism prevailed, protest was not only considered impossible, it never even crossed the minds of most people. Even determined activists who braved the streets knew that they could be arrested and tortured. So when country after country was overtaken by protest I had to ask: What had changed? Why now? I set off to Egypt to find out.

WHY EGYPT?

While I was intrigued by the domino effect of Arab Spring protests in 2010 and 2011, I found that the most productive way to begin to answer my question of why people protest under a repressive regime was to study one country in depth. Rather than conduct more superficial research comparing states, I concluded that taking the time to understand protest cycles in Egypt, a country I had come to know well, might offer greater insights into the processes of individuals' decisions to protest or not to protest that could be applied to other places. While each Arab Spring country has its own history, conditions, and political dynamics, each also demonstrates commonalities with the Egyptian case. Grievances related to police brutality, the economy, and/or corruption were factors in all of the countries where the populations ousted their leaders. As in Egypt, youth in many Arab Spring countries used social media as a means of mobilization and protest organization. Finally, state violence against protesters was present in varying degrees across the board. In this book, I discuss these key structural elements and many more as they relate to the Egyptian case. However, my findings may be applied to understanding decision-making processes to protest in countries from Tunisia to Syria. It is my hope that the methods and framework of analysis used in this study, which are outlined in the first chapter, may contribute to the work of scholars conducting similar studies in other Arab Spring states.

There are unique qualities about the Egyptian case that make for fascinating research. Historically, there are very few instances of mostly unarmed protesters removing their country's president twice within a short period of time. The closest example to the Egyptian scenario is Kyrgyzstan's Tulip Revolution, which deposed President Askar Akayev in 2005, and the Second Kyrgyz Revolution, which removed President Kurmanbek Bakiyev in 2010. In both the Kyrgyz and Egyptian cases, the people were able to remove the second president more quickly than the first. When a population lives under authoritarian rule for an extended period of time with minimal public challenge to the regime and then removes its president through popular protest, one should take note. However, when it occurs a second time within a few years, or in the Egyptian case, two years, there has clearly been a dramatic shift in political opportunity structures, mobilizing structures, framing processes, and the psyche of the population. A second uprising also indicates a failure to meet protesters' initial demands.

Studying protest decision-making in Egypt provided me with two large events within a relatively short time frame in which (1) there was a clear intention to overthrow the government and (2) interviewees had to decide to protest or not protest. The Egyptian case also allowed me to examine how variables, such as political opportunity structures and mobilizing structures, change over time. Thus, Egypt was an ideal setting for my study.

THE CHALLENGES OF DOING RESEARCH IN A TUMULTUOUS MIDDLE EAST

There were numerous challenges to data collection due to government restrictions, high levels of suspicion of foreigners during the time of my fieldwork, and mass political violence. In Egypt, all large-scale research projects must be approved by the Central Agency for Public Mobilization and Statistics (CAPMAS), a government agency that oversees projects such as survey research within the country. The problems that may arise when attempting to register one's research with CAPMAS include the agency's refusal to approve a study, its refusal to approve all the questions in the study, or a prolonged approval process lasting up to two years. If one looks at the World Values Survey for Egypt, certain questions from the survey were omitted when data was collected in Egypt, possibly because the government would not approve them. Even if a large-scale project were approved by CAPMAS, the government's mere knowledge of the project would put both the researcher and interviewees in danger of being watched by a government minder. The unpredictability of the government's reaction to the project over time because of changing political circumstances could leave interviewees in the vulnerable position of being subject to arrest and torture due to political engagement. Additionally, the presence of a government minder would violate the anonymity of the human subjects in the study, thus violating policies of the Institutional Review Board (IRB). While smaller scale, in-depth interviews were the best way to examine my research topic, it would have been helpful to then continue by testing the findings on a larger scale using survey research. Unfortunately, impediments, including those presented by CAPMAS, made survey data collection on a larger scale too difficult. Additionally, time and financial constraints on the book project made conducting surveys impossible.

After the first month of my second round of fieldwork, a military coup took place in Egypt beginning on July 3, 2013. The coup had repercussions on my study, as well as on its funding. The Boren Fellowship Program, which was funding my research, evacuated me from the country. I was told that I could use the fellowship money to study Arabic in another country, but if I wished to return to Egypt, I would have to pay back the money and return with no financing, since the Egypt program had been canceled due to political unrest. Because I chose to return to my research site and complete my study without outside funding, the amount of money I could devote to research assistants, travel, and other interview considerations had to be recalculated and reduced.

The issue of researcher safety in respect to both the government and interviewees played a part in determining where and with whom I conducted interviews. At various points during my fieldwork I had to confront the possibility of being put in danger by my interviewees. In 2012, Egyptian state television had run advertisements warning Egyptians about foreigners being spies (El-Shenawi 2012). These advertisements contributed to a wave of xenophobia, and on two occasions in the middle of interviews I was questioned and accused of being a spy. One interviewee asked if I had cleared my project with the Ministry of the Interior, stopped me in the middle of the interview, and threatened to call the police. Additionally, a local journalist had warned me of instances when foreign journalists were mobbed and threatened when conducting interviews in public settings.

Even more disconcerting was the possibility of being arrested for conducting research. In Egypt, research is not technically illegal. However, the government has been known to arrest researchers or haul them into the police station on suspicion of spying. A few months before I began my fieldwork, an American colleague of mine was meeting an interviewee in Al-Mahallah al-Kubra. He was arrested and falsely accused of spying and paying children to throw rocks at the police, after which he was held and questioned in an Egyptian jail for 56 hours. He was then questioned and charged by the Al-Mahallah al-Kubra general prosecutor, his photo and information were circulated in the newspapers, and he endured a travel ban for almost a year that prevented him from leaving Egypt. Additionally, the house of a colleague who was arrested along with him was raided and his belongings were confiscated. Egyptian authorities will usually not physically harm American detainees. However, another of my American colleagues who was arrested by Egyptian authorities reported being subjected to psychological torture and witnessing firsthand the torturing of Egyptian youths. In view of the risk posed by the possible objections to my research by the Egyptian government because I was conducting interviews, either my research assistants or I had to scout out interview locations to ensure the personal safety of all involved and, as much as possible, interviewees had to be checked out to make sure they would not pose a threat to me. With such a large number of interviews, this process was not always fully successful. Fortunately, I was able to complete my project without government interference.

The next problem I faced was high levels of political violence and sexual assaults against women at protest sites during the time of my fieldwork. From the time of the 2011 Revolution onward, there was an epidemic of sexual assaults on female protesters. At one protest in Tahrir Square, there were eighteen confirmed attacks on women with six requiring hospitalization (el Sheikh and Kirkpatrick 2013). Women were attacked by mobs, had their clothes violently torn off of them, and were sexually assaulted in the middle of the Square. Because of the threat of sexual assault, whenever I conducted fieldwork at a protest site, I had either one or two large men accompany me as bodyguards. However, I limited the number of protests I attended because there had been too many instances of women being gang-raped at demonstrations. In reality, two men were no protection against a mob.

Regarding political violence, my residence happened to be located on a main protest route where protesters marched by on a weekly, and sometimes daily, basis. While my location afforded me a prime view of the events, it also placed me in a center of political violence. Throughout the summer of 2013, there were days when I was unable to leave my home because there was continuous shooting taking place, either on my street or close by. One day as I ventured outside my home, I saw government tanks shooting warning shots at protesters only one street away; I was subsequently tear gassed when the wind blew the gas aimed at protesters in the opposite direction. To give an idea of the magnitude of violence, on October 6, 2013, tens of anti-coup protesters were killed by the regime on my street and the streets surrounding my home (Kingsley 2013d). I was never fully sure if my area would remain safe for an entire day, or whether violence might erupt in an area where I was doing research. One week after I completed my fieldwork at the Raba'a al-Adawiya sit-in in Nasr City, the government violently cleared the protests and killed over 1,000 protesters. Human Rights Watch stated that it was the largest mass killing of protesters in a single day in history (Human Rights Watch 2014). Another day I went to Ain Shams University to meet a few interviewees but had to relocate my interviews because of protests taking place on the campus. The immense amount of violence slowed down my research considerably because there were many days when it was too unsafe for either my interviewees or me to go outside.

Following the August 14, 2013 dispersal of the Raba'a al-Adawiya sit-in, the military implemented a nationwide curfew that began at 7:00 p.m. and ended at 6:00 a.m. While over time the length of the curfew was reduced, the fact that people had to be home by a certain time posed serious challenges to my research. First, many interviewees could not meet with me because by the time they finished work they had just enough time to make it home before the curfew went into effect. Second, I had to cut interviews short in order to arrive home before curfew myself. If I was unable to make it home before the start of curfew, I had to remain in my interview location overnight.

Other potential difficulties in my research were post-revolutionary preference falsification (Kuran 1991), memory loss, and time period. Following a revolution that leads to the successful overthrow of a president, there is always the potential for individuals who were pro-regime to say that they were anti-regime after the fact. Additionally, as time progresses, individuals often forget important details. During the interviews I conducted in 2013, when asked what television networks they watched during the Revolution, many respondents said CBC. However, my research assistant pointed out to me that CBC did not air in Egypt until July 2011 (Dubai Press Club 2012, 46). Interview responses may have also been affected by the time period in which they were conducted. Because my interviews took place at a time when the majority of interviewees were highly dissatisfied with the Morsi government that succeeded Mubarak, their perception of the Mubarak regime may have been more favorable than it was in 2011.

The final fieldwork problem that I faced was that my research was cut short in December 2013 because of an untrustworthy research assistant.

When research takes place under a repressive regime, one of the jobs of a research assistant is to ensure the researcher's safety at all times. Thus, a lot of trust is involved and the research assistant must be vetted and recommended by others. Unfortunately, my determination to have a representative sample that included enough women overtook my usually sound judgment and concern for my own safety. When my other research assistants and I had exhausted our contacts with women in the lower class, an acquaintance offered to assist me in obtaining interviews with the additional numbers needed for the project. Toward the end of his work, this acquaintance threatened that if I did not pay him E£8,000, he would go to the police and say that I was a spy. Knowing the grave risks of being accused of spying while researching, I was forced to leave my home in the middle of the night, go into hiding, and terminate my research early by departing the country one week later. While I only completed 170 of my 200 intended interviews, I was fortunate to have preserved my personal safety, since both my family and I were receiving threatening messages during this precarious time.

Despite the many challenges outlined above, my time conducting research in Egypt was very special. Egyptians are rightly known for their hospitality, and the way that interviewees so warmly welcomed me into their homes and into their family lives was an experience that I will never forget. From invitations to *iftar* dinners during Ramadan to dancing and chatting with women in their living rooms, I had many days of joy and laughter. I will especially remember the district "tough guy" who allowed me to conduct interviews in his barber shop. While many in the area feared him, to me he was a gentle giant. Any time I walked into the shop, he would immediately find me a comfortable place to sit and insist on running across the street to buy me food and drink. The friendships I made will last a lifetime, and the immense amount of support I received from so many Egyptians throughout the process demonstrated their sincere kindness and selflessness. There are no people like Egyptians. *Masr om el donya.*

ACKNOWLEDGMENTS

This book was a six-year project that evolved out of my PhD dissertation, and over that time period I was fortunate to have many people support my efforts.

First and foremost, I thank my advisor, Jan Kubik, for his guidance and contribution to my intellectual growth. In the courses I took with him and during our collaboration on my dissertation, he generously shared his vast knowledge of social movements. The way he consistently pushed me to think about, and then rethink, concepts and ideas made me feel as though I were having sessions with a gym trainer for the mind.

I also want to thank my committee member, Paul Poast, who spent hours of his free time working on my game theory model with me. Paul is known for always going above and beyond to help students, and I was fortunate to benefit from his expertise in research design and methods. In addition to the academic support I received, there are no words to express my gratitude to Jan and Paul for their unfaltering support when I was in the field. During the military coup and ensuing political violence, Jan and Paul were always quick to answer my emails or Skype me whenever I had a question or concern about the viability of my project, given the political circumstances, or about my safety.

I would also like to thank committee member Roy Licklider for the thoughtfulness and kindness he has shown me, from sending me articles pertaining to my research topic to attending my conference presentations. I am beyond appreciative for his willingness to take on my lengthy dissertation at such short notice and for providing constructive comments on my work.

I must also give many thanks to outside reader Maye Kassem. Maye has been by my side in my academic journey since 2007, when she agreed to be my master's thesis advisor at the American University in Cairo. Maye wears many hats. She has played the roles of professor, advisor, dissertation reader, and mentor, but, most important, she has become family. In addition to advising and supporting me throughout my fieldwork, she also provided emotional support and a safe haven when my project began to pose risks to my safety.

In addition to my dissertation committee, I am also indebted to a number of other professors. I would like to thank Alvin Tillery for being in my corner for the past seven years. I am incredibly lucky to have such an amazing mentor whose unwavering support and belief in me has helped form who I am as a scholar today. Alvin has been selfless with his time and advice and I am forever grateful. I am also indebted to Douglas Blair for sparking my interest in game theory and to my Arabic teacher, Mona, for preparing me linguistically before I embarked on my fieldwork. My development as a political scientist was shaped through my coursework with Eric Davis, Daniel Keleman, Jack Levy, Beth Leech, Andrew Murphy, and Manus Midlarsky. In addition to professors, I would not have graduated without the dedication of Graduate Administrative Assistant Paulette Flowers-Yhap. Ms. Flowers-Yhap worked tirelessly to answer all of my questions, provide me with information, and take care of appointments, forms, and due dates. She is the superwoman of the Rutgers University Department of Political Science.

I completed the revisions for this book during my first semester teaching at Hamilton College. I am grateful for the support of many colleagues including Alan Cafruny and Jaime Kucinskas, who provided much needed advice and took the time to discuss and read sections of my work.

My research would not have been possible without my research assistants, Diaa and Mostafa. These two men put their own security at risk to make sure that my fieldwork was completed and went to great lengths to ensure my safety. They put countless hours into this project, and their linguistic expertise and knowledge of Cairo were vital to this study. Diaa and Mostafa, I am forever indebted to you. I am also thankful for my other research assistants, Dina, Ahmed, Karim, and Zina.

Throughout this process, a number of friends have helped to make this project come to fruition. I am thankful to Isabel Esterman, Jano Charbel, Derek Ludovici, and Lewis Sanders IV for the long nights talking about Egyptian politics, information provided on the Revolution and transitional period, and, most important, friendship. We have been through so much together and you all know what you mean to me. I must also thank Derek Ludovici for the dissertation brainstorming sessions and critiques of my project. I would like to thank Gudrun Kroner and Karell Inga Valdez for so graciously welcoming me into their home on short notice when I was evacuated from Egypt, and I would like to thank Robert Wilson for providing his home as a space in which to write my book. I am also grateful to Hanan Kashou for assistance in translation and encouragement throughout the dissertation process and Farah Jan for her advice and reassurance. This project would not have been what it is without the unconditional friendship, advice, knowledge, and assistance of Dina. Your light shines throughout the pages of this book.

It was my parents who instilled the passion for learning in me at an early age. Thank you for your endless love and guidance. Thank you for supporting my decision to continue with my fieldwork when so many people suggested I abandon the project. Thank you for believing in me. Additionally, I especially want to acknowledge my grandparents, Manson A. Donaghey and Fay Donaghey, for emphasizing the importance of education through generations in our family. As a prominent educator of his day, my grandfather is still the person to whom I turn for advice on pedagogical matters.

Finally, I want to thank all my interviewees for participating in this project. They welcomed me into their homes, took hours out of their day to speak with me, and opened up to me not only on the political level but also on the personal one. Many expressed to me that their main hope was for a better Egypt; that is my wish as well.

K.D.J.

Contesting the Repressive State

1

Introduction

Kareem[1] leaned over the lunch table, looked directly into my eyes, and with audible frustration in his voice said, "Before, Mubarak took freedom out of the people; now, people are taking freedom out of themselves." He had articulated what was often left unspoken, a perspective held by many revolutionaries who were disappointed by the final outcome. As we sat in the trendy Zamalek restaurant, with its peach-colored walls and ornate Moroccan-style lamps, Kareem began to rehash the past four years of exhilarating protests, the pain of losing friends martyred by government forces, and the ouster of two presidents, all culminating in the Egyptian people's electing a president who was arguably more repressive than the one many had risked their lives to remove in January 2011. For some, the absence of protest rang louder than the chanting in the streets. The silence represented revolutionary exhaustion and defeat. It also reflected fear and a belief that a military strongman was preferable to the chaos that had threatened their own country and actually overtaken Syria. The people who had demanded the downfall of the regime had now conceded to the 2013 protest law, abandoning protest as a means of political contestation, if in fact they were dissatisfied with the current regime, which many were not.

It had not always been this way. There was a time long gone, a time when Egyptians were just beginning to find their voices. "Hosni Mubarak is just like Sharon," protesters cried as they challenged the central security forces around Cairo University. This was not the 2011 Revolution. It was 2002 and people were demonstrating in support of the Palestinian Second Intifada. At the time it was rare to hear protesters cross the red line and include the Egyptian president's name in their chants, but an anti-regime dimension was slowly creeping into the vocabulary of opposition.

It was in 2000 that the current generation of youth mobilization in Egypt began, when groups such as Kefaya, also known as the Egyptian Movement for Change, and the Revolutionary Socialists protested in support of the Palestinian Second Intifada (Lynch 2013, 57). In 2004, Kefaya held its first anti-regime protest in front of the Journalists' Syndicate in Cairo. This demonstration marked the first time that the chant "down with Mubarak" was heard in public. It was unheard of to denounce the government openly, and the act was significant as a step toward "breaking the barrier of fear." The group, which comprised students, young professionals, and the unemployed, had an estimated membership of 500, with 50-100 core activists in Cairo (Onodera 2009, 49). Kefaya activists gained international recognition on May 25, 2005, now known as Black Wednesday, when Egyptian security forces violently attacked protesters in front of the Journalists' Syndicate in Cairo. By this time their demands had become more clearly defined and included a call for free elections, termination of the emergency law, blocking Gamal Mubarak from succeeding his father as president, and an end to the domination of politics by President Mubarak and his National Democratic Party (NDP) in the lead-off to the Egyptian parliamentary and presidential elections.

The April 6th Youth Movement was founded in 2008 in support of the workers strike in al-Mahallah al-Kubra. Attracting over 70,000 members on its Facebook page by the beginning of 2009, the movement called for people to stay home and wear black in support of the striking workers. While the group had a large number of online supporters, the actual number that protested in the streets was much smaller, with about 50 activists demonstrating in Cairo. On July 23, 2008, 25 April 6th activists were detained when they marched in Alexandria. Later, on November 4, 2008, members of the group attempted to protest in various parts of central Cairo to celebrate a National Day of Love, but facing plainclothes police they moved to Al-Azhar Park, where they were eventually arrested and their cardboard banners and plastic hearts meant for distribution were confiscated (Onodera 2009, 53-54).

The We are all Khaled Said Facebook page was created in 2010 following the death of Khaled Said, a young businessman from Alexandria who had been dragged out of a cafe and beaten to death by the Egyptian police after he posted a video online exposing police corruption (Giglio 2011, 15). Originally set up by Egyptian political activist and journalist Abdul Rahman Mansour, the page was eventually administered by both Mansour and Google executive Wael Ghonim (Khamis and Vaughn 2012, 150). The page organized a series of silent stands against the regime where participants stood on the corniches in Alexandria and Cairo wearing black. The first stand was called "A Silent Stand of Prayer for the Martyr Khaled Said along the Alexandria Corniche." While the silent stands brought hundreds into the streets, the demonstrations were focused on justice for Khaled Said and sending a message to the Interior Ministry, not bringing down the regime.

When we look at political mobilization in the years leading up to the 2011 Egyptian Revolution, we see a large disparity between the number of people politically participating online and the number of individuals protesting in the streets. During one silent demonstration organized by the We are all Khaled Said Facebook page when the numbers in the streets were limited, Wael Ghonim posted, "Where are the people who said they were coming? Where are the 10,000 men and women?" (Ghonim 2012, 76). What remains unclear is, after years of organized protests by opposition activists that failed to draw significant numbers, why and how on January 25, 2011, and the following 17 days thousands of Egyptians suddenly took to the streets against the Mubarak regime. That is: Why do people protest?

This book is organized chronologically and touches on why and how people make the decision to protest or not protest during different periods of the revolutionary process in Egypt. To be even more specific, the study asks: Why and how do individuals who are not members of political groups or organizers of political movements choose to engage or not engage in anti-government protest under a repressive regime? In answering the question, I argue that individual decisions to protest or not protest are based on the intersection of three factors: political opportunity structures, mobilizing structures, and framing processes. I further demonstrate that the way by which these decisions to protest or not protest take place is through emotional mechanisms that are activated by specific combinations of these factors. As subsets of the larger question posed in this study I ask how and whether (a) social media acts as a stepping stone to on-the-ground political action, (b) government repression during revolutionary protests encourages or discourages revolutionary bandwagoning, and (c) real and perceived changes in political opportunities following revolutionary protest affect protest mobilization.

The goal of the book is to investigate the relationship between key structural factors and the emotional responses they produce. The study aggregates the responses of interviewees and identifies patterns in those answers about some of the most salient structural elements during different periods of the revolutionary process that activated particular emotional mechanisms leading to decisions to protest or not protest. In this work, I am primarily interested in initial decisions to protest, rather than protest-sustaining mechanisms. The study does not seek a single causal variable for protest nor does it aim to uncover multiple interacting variables that lead to protest. The purpose of this work is to demonstrate the connection between structure and decision-making processes guided by emotion.

THE THEORETICAL APPROACH: RATIONAL CHOICE, COLLECTIVE ACTION RESEARCH PROGRAM, AND THE COLLECTIVE ACTION DILEMMA

Social movements have been studied from a number of angles. One large divide in the field has been characterized by Mark Lichbach (1998) as one between the Synthetic Political Opportunity Theory (SPOT) approach and the Collective Action Research Program (CARP) approach. While the SPOT approach, made popular by Doug McAdam, Sidney Tarrow, and Charles Tilly, dominates the field and focuses on structure and political processes, the less popular CARP approach, which has its foundations in Mancur Olson's 1965 work *The Logic of Collective Action*, centers more on rational action by individual actors. What this book aims to do is marry the two approaches, as suggested by Lichbach, to understand how individuals make rational decisions based on actual and perceived structural factors.

Rational choice is the framework for understanding and formally modeling political behavior. It may be preferable to view rational choice as an approach rather than a theory, as there is no single theory or unambiguous standard for rational choice (Green and Shapiro 1994, 13). The rational approach, referred to by Lichbach as CARP, examines the cost-benefit calculations that individuals make before taking action.

The collective action dilemma, which is the question of how to produce the public good when individuals can receive the benefits produced by the group without actually joining, is at the core of my study. My book aims to advance research on the collective action dilemma by examining protest mobilization leading up to and during the 18 days of the 2011 Egyptian Revolution, the transitional period led by the Supreme Council of the Armed Forces (SCAF), and the four days of the June 30, 2013, uprising in Cairo, Egypt. Solving the collective action dilemma implies looking at both protesters and non-protesters, yet some works still do not delve deeply enough into the decision-making processes of non-protesters. One of this project's contributions is the extensive time spent on interviewing and researching individuals who did not protest in order to understand the differences between the two groups. This work provides an empirical study of protesters and non-protesters in Egypt, testing the predictions of decision models regarding anti-government protest under repressive regimes.

In this study, I explore individual decision models of collective action, where payoff matrixes of collective action treat the group as a unitary actor. I will also rely on simple threshold models. Such models of group action are founded on the idea that each person's propensity to protest is a function of the number of others who are already protesting (Oliver 1993, 289). In individual decision models, equations for the net payoff of participating in collective action as a function of the benefit of the collective good, the benefit of selective incentives, and the costs of participation are often produced, but "authors rarely manipulate these equations mathematically to produce derivations or new results, but instead use them heuristically to organize a term by term verbal discussion of the determinants of participation" (Oliver 1993, 278). The level of interest in a collective good is often operationalized with attitude scales measuring the intensity of opinion about a collective issue (Oliver 1993, 278). What needs clarification in threshold models is how the first individuals at a protest make the decision to take to the streets and how preferences are ordered in making cost-benefit calculations. In chapter 3, I explain how Facebook informs individuals about how many others will protest before a protest event even commences. In chapter 4, I outline the emotional mechanisms that help to order individual preferences in response to government violence.

Emotions as Causal Mechanisms in Rational Decision-Making

In order to understand how individuals make the decision to protest or not protest, it is necessary to examine causal mechanisms. For this book, I draw on Barbara Koslowski for my definition of causal mechanism. "A causal mechanism is the process by which a cause brings about an effect. A mechanism is a theory or explanation, and what it explains is how an event causes another" (Koslowski 1996, 6).

In simple terms, causal mechanisms are the black box between the independent and dependent variables. If x is the independent variable and y is the dependent variable and x causes y, then the causal mechanism is how x causes y (Kiser and Hechter 1991, 5). This explanation identifies not only what a causal mechanism is but also how causal mechanisms relate to variables. Variable-based research and causal mechanism research are complementary, and their combination produces a more complete explanation of causality. Without causal mechanisms, we do not know how the independent variable causes the dependent variable.

While some scholars view causal mechanisms as unobservable entities (Mahoney 2001; George and Bennett 2005), I do not concur that causal mechanisms are always "unobservable." I would argue that there are indicators and proxies for some mechanisms that can be observed. Eva Bellin's (2012) research on the Arab Spring cites the emotional triggers of anger, fear, and euphoria as mechanisms compelling ordinary citizens to take to the streets. While emotions are not observable, the manifestation of the emotions, such as angry graffiti writing, angry signs, the content of chants, and the burning of buildings are indicators of particular emotions.

Some scholars believe that rational choice models produce the best results because they posit strategic rational reasoning (usually treated as an unobservable entity and represented with the help of a utility function) as the mechanism that directly generates behavior (Mahoney 2001, 581; Hedstrom and Swedberg 1998). In rational decision-making models, individuals have ordered preferences and make cost-benefit analyses accordingly. Within the approach used in this study, I argue that among the causal mechanisms that lead to the decision to protest or not protest are emotions; emotional mechanisms help to order preferences.

Early works on emotions within the context of social movements characterized emotions as irrational, causing individuals to be impulsive and irritable (Le Bon 2002). In these works, individuals were driven to frustration, and emotions were reinforced by crowd dynamics. The pathologizing perspective on crowds that saw reason and emotions as antithetical was usually grounded in the theories of Sigmund Freud (1959).

More recent scholarship does not see collective action and emotions as incompatible. "Instead, they are simultaneously rational and emotional processes that structure, motivate and form the basis of strategic action" (Sin 2009, 90). Emotions operate to meet situational challenges by raising the saliency of one desire or concern over another, meaning "emotion helps select among competing desires" (Petersen 2002, 17-18). Emotions are a crucial element in the decision-making process. They help define goals and motivate individuals to take action toward them (Jasper 1998, 421). Therefore, in this study, emotions will be examined as causal mechanisms in individual decision-making to either protest or not protest.

In her analysis of the Arab Spring, Wendy Pearlman claims that the fact that Egyptians were feeling subjects does not indicate that they were not also strategic. "Emotions affected protestors' appraisals of changing circumstances and willingness to assume risk" (Pearlman 2013, 399). This finding is consistent with that of Antonio Damasio (2003), who ran clinical tests on patients with damaged ventromedial prefrontal cortexes and found that an important aspect of the decision-making process is that an individual compares potential alternatives with emotions and feelings from similar past situations. Thus, emotions are part of the learning process and are rational. In chapter 3, I present the emotional mechanisms that lead individuals to participate politically online and those that draw individuals offline and into the streets. In chapters 4 and 5, I outline the emotional mechanisms activated by government violence against protesters that motivate individuals to protest against the regime. Later, in chapter 5, I explain the emotional mechanism produced as a result of a revolutionary victory and its effect on protester empowerment.

Synthetic Political Opportunity Theory

Rationalist models need to be complemented with approaches that consider structural factors. Lichbach argues that political causes of collective action remain uncovered if we do not explain the "key operative and inoperative CA processes" (Lichbach 1998, 410). Thus, contexts, structures, and institutions need to be investigated to understand how they shape the competing interests of the regime, dissident entrepreneurs, dissident followers, and dissidents' allies and opponents. Only then can we achieve a fuller explanation of how collective action processes begin, are maintained, and end.

SPOT is a structure-oriented approach focusing on contentious politics, collective action, and collective mobilization (Tilly and Tarrow 2007) that combines resource mobilization and political process approaches. Resource mobilization theory focuses on the resource capacity of states and their challengers and assumes that social movements are rational responses to conflicting interests and injustices (Tilly 1978). This approach looks at the question of participation based on cost-benefit calculations. In resource mobilization theory, which may be merged with the rational choice approach, institutional politics and political variables become central to explanations of collective action. The relationship between state actions and individual decisions to protest are thoroughly examined in chapters 4 and 5.

In the political process approach, social movements are "triggered by the incentives created by political opportunities, combining conventional and challenging forms of action and building on social networks and cultural frames" (Tarrow 1994, 1). Three important aspects of this approach that are relevant to this study are political opportunity structures, mobilizing structures, and framing processes.

Political opportunity structures are the particular set of variables that explain the variations in how movements pursue strategy. These structures are composed of "specific configurations of resources, institutional arrangements and historical precedents for social mobilization, which facilitate the development of protest movements in some instances and constrain them in others" (Kitschelt 1986, 58). An important point acknowledged in this study is: "No opportunity, however objectively open, will invite mobilization unless it is a) visible to potential challengers and b) perceived as an opportunity" (McAdam, Tarrow, and Tilly 2001, 43). In chapter 7, I present another perspective on political opportunities. In this case, these opportunities are perceived by the opposition as being open, but in "objective" terms these are, in fact, short-term openings created by a segment of the regime in order to overthrow another part of the regime with the intent of closing opportunities in the long run.

McAdam reminds us that "the kinds of structural changes and power shifts that are most defensibly conceived of as *political* opportunities should not be confused with the collective processes by which these changes are interpreted and framed" (McAdam 1996, 25-26). The two are related, but they are not the same. Treating them separately allows us to preserve definitional integrity and also allows us to discern a particular empirical phenomenon where collective action occurs even though there has been no significant change in the relative power position of challenging groups (McAdam 1996, 26). This concept is most important in the case of the 2011 Revolution, when actual relative power positions were not altered but the opposition still mobilized. Additionally, political opportunities should be seen as a dependent variable, not only an independent one. While opportunities open doors to political action, movements may also create opportunities (Gamson and Meyer 1996, 276). Chapter 5 examines how the 2011 Revolution changed political opportunities, creating new spaces for political dissent which in turn altered repertoires for contention leading up to the June 30th uprising.

Institutions pose both constraints and opportunities for individuals. Reacting to institutions, individuals may act in a culturally uniform manner, not because of shared experience, but because they must confront the same institutional hurdles. Thus, social movements are shaped by the institutions they confront. The way in which political opportunities shape repertoires for contention and mobilizing tactics will be highlighted in chapter 3, which examines the use of social media as an avenue for dissent under an oppressive regime. It is important to focus on people countering repressive political structures because studies on protest under such regimes have been limited, relative to those exploring democratic systems, in terms of the extent and type of data collected due to the restrictions and risks associated with such research.

In this study, mobilizing structures are "collective vehicles, informal as well as formal, through which people mobilize and engage in collective action" (McAdam 1996, 3). As we have observed in the previous paragraph, the types of mobilizing structures that develop are often shaped by political opportunity structures. Scholars examining mobilizing structures focus on the ability to raise material resources and mobilize dissent.

Movement structures are the mechanisms and organizational bases that collect and use the movement's resources (Rucht 1996, 186). Hanspeter Kriesi's discussion of mobilization includes distinguishing between four types of formal organizations: social movement organizations (SMOs), supportive organizations, movement associations, and parties and interest groups (Kriesi 1996, 152). The type of formal organization that is relevant to this study is the SMO. The two criteria that distinguish SMOs from other types of formal organizations are: "(1) they mobilize their constituency for collective action, and (2) they do so with a political goal, that is, to obtain some collective good (avoid some collective ill) from authorities" (Kriesi 1996, 152). Social movement organizations and their ability to mobilize dissent online and in the streets are explored in chapter 3, in relation to the January 25th Revolution, and in chapter 7, regarding the June 30th uprising.

While mobilizing structures of SMOs are important, this study goes further to explore mobilizing structures as they relate to unorganized networks. This book examines friendship and work networks in the streets and online that aid in the mobilization process. In the past few years, a growing literature on mobilization through online networks has developed (Siegel 2009; Allagui and Kuebler 2011; Herrera 2014). I explore how friendship networks on Facebook mobilize dissent both in conjunction with SMOs and independent of them.

Frames in collective action are the outcome of negotiating shared meaning. Framing can also be viewed as a purposeful activity where actors use frames for mobilization. These frames are geared internally toward movement activists as well as externally toward bystanders and opponents (J. McCarthy 1996, 149). In order for frames to be effective, they must resonate with the people toward whom they are directed. Frames perform a transformative function in mobilization for collective action by "altering the meaning of the object(s) of attention and their relationship to the actor(s), as in . . . the transformation of routine grievances or misfortunes into injustices or mobilizing grievances in the context of collective action" (Snow 2004, 384). In collective action framing, a group negotiates an understanding of a problem that needs to be addressed, decides whom to blame, posits alternative arrangements, and urges others to act together to effect change.

This study relies on a definition of framing by Dalia Fahmy that claims, "A frame is an interpretive framework that makes events meaningful, and thus is able to organize experiences, guide action, and affect behavior" (Fahmy 2011, 22). The relevance of frames to this study is that the way in which a political movement frames grievances may determine an individual's cost-benefit analysis when calculating whether or not to protest. I examine how movement frames in petitions and on Facebook define grievances, attribute them to the political order, and suggest the necessity for modifying the political order through collective action. I also outline how frames are used to produce a new collective national identity.

Synthesizing Synthetic Political Opportunity Theory and the Collective Action Research Program

Lichbach outlines the structure-action problem, or how to interrelate the micro (individual), meso (group), and macro (societal) levels of analysis (Lichbach 1998, 403). His solution to this dilemma is to integrate the SPOT and CARP approaches. SPOT is strong on structure and weak on action, while CARP is strong on action and weak on structure (Lichbach 1998, 412). Thus, when merged, the CARP and SPOT approaches are complementary, where CARP provides the action and SPOT the structure.

In Part I, this study takes on Lichbach's challenge to integrate the SPOT and CARP approaches. The book is rooted in the CARP approach because I investigate individual decisions to protest or not protest. I explain how people decide to protest by examining individuals' cost-benefit analyses, including preferences, and how emotions help to order preferences. At the same time I answer why people protest by exploring the manner by which political opportunity structures, mobilizing structures, and framing processes affect individuals' decisions. "Structure without action has no mechanism; action without structure has no cause" (Lichbach 1998, 415). Using the CARP approach allows me to look at the mechanisms involved in the decision-making process, while the SPOT approach provides me with the causes of those decisions. In Part II, which discusses the SCAF transitional period and June 30th coup, I focus primarily on changes in political opportunity structures and the discrepancy between perceived and actual opportunities. The reason for this shift toward a SPOT-centered approach is that, while emotions and individual decision-making still provided explanations for protest, I found that the changed political opportunity was the most important factor that influenced the dynamic of the movement during that particular time period.

DEFINING EVENTS

The importance of definitions is that they set the parameters for the theoretical context in which political events are examined. Inconsistencies in definitions may lead to the mislabeling of events or the inability to merge varying works into a greater body of scholarship. There has been much debate surrounding how to label the 2011 Egyptian protests against Mubarak and more of an argument concerning what to call the June 30th protests. Were they revolutions, coups, or some type of uprisings? Thus, an exploration and delineation of the term "revolution" is necessary in order to place this study within the appropriate context.

One of the principal arguments concerning the definition of revolution centers on the issue of actual change versus effort to change. Those who define revolutions by their outcomes, such as Theda Skocpol (1979), believe that revolutions occur when structural change takes place, whereas rebellions happen when people attempt to change the system but do not succeed. For Skocpol, sociopolitical transformation, meaning actual change of the state and class structure, or at least the state structure, constitutes revolution, whereas failed attempts to do so fall into another category, rebellion.

Other scholars, such as Jack Goldstone and Timur Kuran, do not see actual change as a necessary element of revolution; merely the attempt to transform the system is sufficient. Goldstone's focus on efforts to change values and institutions sees revolutions as "an effort to transform the political institutions and the justifications for political authority in a society, accompanied by . . . mass mobilization and noninstitutionalized actions that undermine existing authorities" (Goldstone 2003, 54). Following this line of thinking, Kuran's definition of revolution denotes "a mass-supported seizure of political power that aims to transform the social order. By this definition it is immaterial whether the accomplished transfer of power brings about significant social change" (Kuran 1991, 13).

The differences between these two approaches to defining revolution are significant and have wide-ranging implications. Kuran and Goldstone's definitions allow scholars to identify revolutions from the time an uprising begins. If the stated aim of the people is institutional change and they revolt against the government, then revolution must be occurring. Skocpol's definition makes identifying revolutions much more difficult. How do we know when institutional change occurs? For how long does that change have to last for it to be called institutional change? While Skocpol's definition may be helpful for understanding revolutions that took place decades or centuries earlier, it may be more problematic for those studying more recent revolutions such as the fall of many former Soviet states or the recent Middle Eastern uprisings. If scholars intend to begin academic work on these movements, how long would they have to wait before they could place them into proper context?

In my study, I subscribe to Kuran's definition of revolution. Thus, I argue that January 25, 2011, was a revolution because the aim of the protests was to change not only the president but also the social order and political institutions within Egypt. Despite the reality that political institutions were not transformed and many remnants of the old regime remained, the fact that the people tried to change the system allows me to call what occurred in January and February 2011 a revolution.

Some scholars would challenge my definition of 2011 as revolution because it led to a military takeover of the country by SCAF prior to Morsi's election (Stein 2012). I would argue that while there were some elements of a coup in 2011 in that the military, as unelected officials, took over the transitional period, a military transitional government does not override the fact that in January and February 2011, the Egyptian people were protesting in an attempt to achieve regime change. Additionally, SCAF eventually stepped down and permitted presidential elections to be held in 2012, though they did make some attempts at a last minute power grab through a supplementary constitutional decree right before those elections.

Defining the June 30, 2013, protests is a bit more difficult. While there were a number of anti-regime activists protesting for regime change, the vast majority of individuals I interviewed were not demanding a transformation of the system; they only wanted to remove the president. Based on Kuran's definition, June 30th cannot be considered a revolution. The uprising was also facilitated by the military and Ministry of the Interior, which provided tactical and logistical support to the Tamarod movement. Thus, I define June 30th as a popular participatory veto coup through opposition cooptation.

DATA SOURCES AND COLLECTION METHODS

In this study, I examined a number of secondary sources. In order to provide historical background and theoretical context, I used books and academic journal articles. Reports and documents from international organizations, nongovernmental organizations, research institutes, and governments were utilized to establish facts and obtain statistics on the Egyptian economy, police brutality, and corruption. I viewed newspaper articles to establish factual timelines of the 2011 Revolution and 2013 uprising; they were particularly important for documenting events during the Morsi presidency and the June 30th protests, as there were few academic sources touching on that time period.

The data collection methods I employed to obtain primary sources for my study were open-ended interviews, structured interviews, informal conversations, participant observation, and nonparticipant observation. In addition to the fieldwork I conducted in Egypt between 2004 and 2008 while studying at the American University in Cairo, I began my preliminary research on the uprisings during the 2011 Egyptian Revolution.

Each day I read newspaper articles to locate names of activists, found the activists on Facebook, and established contact for interviews I intended to conduct when I began my field research. In April 2011, I interviewed Srdja Popovic, who trained the April 6th Youth Movement in nonviolent protest tactics, to understand group mobilization methods and framing processes. From 2012 through 2013, I conducted more than 170 structured interviews with members of the lower and upper classes in 46 districts of Cairo who either protested or did not protest in the January 25th Revolution. One hundred fifty-nine of those interviews also covered questions on the transitional period and the June 30th protests. I conducted additional unstructured interviews in July and August 2014, as well as in February 2016.

Initial research on the January 25th Revolution by many scholars has been based on a few elite interviews and discussions with activists (Khamis 2011), who often do not reflect the perspective of the general population. This study uncovers the experiences of a more diverse and representative sample by interviewing a large number of non-activists. The importance of including negative cases is that the explanatory theory being tested implicitly includes predictions about cases where the phenomenon is present and cases where it is not. The criteria for my interviewee selection were that each individual could not have been a member of a political group or an organizer in a political movement before January 25th and that he or she had to be an Egyptian citizen whose primary residence was Cairo at the time of the January 25th protests.

The large number of cases under investigation places my project in the category of a medium-N study. While the number of cases under investigation is not random or large enough to engage in regression analysis and establish statistical significance for my findings, I am able to calculate percentages of like responses to estimate—in a preliminary fashion—the distribution that may exist in the population at large. No better estimates exist.

Due to government restrictions and the extreme level of political violence that took place during the time of my field research, it was impossible to obtain a random sample without putting my safety or the safety of my interviewees in jeopardy. Additionally, in order to collect a random sample I would have needed to have full information on the universe from which I was sampling. It would have been extremely costly to obtain such knowledge and to sample properly based on this knowledge. However, throughout the interviewing process I attempted as much as possible to obtain variation based on gender, age, area of the city, and social class. In addition to snowball sampling, interviews were obtained through my extensive contacts in the upper and lower classes and the contacts of my research assistants.

Being unable to draw a statistically representative (random) sample, I turned to other methods of sampling, particularly theoretical sampling. The purpose of theoretical sampling is to uncover "categories and their properties" in order to place their interrelationship into a theory. In statistical sampling, the researcher obtains evidence on distributions of people in the categories for the purpose of descriptions and verifications (Glaser and Strauss 1967, 62). Instead of probability sampling, I engaged in purposive sampling, a non-probability form of sampling that does not aim to sample participants on a random basis. The aim of purposive sampling is to sample participants in a strategic way, so that individuals sampled are relevant to the research questions that are posed (Bryman 2012, 418). The types of purposive sampling that I performed were "maximum variation sampling," a type of sampling that aims to ensure a wide variation in terms of the dimension of interest (Bryman 2012, 419), and snowball sampling, a non-probability sampling technique where existing interviewees recruit new subjects from among their acquaintances. Snowball sampling is often used when probability sampling is not feasible or is impossible (Bryman 2012, 424).

Theoretical saturation in purposive sampling occurs when the researcher samples theoretically until a category is saturated with data, meaning there does not appear to be any new or relevant data emerging from an interview category, the category is well developed in demonstrating variation, and the relationships among categories are validated and well-established (Strauss and Corbin 1998, 212). At the end of my research I was reasonably sure that I was reaching theoretical saturation.

The majority of my interviewees were under the age of 40 at the time of the January 25th Revolution, which is consistent with the country's demographics where the median age is 25.1 (Central Intelligence Agency, n.d.). Additionally, there are more interviews from the lower class than the upper class, which also corresponds with the country's demographics where 48.9% live below the poverty line (Sabry 2014) and many more live just above it.

The participant observation in which I engaged included observing weekly anti-Morsi protests in Cairo in 2012 and 2013, pro-Morsi demonstrations in 2013, and the marches to Tahrir Square from June 28th through July 3rd 2013. I conducted field research while attending the November 27, 2012, protest in Tahrir Square against Morsi, the anti-Morsi protests in Tahrir Square on July 1, 2013, which was the second official day of the June 30th uprising, the July 26, 2013, pro-military demonstration in Tahrir Square, and the Rabaa al-Adawiya sit-in in August 2013. I was able to obtain data through nonparticipant observation of Facebook group pages and individual Facebook pages, where I viewed political discussions and wall posts. One of the purposes of examining Facebook content was to uncover methods for raising political awareness and political participation online.

ORGANIZATION OF CHAPTERS

The book has eight chapters. The arguments and evidence are organized into two parts based on time period. The first part explores why and how individuals made the decision to protest or not protest in the January 25th Egyptian Revolution, focusing on grievances and structural issues, social media, and government violence against protesters. The second part examines the revolutionary transitional period, focusing on protest dynamics under the military transitional rule, institutional problems and leadership decision-making under SCAF and the Morsi government, individual grievances during the rule of President Morsi, and political opportunities and individual decision-making that led to participation in the June 30, 2013, protests and subsequent military coup.

The organization of my book is as follows: Part I, "The Downfall of Mubarak," is composed of chapters 2 through 4. The purpose of this section of the study is to outline Mubarak's ouster, beginning with grievances and mobilization leading up to the Revolution, and continuing with protest mobilization during the Revolution. Chapter 2 provides background for the 2011 Revolution by highlighting the grievances of the upper and lower classes regarding economic factors, police brutality, and corruption. The purpose of the chapter is to explain why a large portion of the Egyptian population was unhappy with the Mubarak regime in the years leading up to the Revolution and where they attributed the blame for their plight. The chapter also demonstrates how social movement organizers frame grievances in a manner that leads to successful protest mobilization. Throughout the chapter, I provide rich description and examples based on field notes and interviews, including victims of police brutality, the economically deprived, individuals who were hurt by corrupt practices, and those who benefited from the Mubarak system. Chapter 3 contributes to the emerging literature on social media and protest by presenting a model of how individuals move from being nonparticipants to online participants to protesters on the street. The chapter explores the role of social media in protest participation, using interview data, tables, and models to demonstrate how sources of information affected individual mobilization leading up to the revolutionary protests. The chapter shows how Facebook facilitated the building of a politically conscious civil society leading up to the Revolution, contributed to reinforcing grievances and mobilizing opposition to the regime, and lowered the threshold for engaging in political participation. In this chapter, new theoretical concepts, such as "online preference" and "revolutionary bandwagoning online" are presented. Chapter 4 also uses qualitative data and interviewee accounts to explain how government violence affected protest mobilization. The chapter examines rational altruistic decisions to protest and the emotional mechanisms that produce such decisions. I focus on the emotion of "moral shock" in the face of government violence and feelings of "collective national identity" as motivators for protest.

Part II, "The Transition and Downfall of Morsi," comprises chapters 5 through 8. The aim of this segment of the book is to examine the relationship between protesters and the military government during the transitional period, as well as to explain why and how Morsi's presidency came to an end. Chapter 5 explains how changes in political opportunity structures following the 2011 revolutionary protests affected subsequent anti-regime mobilization and the dynamics between the military transitional regime and those who contested it. I introduce the post-revolutionary emboldening effect emotional mechanism and demonstrate that changes in political opportunities created during the 18-day uprising altered repertoires of contention and reconfigured the power relationship between the regime and its opponents. The chapter also claims that particular elements of protest dynamics under SCAF led to a relatively quick transition to civilian rule. In chapter 6, I outline the individual grievances arising from political, economic, social, and religious conditions under the government of Mohamed Morsi that became the foundations of opposition to his rule. The chapter relies on interview data and fieldwork conducted in Egypt during the year of Morsi's presidency. In chapter 7, I identify the discrepancy between real and perceived political opportunities and the effect this gap had on political mobilization for the June 30th protests. The chapter relies on interview data and fieldwork conducted during the 2012 anti-Morsi protests, the 2013 coup, the months following the coup, and at protests in Tahrir Square and in the Rabaa al-Adawiya sit-in. In addition to outlining the politics surrounding Morsi's 2012 constitutional declaration, the subsequent protests, and how the Tamarod movement mobilized mass protests against Morsi that took place on June 30, 2013, the chapter also presents the intricate details and step-by-step process of the 2013 military coup. The chapter explains post-coup politics, including the designation of the Muslim Brotherhood as a terrorist organization, the military's mobilization of the public against the Muslim Brotherhood, the Rabaa al-Adawiya massacre, the cult of General el-Sisi, the 2014 constitutional referendum, and the 2014 presidential elections. In chapter 8, the concluding chapter, I summarize the arguments, discuss them within the context of the literature on protest mobilization, and explain the theoretical implications of the book.

PART I

The Downfall of Mubarak

2

Grievances against the Mubarak Regime

Fatima was in her mid-fifties, but she looked and felt much older. Her life of personal hardships had left her drained, and she had developed diabetes from the poor eating habits common in Egyptian society. Walking was difficult because of the constant swelling in her ankles, and multiple trips to the doctor and various medications from the pharmacist had failed to alleviate her pain. Fatima spent most of her days sitting in the dark on the faded pink and black striped satin sofa of her two-bedroom ground floor apartment smoking her Cleopatra cigarettes and coughing. When she ran out of smokes, she would lean out the one window in the house with a handful of Egyptian pounds and beckon to the boys playing in the street to come closer. She would hand the money to one of the boys and ask him to buy her another pack. Ten minutes later, he would return clutching the soft gold container of cheap cigarettes.

Fatima was the widow of a low-level police officer. On the rare occasion that a new guest came for a visit, she delighted in dusting off the black and white photo of her husband and demonstrating his likeness to Egyptian actor Omar Sharif. Fatima lived for her two sons. She chose to sleep on the floor of the living room in order for each son to have his own bedroom. Her younger son, Adel, was in art school, and she was always eager to show off his sketches, but her pride and joy was her older son, Ahmed, who had graduated with a degree in physical education and worked as a fitness trainer. Every morning Fatima woke up early to help Ahmed get ready for work. She prepared beans and eggs in the cramped, cockroach-infested kitchen, ironed his work uniform, and waited on him hand and foot. After Ahmed left the house, Fatima would wash the dishes in the bathroom sink, which provided the only running water in the house. Ahmed was the sole breadwinner in the house, and Fatima both depended on him and feared him because of his violent temper.

Ahmed worked in an upscale gym in Zamalek. The monthly membership fees were exorbitant by Egyptian standards, but Ahmed only took home $80 per month, even though he worked six days per week, 12 hours per day. He knew that he was being exploited, but there was nothing he could do about it. He was lucky to have a job. Every month Ahmed would send his resume to hotel gyms and other positions that were higher paying, but time and time again he was rejected. While he had the right qualifications and experience, he had the wrong address. In Egypt, economic mobility was difficult; employers judged applicants based on their area of residence, and Ahmed was from one of the poorer areas of Cairo. When possible, fancy gyms preferred to hire from the middle class.

Ahmed's fortunes began to change when he met a young foreign woman named Ellen at the gym one day. With his good looks and charm, he convinced Ellen to marry him after only a few months, and she paid for them to move to a more affluent area of Cairo. With his wife's help, Ahmed was able to secure a position at one of the top gyms in the city, but he soon learned that escaping his socioeconomic class was more difficult than he had thought.

Every day Ahmed finished work around 11:30 p.m. and immediately returned home for dinner, or at least called to say that he would be late. One evening he did not come home. By 1:00 a.m., Ellen decided to call and check on him, but his phone continued to ring with no response.

With dinner prepared and no husband to feed, Ellen sat on her sofa dialing her husband every half hour, becoming more and more worried as time passed. Finally, around 5:30 a.m., Ahmed showed up at their door looking exhausted. When Ellen asked him where he had been and what had happened, he told her that he had been detained by the authorities and taken to the police station. Knowing that her husband was not one to be involved in illegal activity, Ellen confusedly asked why. Ahmed told her that because he had been walking around Maadi late at night with a national ID that indicated he was from Sayeda Zeinab, they assumed that he was up to no good and decided to take him in.

Although many people expressed dissatisfaction with the Mubarak regime because of the lack of freedom, the poor education and health systems, and the January 2011 Alexandria church bombing, this chapter focuses on the three areas of dissatisfaction most cited by both lower- and upper-class protesters: economic grievances, anger over police brutality, and frustration with corruption. As in Ahmed's story from 2004 to 2006, too many Egyptians faced poverty, corruption, and arbitrary arrest, among other plights. In almost every category of complaint, the reasons for lower- and upper-class resentment against the Mubarak regime coincided, demonstrating that the two classes had very similar experiences in their confrontations with the regime and that the toxicity that characterized Mubarak's rule had permeated all levels of society.

THE ECONOMY

Leading up to the Revolution, one of the greatest concerns for both lower and upper classes in Egypt was the poor state of the economy. While country reports produced by the International Monetary Fund (IMF) and Bloomberg projected a relatively positive outlook on the Egyptian economy regarding resilience to the world financial crisis, financial market conditions, and economic performance (International Monetary Fund 2010), prospects for areas of the economy that affected everyday life, such as inflation and employment rates, were dismal.

During 2007/2008, the Egyptian economy performed at a high level, expanding at 7.2% compared to 3.5% during 2000/2001 (Ghanem 2010, 11). In the third quarter of 2010, the Egyptian economy was still expanding by 5.6% (Wahba and Shahine 2010). However, Egypt was also undergoing a serious liquidity crisis due to the loss of hard currency from declining tourism. Foreign exchange reserves had shrunk from $30 billion to $15 billion because of the government's inconsistent policies on the Egyptian pound, which had been devalued many times (Elaasar 2010). Estimated losses in the tourism sector ranged from $2 to $3 billion, and the airline and shipping industries had been hit by a 50% increase in insurance premiums (Elaasar 2010).

Adding to these serious market concerns was the problem of extremely high inflation, which had a direct impact on the domestic population and its ability to meet basic needs. There had been a series of inflation spikes in the decade leading up to the Revolution. In 2003–2004, inflation rates increased due to a huge devaluation of the Egyptian pound; in 2006–2007, inflation spiked because of the avian flu outbreak; and in 2008, inflation hit a high of 18.3% (IndexMuni 2011) because of the world commodity price increase (Moriyama 2011, 5). By the 2010/2011 fiscal year, inflation sat at 10.2% (United Nations Economic Commission for Africa 2013, 4).

Another complication for Egypt was the youth bulge and the inability of the Egyptian workforce to absorb the growing number of recent graduates. The United Nations Development Program (UNDP) defines youth as those belonging to the 18 to 29 age group, which represented approximately 20 million members of the Egyptian population. A 2006 census reported that 25% of the Egyptian population fell into the youth category (Handoussa 2010, 35). Over the course of Mubarak's almost 30-year rule, the country's population increased by 90%, from 45 million to 85 million (Roudi-Fahimi, El Feki, and Tsai 2011), but job creation did not keep up with people creation.

In 2006, more than 80% of the unemployed were under age 29, and 82% of the unemployed had never held a job before (Handoussa 2010, 148), implying that there was a labor market insertion problem in Egypt, with youth being unable to transition from study to work. In 2010, the unemployment rate in Egypt stood at 9.7% (Indexmuni 2011). Approximately 90% of those unemployed were under the age of 30 (Handoussa 2010, 6), and many who were not unemployed were underemployed. While it is usually assumed that when young individuals complete their schooling they will transition into the workforce, 58.5% of 18- to 29-year-olds were out of the workforce (Handoussa 2010, 38); they were not considered to be unemployed because they were not even seeking employment.

The demographics of youth unemployment in Egypt may surprise those who assume that unemployment is a problem principally for the lower classes. "Unemployment is highest among youth who come from households in the fourth wealth quintile, slightly drops for those in the highest wealth quintile, and is lowest among youth who come from households in the lowest wealth quintile" (Handoussa 2010, 139). The explanation for this distribution is that graduates from the upper classes can afford to wait for suitable employment, often with the support of their parents, while those from the lower classes are more willing to take any job available to them, thus having a lower reservation wage. Those in higher socioeconomic brackets expect to obtain positions in the formal economy, while those in the lower socioeconomic brackets are more willing to take work in the informal sector rather than remain jobless. Diane Singerman, who studied popular quarters in Cairo, observed, "Two-thirds of the men and women in the community I studied were supported by the informal economy in either their primary, secondary, or tertiary economic activity" (Singerman 1995, 176), and in 2006 Salwa Ismail noted the "growing informalization of the labor force" (Ismail 2006, 4). However, employment does not mean wealth. While poor youth have higher employment rates, they still subsist on meager wages and are more often underemployed than their counterparts in the upper classes.

The number of Egyptians living below the poverty line of $2 per day rose from 17% in 2000 to 22% in 2010 (Roudi-Fahimi, El Feki, and Tsai 2011). However, nearly half of Egyptians were living under or just above the poverty line. To understand the economic grievances of lower-class Egyptians, it is important to highlight the daily challenges they endured and the exasperating conditions that impelled a person to face the danger of protest against an armed regime.

It should be understood that in my interviews I posed questions to elicit what led people to the point of participating in the Revolution. Although the grievances described were attributed to the failures of the Mubarak regime, many of them, particularly those related to the economy, were ongoing at this period of instability following the uprising.

As part of my research, I took a number of trips to El-Baragil, an area of Giza at the edge of Greater Cairo. I was fortunate to find a taxi that would take me there, as usually only tuk-tuks would agree to navigate the rough, unpaved roads and narrow streets. On one occasion, we made our way to my destination, maneuvering to avoid flooded streets. A man riding a horse behind us seemed to be having an easier time, eventually passing us on the road. When I arrived at the home where I was supposed to conduct a number of interviews, I climbed the stark stairwell with eroding walls to the small apartment and headed to the cramped sitting room where women representing three generations awaited me.

As I held a young woman's baby in one arm and wrote with the other, we spoke about economic hardships. Prior to the Revolution, the woman's husband had been "unfairly" arrested, which had made her situation even more difficult than most because of the financial burden. In the lower classes, while economic conditions have forced many women to enter the workforce out of necessity, women's employment is often frowned upon. As another middle-aged woman explained, "We are housewives for real men. We don't have to think about politics or money," implying that the men of the family could financially support their families, allowing the wife to stay at home. The majority of people with whom I spoke from all classes reported having mothers who were housewives and/or being housewives themselves. However, this self-reporting of employment status can be deceptive. In the lower class, the need for a woman to work is sometimes viewed as shameful for the husband who cannot support the family on his own. Thus, women will often categorize themselves as housewives even when they perform some type of work in the informal economy, such as domestic service, food vending, or raising poultry. In the case of women whose husbands have been detained, the women either become the sole family breadwinner or place additional stress on extended family to care for them.

The difficulties related to a husband's arrest were revealed again when I interviewed a young woman in a local cafe in Haram. Sitting and sipping my tea, I had just completed my scheduled interviews for the day when a woman like no other I had witnessed entered the room. Everyone in the cafe turned around to stare at her hot pink, skin-tight *abaya* (robe) and black *niqab* (face covering). Curious, I enlisted one of my companions to approach her and ask if I could interview her, and she agreed. Removing her *niqab*, she sat down and we began to speak. Through my interview and a discussion my companion had with her afterward, I learned that before the Revolution she had worked as a belly dancer in a cabaret and her husband had served as her manager. When her husband was detained indefinitely by the police, she was forced into prostitution to survive.

Other women facing financial hardship made different choices from accepting what Egyptian society viewed as "immoral" employment. I spoke to the 20-year-old sister of a cabaret worker who had chosen not to enter her sibling's profession, explaining that she had at one point sold her kidney to make ends meet. Having grown up on the streets, she believed that her desperate economic and living conditions, which she blamed on the Mubarak regime, had pushed her to do things she otherwise would have never contemplated.

Interviews with lower-class men usually took place at their worksites or at street cafes. Many were students, unemployed or underemployed, and had plenty of time to converse. They discussed the societal pressure to serve as breadwinners, and many claimed that under Mubarak people had been unable to survive economically. One young man explained, "I wanted to live a better life. Work, eat good food, have money." Fulfilling the basic need of eating had often been difficult, and many of the poor would drink tea with copious amounts of sugar to stave off hunger. An unemployed youth related, "People were walking in the streets hating themselves. What will I eat today? Mubarak was a thief, just telling people there was stability in Egypt but in a loser way," and another young man knew many people without enough money to eat who would inquire, "Where is Nasser?" reminiscing about the populist president of the 1950s and 1960s who was known for distributing subsidies. One of the heart-wrenching stories was related by a 21-year-old student from Shubra. One day he was in the market with his mother buying tomatoes and they came across an old woman crying. The old woman said, "Mubarak is eating and he's good so *Alhamdullillah*." The aging woman was starving, but at least the president was eating well.

Many men complained of underemployment or their inability to obtain work commensurate with their education level. Young people who had graduated from university were working at any job they could find, not necessarily one in their field. Examples were an engineer washing plates in the tourist resort of Sharm El Sheikh and his friend with a PhD who drove a microbus for a living. One young man said in exasperation, "I wanted a better life. I have a good degree and think I should have a better position. I wanted to change my level." A mother from a poor family in El-Waily was distressed because her sons had no job opportunities after graduating with advanced degrees, and a young man recalled that when he graduated from university he dreamed of a job he knew he would never obtain. "I saw how [the Mubarak regime] killed the dreams of young people."[1] Many complained of favoritism as a barrier to employment or advancing their status. "An engineer's son became an engineer; a doctor's son became a doctor. Wealth was passed on and there was nepotism."

The inability to afford marriage was another concern for many men. In Egypt, marriage is an expensive process. In order to marry, a man is expected to pay for the wedding, offer the woman a *shabka* (jewelry gift) and *mahr* (dowry), and provide the marital residence. In 2008, the average cost of marriage in Egypt was almost the same as the average per capita annual income, $5,460 (Roudi-Fahimi, El Feki, and Tsai 2011). While families often assist with, or fully cover, the expenses, the exorbitant cost of marriage combined with high unemployment levels led many young people to wait longer than ever before marrying. A 21-year-old man from Sayeda Zeinab who worked at a media company expressed in an almost desperate tone, "I have to get married. I have to have children, good hospitals.

I need basic things. The rights of the people are not dreams. These are their rights."

Dissatisfaction with the economic situation was not limited to the lower classes. Young, affluent Egyptians also lamented the employment situation, among other grievances. However, in contrast to the location of my interviews with the lower classes, discussions with the upper classes took place in posh Nile cafes, luxury apartments, and villas in newly built compounds. Of course, there was the occasional young man who preferred the local street cafe, but for the most part, I noticed that when I offered to cover the bill, the cost had changed from E£5 to E£50.

The lifestyle of upper-class youth was more than comfortable. A typical week included frequent trips to upscale cafes, where friends gathered to drink pricey juices and smoke hookah. Long weekends were passed traveling to beach resorts, such as Sharm el-Sheikh and the North Coast, where families either owned their own beach houses or were able to afford resort hotels. However, looks can be deceiving. Given the poor economic situation, the affluent habits of the upper-class youth were supported by parents, not by their own incomes. Other than a few from the very upper echelons with connections, it was almost impossible for these youth to find decent-paying jobs, despite their families' having invested thousands of dollars in foreign educational institutions. One young man, whose family owned an apartment in Mohandeseen and a massive villa on the outskirts of Cairo and who had been educated abroad, was elated when he finally received a job offer from an international company that paid E£3,500 (approximately $500) per month. With a lifestyle that included trips to Europe and riding around Cairo on his motorcycle, that type of pay would only serve as pocket money. Thus, the socioeconomic status of these young people was defined principally by the positions their parents held and the assets their parents owned. Even when an upper-class man was unemployed or underemployed, he was still able to marry because his family would cover the related expenses; however, for the middle class, things were more difficult.

Members of both middle- and upper-middle classes who were about to enter the workforce expressed anxiety about securing a position following graduation, particularly after witnessing the failure of so many of their friends. An unemployed upper-middle class youth complained that there were either no job opportunities or salaries were low, asserting that under Mubarak "you had to be connected to someone to get a job, even if you were the best one for the position." A 20-year-old student from Dokki articulated, "A simple guy couldn't find a job, raise his social status, or get married," and a 30-year-old man whose father was a military officer explained that after completing university he found that there were no jobs. He had graduated with a degree in business administration and English but was unable to find a position in his field. Eventually, he had to take any job he could get. He and his friends could not afford to marry because of low incomes, and the rents for flats were at minimum E£2,000 per month. "Every year the rent was more and more and [my friends] don't have the income to pay it. Private companies pay better than the government, but they still don't pay enough to keep up with inflation." He then used words that were repeated frequently by Egyptians. At the time of Mubarak, "The people didn't have their rights."

In addition to the grievances of the upper classes about unemployment and low pay, a running theme was their sympathy for the lower classes. Some members of the upper class were uncomfortable with the vast income disparity between the rich and poor in their country. Passionately describing the political and economic situation in the time of Mubarak, a young doctor said, "It's not fair. The economy was terrible . . . and all the money was in the hands of 1% of the population while the other 99% were almost starving." A young man from Dokki who worked in real estate reiterated the sentiment, saying, "The people were getting weaker and the country was dealing with people like they were slaves. The poor were like slaves and the upper classes were the owners of the country. The middle class were lost with what to do." Another student explained, "I wasn't hurt by the Mubarak regime, but I worried about the lower class." The general feeling was that the country had been becoming one of rich and poor with a rapidly dwindling middle class.

The empathy and solidarity that the upper class demonstrated for the plight of the lower class was the reason why one lower-class man had decided to protest in the Revolution. At the beginning, he had thought the Revolution was going to be a joke. On January 25th, he had made his way to Tahrir Square out of curiosity. He had approached a "posh" upper-class young woman in the Square and asked, "Why are you here?" She had replied that maybe the poor people did not have time to speak, so she would speak for them. Her words had inspired him, and following the encounter he had been hopeful.

POLICE BRUTALITY

It is no secret that the Egyptian police have a history of torturing detainees. In his autobiography, Anwar al-Sadat, reflecting on his time as vice-president of Egypt under Nasser, wrote, "In the first four years of revolutionary rule, when the Revolutionary Command Council wielded all power, there were mistakes and violations of human rights but these were limited in scope. It was after 1956 that they began to acquire huge dimensions" (el-Sadat 1977, 209). The torture of communists and Islamists was widespread in the 1960s but lessened at the end of the 1960s and into the 1970s. However, with the 1981 assassination of President Sadat, torture made a comeback as a tool of the state (Human Rights Watch 2011b, 13).

The backdrop to the Egyptian state practice of torture is an emergency law that has been in place for the majority of the past one hundred years, and consistently since 1981 when Mubarak came to power (Reza 2007, 534). With the assistance of emergency law, the General Directorate for State Security Investigation (SSI) was able, in the period leading up to the Revolution, to use extralegal means to extract information from and punish prisoners and arbitrarily detain citizens. Emergency law "gives the executive—in practice the Interior Ministry—extensive powers to suspend basic rights by prohibiting demonstrations and detaining people indefinitely without charge" (Human Rights Watch 2011b, 10). The SSI, which was under the direct control of the Ministry of the Interior, was an internal-security agency whose number of employees, soldiers, and officers was unknown and considered to be a state secret. The agency "maintains a system of nationwide surveillance, using both its own plainclothes agents and a network of informers, some of whom appear to be recruited while in custody" (Sherry 1993).

The list of abuses in Egypt has been long and varied and includes intimidating or recruiting police informers, punishing a citizen as a favor to a third party, pressuring individuals to forfeit property, punishing those who challenge police authority, obtaining information or confessions illegally from detainees, intimidating individuals because of their sexual orientation, religious beliefs, or political beliefs and activities, and abusing women and children related to suspects, in what some describe as a hostage-taking policy (Human Rights Watch 2011b, 16).

Police brutality in Egypt has taken many forms, including threatening victims that their families will be killed and interrogating prisoners while they hear the screams of fellow inmates being tortured nearby (Amnesty International 2007b, 18). Victims of torture are threatened with re-arrest if they lodge complaints against their abusers (Amnesty International 2009). In a Human Rights Watch report on the persecution of homosexuals in Egypt, men who were imprisoned because of their sexual orientation reported being administered electric shocks on their genitals, limbs, and tongue, raped by other prisoners, "whipped, beaten, bound and suspended in painful positions, splashed with ice-cold water, and burned with lit cigarettes" (Reproductive Health Matters 2009, 173). Describing torture methods, Virginia Sherry related:

> Detainees, usually stripped to their underwear or totally naked, and almost always blindfolded, endure beatings with sticks and other hard objects; electric shocks on sensitive body parts, sometimes while doused with water; forced standing for long periods, often in front of an air conditioner; hanging by the wrists or other forms of painful suspension; and harsh psychological torture, including threats of sexual violence against themselves or female family members. (Sherry 1993)

One young man who had participated in the storming of Amn al-Dawla (State Security) offices during the Revolution claimed to have found

Tasers, torture devices, and prison cells in the building. He described the offices as "the Middle Eastern Guantanamo Bay."

While the important role of videos and photographs of torture in fomenting dissent has been rightly examined, this part of the chapter focuses on firsthand experiences of abuse and torture. When asked if there were any stories in the news prior to the Revolution that bothered them, the number one answer for both upper and lower classes, both protesters and non-protesters, was that of Khaled Said, the young Alexandrian man tortured and killed by police. However, as one student from Shubra put it, "I didn't need the news; I saw it with my own eyes."

Many writings on the Revolution have cited police brutality as one of the primary grievances of protesters (Lesch 2011). In my research, I found a complex phenomenon that extended beyond torture to include arbitrary arrest, abuse of power, corruption, and the targeting of specific populations. What was surprising was the similarity in experiences of confrontations with the police that upper- and lower-class Egyptians faced. The stories of the upper and lower classes coincided most closely when describing the arrests of friends, family members, or acquaintances on the grounds of being Islamists or suspected Islamists. Accounts of police abuse of power and police brutality were also similar. Where class narratives began to diverge was in the area of arbitrary arrest. Members of the lower class were much more likely to report being subjected to arbitrary arrest than those in the upper class.

Many of the lower-class accounts of police brutality described interactions that did not take place in prisons but instead on the streets. Police acted with such impunity that they did not even feel the need to hide their actions from public view. An older man, Nabil, had been involved in frequent disputes with another man from his area. Unfortunately for Nabil, the man with whom he had disagreements had police connections. One day the police showed up at Nabil's shop, beat him up, and tortured him in his own store. Similarly, a young man from Bassatine related that there was a man from his neighborhood who had owned a small supermarket where the police used to take items without paying, but the shop owner was too afraid to say anything. One day the shop owner had had enough and began to fight with one of the police officers. In retaliation, the officer went to the shop owner's house and hit the man's sister. This story came to an ugly end when the shop owner shot the police officer for disrespecting his sister. Relating an account of police abuse at a demonstration site, a man from Hadayek El-Kobba described coming across a protest downtown and observing a police officer dragging a woman by her hair. When the man had tried to intervene, the officer had confronted him, saying, "If you interfere, I'll take you instead."

Worse than the cases of public displays of excessive force was the story of a young man who had been arrested during the Revolution by military police. While this chapter aims to explain grievances leading up to the Revolution, I believe this particular story of arrest and torture provides important information on Egyptian torture practices.

This young cafe employee, who reported that he had attended the January 25th protests to observe, but not participate, had been picked up by the military police and taken to military prison. While in custody he, along with many others, was repeatedly administered electric shocks. He was wearing boots with thick rubber soles, which caused the police difficulty because the shoes protected him from the electricity. After the young man had been subjected to repeated shocks, his head was bashed numerous times by his torturers, and he was left with an indentation in his head where his skull had been fractured. Following his stay in military police custody, he had been transferred to a military hospital where he had received top-notch care. Before releasing him back on the streets, his captors tried to ensure that there were few or no signs of the torture that had taken place. This story demonstrates that torture was institutionalized in Egypt and practiced by both the police and military.

While many might assume that only the lower classes were subjected to police brutality, there were just as many stories involving the upper class. A young filmmaker in his early twenties, who resided in Dokki, related that he had been attacked by the police on multiple occasions. One evening he had been with his American girlfriend in Muqattam. A police officer had stopped the couple and become angry and impatient when the man persisted in interpreting to his American friend. The police officer had kicked him and pulled hair out of his head.

Interviews unveiled other stories of police brutality toward the upper classes, many accounts concerning involvement in political activity. A female school director angrily related that a journalist friend of hers had been arrested and sodomized by the police for his political activism. A friend of an engineering student had been beaten by police at a protest in front of the Journalist Syndicate, and a middle-class pharmacist explained, "I had friends who protested before the Revolution and got arrested; some got out and some disappeared." Finally, a young film editor described that not only had one of his friends been taken to a police station and tortured but that later, during the Revolution, he himself had been detained by military police and had witnessed young boys being tortured in front of him.

These stories speak to police brutality based on abuse of power against everyday citizens going about their business and the targeting of secular anti-regime political activists. In the next section, I examine how police specifically sought out Islamists and suspected Islamists from both the lower and upper classes for detention and torture.

ISLAMIST TARGETING

The most well-known and influential Islamist group in Egypt is the Muslim Brotherhood. Founded in 1928 by elementary school teacher Hasan al-Banna as a reaction to what he saw as the lack of religion and morality in society, the group transformed into a political organization by the end of the 1930s, supporting the monarchy of King Faruq (Fahmy 2011, 84) and fielding its first candidates for parliament in 1941 (Davis and Robinson 2009, 1306). By the late 1940s, the organization aimed to implement Islamic law in Egypt (Onians 2004, 78).

Although there have been times in the twentieth century when the Muslim Brotherhood has experienced relative freedom to organize, members of the group have also been subjected to state attacks, such as the 1949 assassination of al-Banna by state agents in response to the Brotherhood's assassination of Prime Minister Mahmud Fahmi al-Nuqrashi, who had attempted to dissolve the Brotherhood in 1948 (Davis and Robinson 2009, 1306). According to Fahmy, "The initial relationship of the Brotherhood with Nasser's regime was a close and mutually beneficial one" (Fahmy 2011, 87). However, in 1954, the Muslim Brotherhood became a banned organization after one of its members attempted to assassinate President Nasser. More than 4,000 Muslim Brotherhood members were arrested, thousands went into exile (Onians 2004, 78), and a number of its leaders were executed (Kepel 1995, 110).

When Sadat assumed power in 1970, he needed Brotherhood support against Nasserite leftists and radicals, so he freed Brotherhood prisoners (Kepel 1995, 111) and leaders such as the General Guide Hudaybi and Sister Zainab Ghazali on condition that they would engage only in limited political activity (Sattar 1995, 18). However, after Sadat accused Muslim Brotherhood General Guide Tilmisani of trying to overthrow his regime, the president had Tilmisani arrested, along with hundreds of activists. Muslim Brotherhood publications were banned, and ten Islamist societies were dissolved (Sattar 1995, 19). This confrontation with Islamists led to Sadat's 1981 assassination by members of al-Jihad group.

Noman Sattar describes the Egyptian regime's approach to Islamists as "confrontation-suppression-accommodation" (Sattar 1995, 10). While Islamists were arrested en masse following Sadat's assassination, in 1984 they won eight seats in the People's Assembly. The following year, Islamists were again confronted by the regime when the government sealed off a mosque that was supposed to serve as the starting point for a march, denied the group a march permit, and detained five hundred expected demonstrators (Reza 2007, 546).

The Mubarak regime, like those before it, had a schizophrenic relationship with Islamists. After the 1997 Luxor massacre, the government crushed the military capabilities of al-Jihad, al-Gama'a al-Islamiyya, the group responsible for the terrorist attack, as well as other fringe groups, arresting or killing their leaders. However, between 1997 and 2000, the government released approximately 8,000 Islamist prisoners belonging to al-Gama'a al-Islamiyya, the purpose of which was to "reward its recent positive behavior and punish Jihad" (Gerges 2000, 596).

While the Muslim Brotherhood was a banned organization, 88 members were elected to the People's Assembly in 2005 as independents; however, when members of the group won almost 20% of parliamentary seats that same year, the regime arrested thousands of Brotherhood members, confiscated the group's assets, and passed a constitutional amendment that banned "any political activity based on a religious point of reference" (Rutherford, Cook, and Wawro 1976, 5). According to Al-Awadi (2005), Mubarak was threatened by moderate Islamists' ability to provide social services to the poor through their organized networks, thereby challenging state power. Thus, the Mubarak regime attempted to diminish Brotherhood influence through launching an offensive campaign against the group (Al-Awadi 2005, 62).

An Amnesty International report expressed concern that detainees were being held for political beliefs and membership in unauthorized Islamist groups. They also worried that Islamists were at risk for torture, particularly at SSI headquarters in Lazoghly Square, Cairo, and other SSI branches (Amnesty International 2007b, 18). The ongoing relationship between the Egyptian state and Islamists is best described by Tarek Masoud:

> Islam is both avowed enemy and jealously defended state religion. Police routinely arrest Muslim radicals who would overturn the political order and establish a state based on their faith; but they also arrest those who would offend that faith. This is not merely a case of the Egyptian government throwing its Islamist opponents a few bones in an attempt to quiet them down. It is part of a repressive state's attempt to make up for what it lacks in democratic legitimacy by wrapping itself in the mantle of Islamic legitimacy. (Masoud 1999, 128)

When people were asked if they or someone they knew had been hurt by the Mubarak regime, a frequent answer was, "Yes. . . . for having a beard," a metaphor for being an Islamist. Sitting in a cafe across from Ain Shams University, a student described an incident involving his father, who sported a beard. One day his father was outside fixing his car when a microbus stopped and an officer from State Security got out. The officer approached his father and demanded that he produce his national identification card. The father asked, "Who are you?" and the officer replied, "I'm an officer from State Security." After inspecting the father's ID, the officer asked to see the phone numbers in his mobile phone. When the father inquired why, the officer said, "There are a lot of terrorists with beards." Another affluent man in his mid-twenties related that a friend from college had been "disappeared" for three years for being religious and suspected of knowing members of al-Qaeda. When he finally came home "he didn't know anything about our religion."

While some individuals suspected of Islamist affiliation were plucked off the streets by the security services, a more common practice was the targeting of frequent mosque-goers. A tour operator related the story of his friend, a man in his late thirties, who had been arrested for praying *fajr* (morning prayer). One morning the friend went to the mosque to pray and the police stopped him and asked if he was a member of an Islamist organization. Despite replying in the negative, the friend was arrested for being a suspected Islamist. In Egypt, those who pray *fajr* at mosque are viewed by the authorities as being potentially too religious. The friend was detained for over a year, and when he was released after the Revolution he was a completely changed man. He no longer spoke clearly and was often disoriented from being exposed repeatedly to electric shock torture. The tour operator was heartbroken by what his friend had been through. They used to go on trips together, and now the tortured man was a ghost of his former self. From an *imam* (preacher) arrested at his own mosque and subjected to electric shock torture to the son of a sheikh who was unlucky enough to be incarcerated after praying at mosque next to men who were being sought on terrorism charges, the number of arrests for being a suspected Islamist was endless.

ABUSE OF POWER AND ARBITRARY DETENTION

The final type of police conduct leading up to the Revolution that I will describe is abuse of power through arbitrary, and what may be deemed unnecessary, arrest. A 2010 report by Amnesty International described how Egyptian authorities used emergency law to detain not only terror suspects but also critics of the regime. Many were held without charges or trial, even when the courts ordered their release (Amnesty International 2010). In a 2009 Amnesty International report, unofficial sources suggested that the number of administrative detainees might have been as many as 10,000, including many who had been held for years without a trial or even charges (Amnesty International 2009).

Oftentimes, following a terror attack, state security conducted mass arrests, not only of suspects but also of family members of suspects, the purpose of which was to force wanted criminals to surrender by holding their wives and children as virtual hostages. In many cases, suspects were held incommunicado for weeks or months, being tortured during that time, and their male relatives may also have been tortured (Amnesty International 2007b, 10). While such arrests violated the constitution, which stated that anyone arrested must be permitted to communicate with the outside world and immediately have access to a lawyer, when it came to state security in Egypt, the contents of the constitution appeared to be more of a suggestion than a set of legal procedures to be followed.

Human rights organizations often focus on illegal police conduct related to detainees being held on suspicion of terrorist activities or for political dissent. However, there is a whole other set of examples, less often discussed, of everyday citizens being arrested due to police abuse of power, implementation of excessive penalties for infractions, and what may be described as lack of investigative competence.

Before the Revolution, Downtown had been a popular hangout for lower-class men who would socialize on street corners and cafes in the Borsa area. A 37-year-old father had gone to Tahrir Square to meet up with his friends. A police car stopped him and his friends and asked what they were doing there. They said they were waiting to meet other friends. The police officer conducted body checks on them and found nothing. Nevertheless, they were hauled off to the police station where they were held for two days. There they were denied the right to a phone call, and their families had no idea what had happened to them. While detained, they were asked if they were with either Kefaya or the April 6th Youth Movement. They were then asked if they liked Hosni Mubarak. As a condition for being released the men were forced to say that they loved the president. Later, they were let go with no charges. The father explained that the police would often pick random people off the streets and arrest them, even higher-class individuals. In his group of friends who had been arrested, at least one of the men was not from the lower class. One of the main reasons that the father had decided to protest in the Revolution was because of his arrest.

Some of the harshest police treatment was directed at the most vulnerable members of society without connections or even family protection. On an August evening, I sat down with a 21-year-old young man in a barber shop who looked much younger because of malnutrition. He had stopped going to school after first grade and had been working as a street vendor in order to survive. His mother had died and his father was unemployed, so he had to fend for himself at a young age. The issue of street vendors in downtown Cairo was a contentious one. Technically, street vending without a license was illegal, but Cairo was full of young men working in the informal economy due to the dearth of formal employment. One could find street vendors all over the city. One day a police officer arrested the young man for selling clothes on the street without a license, and he was held in jail for one week. All he was doing was "trying to be an honest decent guy selling on the street." With little education and no family support, he had had no other options.

Not only were upper-class individuals less likely to be detained than those from the lower class, but they were also more often able to pay bribes or use contacts to avoid arrest or detention. An upper-middle-class PhD student from Maadi explained, "I wasn't in direct confrontation with the police. Class determines the relationship with police. A girl from the upper class was not in direct conflict." Another upper-class student said he was not politically active because he "didn't want to waste time in the police station." However, he knew that if arrested he would be released immediately because he had connections. While on rare occasions members of the upper class faced arbitrary detention, as a rule they did not.

Despite their status, young affluent men were not exempt from police harassment. A young engineer recalled reaching a checkpoint and being asked for his national identification card by a police officer who spoke in a "disrespectful manner." Because of the way he had been addressed, the young man refused to show his ID. A higher ranking officer came over and again demanded to see the ID and wanted to know why it had yet to be produced. In the end, the young man had needed to pay a E£500 bribe before he was permitted to go on his way.

Situations even more precarious included suspected involvement in political activity, which almost guaranteed a problem with the police. A youth from Nasr City who had attended the German University was arrested when passing near a protest site to bring food to a friend who was taking part in the demonstration. The young man was arrested, but his father used his contacts to free him before he was transferred to jail. While those in the upper class were more likely to be able to use bribes and contacts to avoid arrest or to be released from jail quickly, it should be noted that they were not the only ones who had police contacts. There are Egyptian police who come from the lower-middle-class ranks, and one lower-middle-class student explained, "I had connections from a high level, so no one could touch me, but for people with no connections, they could get hurt."

CORRUPTION

During the time under consideration, corruption in Egypt permeated all levels of society, from favoritism by the president in awarding government contracts to friends and associates to the taking of bribes by low-level officials. In 2007, Egypt ranked 105 out of 178 countries on the Corruption

Perceptions Index (Transparency International 2007), and in 2010 it ranked 98, tied with Mexico (Transparency International 2010).

The extent of Egyptian government corruption was exposed after the Revolution when former regime officials and their business associates were investigated on corruption charges. The majority of cases were related to the sale of public assets, particularly land, at below-market prices (U.S. Department of State 2013). Some of the most prominent cases were against Hussain Sajwani, the chairman of Damac Properties, Ahmed Maghrabi, former housing minister, and Ahmed Ezz, CEO of Ezz Steel.

Ahmed Ezz was a steel tycoon with close ties to Mubarak's son Gamal. Involved in both politics and business, he controlled two-thirds of the steel market, was a member of parliament, where he chaired the budget committee, and was an officer and lieutenant in the governing party. Following the Revolution, Ezz was accused of having used his political connections, particularly Gamal Mubarak, to monopolize the steel market. Mubarak's sons were prosecuted for insider trading and corruption; Ezz was charged with money laundering, illicit gains, and rigging the 2010 parliamentary elections.

The corruption case of Ahmed Ezz was one of the more prominent ones, and he and Gamal Mubarak were the two individuals toward whom many Egyptians directed much of their anger. Members of both the upper and lower classes claimed that only a few families were running the country. The situation was described as "thieves controlling the country," "a gang ruling the country," and "a mini Egyptian mafia." However, there were many more instances of deliberate economic mismanagement beyond Ahmed Ezz and Gamal Mubarak. Following the Revolution, the courts found that many companies had been sold at prices below their value, including Shebin Textile, which was estimated at E£600 million but was sold at E£174 million. Al-Nasr Company for Steam Boilers and Pressure Vessels was sold at $17 million, but there were government estimates that valued the company at double that amount. Thus, economic liberalization policies and privatization processes instituted under Mubarak were tainted with extensive corruption. "Privatization meant workers' rights were undercut, companies were sold under value, and Egyptian production was destroyed" (Marroushi 2012).

In addition to the corruption surrounding privatization, there was also a problem of land grabbing and real estate fraud. At the November 12, 2007, parliamentary session, the People's Assembly deputy Gamal Zahran announced that the state had lost some E£800 billion through illicit privatization of Egyptian territories and benefits distributed to senior officials and businessmen, and it was found that the "land mafia" already had seized 16 million feddans of the Egyptian people's land (Schechla, n.d., 4). Later, in December 2011, auditors from the Urban Communities Authority issued report no. 755 claiming that former president Hosni Mubarak, Prime Minister Ahmad Nazif, and other ministers illegally acquired property and granted lands and villas to senior officials, select companies, and elites of other Arab states. These deals, based on direct executive order, led to the sale of property at much less than its actual value, violating Egyptian law (Schechla, n.d., 4). Other corruption headlines included the report by the Egyptian Initiative for Personal Rights (EIPR) that found that poor negotiations and corruption cost Egypt $10 billion in lost revenue between 2005 and 2011 (Mada Masr 2014). These losses derived from export agreements that locked Egypt into selling natural gas at below-market prices.

While most of what has just been described were high-profile cases on the national level, corruption did not escape lower-level officials. According to the U.S. State Department, even U.S. investors continued to report requests for bribes from Egyptian government officials (U.S. Department of State 2013). In a 2008 *New York Times* article, low-level corruption was exposed through a story on state-subsidized bread. An unidentified government inspector explained that the government sold bakeries 25-pound bags of flour for approximately $1.50, and the bakeries were supposed to then sell bread at a subsidized rate, leaving them with a profit of about $10 per sack of flour. However, the baker could also sell the flour on the black market for $15 per sack. After three months, if the inspector certified that the baker used the flour to bake bread, the baker would be refunded $1 per sack. Thus, a baker who used 40 sacks of flour per day over three months would be refunded around $3,300, a portion of which could be shared with the inspector. Given that the inspector was only paid $42 per month, he had a significant incentive to certify the baker's flour usage and then feed his family with the kickback he received (Slackman 2008).

Beyond government indiscretions was a type of corruption that permeated all sectors of society called *wastaa* (influence), a term used widely across the Arabic-speaking world. Many have described *wastaa* as how Egyptian society functions. It can be used to gain employment or a promotion, to be released from detention after an arrest, to have one's paperwork move faster through the government bureaucracy, or even to gain favors in one's local community. One survey found that 40% of Egyptian respondents believed that personal connections were more important than personal skills for securing a job (Roudi-Fahimi, El Feki, and Tsai 2011). In Egypt, a person needed *wastaa* to make his way in the world.

Many Egyptians were directly affected by corrupt practices in the country, from encounters with the police and the demanding of bribes to land confiscations. While descriptions of corruption remained mostly consistent between the upper and lower classes, the one variation that stood out was that corruption had reached such a high level that it prevented many upper-class businesses from functioning at their potential, while in the lower classes, corruption, including lack of *wastaa*, prevented more individuals from obtaining employment or rising in status. However, even the upper classes experienced employment problems due to lack of *wastaa*.

Many members of the lower class were infuriated by corruption related to police actions. The son of a *baweb* (doorman) had worked in tourism sales in a Sinai resort town. The police had tried to force him to become a police informant, and when he refused, he was imprisoned for three months. Another man related that prior to the Revolution he had made his living driving a bus. At checkpoints, the police would often take the man's driver's license and refuse to return it unless he paid them a E£50 bribe.

Other stories of police misconduct included people's observing police taking money from drug dealers and then permitting them to work openly in the neighborhood, and a 50-year-old fruit seller from Kit Kat who complained that police took fruit from her stand without paying when all she was trying to do was make a living and put food on the table. Finally, a 29-year-old unemployed man told of an incident where his father and brother went to the police station to make a complaint against another family. Because the other family was more powerful and had a considerable amount of *wastaa*, the other family made a counter complaint against his family saying that they had guns in their house. As a result, the man's father was incarcerated for one year.

The upper classes had just as many, if not more, complaints about corruption as the lower classes. In addition to stories such as a young man who had drugs planted on him by the police after his arrest for fighting, and the police officer from Rehab whose colleague was demoted and put on probation for refusing to beat protesters in 2005, there were a number of other accounts that made evident the upper class's dissatisfaction with police practices. An older doctor was troubled with the incompetence of the police and their desire to suppress facts to protect themselves. Thieves had broken into his clinic, beaten him up, and stolen from him. The police bungled the investigation, unable to locate either evidence or the attackers. Because the police were embarrassed about how the case was handled, they offered to give the doctor a gun license if he agreed to keep the incident quiet.

Beyond police offences, the grievances of the upper class related mostly to institutional corruption and land confiscations. An upper-middle-class surgeon lost his farm when a prominent businessman bribed officials so that he could take the land for himself for a development project. The surgeon was never compensated for the loss of his land. Another young man faced university corruption. His grades placed him at the top of his class and in a position to receive a teaching assistant job. One of his classmates had *wastaa* and wanted the teaching assistantship, so the university altered the young man's report card, making him fail a course so that his classmate would rank first in his class and receive the coveted position. The young man took his case to court, but lost. In fact, a number of people with whom I spoke had pending cases, or had previously filed cases, against educational institutions or government offices relating to corruption. Some complained that by 2007 the corruption in the country had become so dire that it harmed company owners and their ability to operate their businesses efficiently.

CONCLUSION

Economic grievances are not abstract concepts. They speak to real-world, everyday anxieties about the inability to meet basic needs. To go to bed hungry and be unsure if you can properly feed your children for the next month is a situation that no family wants to face. The majority of Egyptians spent their lives working long hours for little pay, trying to scrape together enough money just to make ends meet. The growing youth population looked to the future and saw no hope for something better. For many, studying hard to be an engineer led to employment as a taxi driver, if one were so fortunate. Even for wealthy youth who were financed by parents, there was indignity in long-term unemployment or underemployment. In a country with strict cultural norms and government laws that deter sexual relations prior to marriage, the difficulty of affording the expenses related to a marital union frustrated many in the younger generation.

In addition to the poor economy, the corruption that grew under the thirty years of Mubarak's rule permeated all sectors of society. In the final decade of Mubarak's presidency, corruption hindered the operations of even upper-class business owners who had once profited under the regime. Corruption led to economic inefficiency and was present in all sectors, from the government bureaucracy to state-subsidized bakeries. It prevented Egyptians without *wastaa* from obtaining jobs for which they were qualified, it created an unfair system of promotions and demotions, it allowed for private land to be seized without compensation, and it permitted the police to act with impunity, shaking down citizens for cash and using their power for their own benefit and that of their friends to the detriment of others.

Most taxing on the individual psyche was living in an environment of fear where parents taught children to keep to themselves, stay out of trouble, and avoid speaking about politics because "the walls have ears." For the lower class, minding this advice did not assure exemption from an arbitrary arrest. They lived with the understanding that they could be plucked off the street at any time for any reason and be imprisoned. Those who were so bold as to engage in political activity, or even publicly demonstrate conservative approaches to the Islamic faith, lived with the knowledge that there was a high probability of arrest. In Egypt, to be incarcerated was to be tortured. Everyone had heard the stories of someone who had been brutalized by the police, but in the years leading up to the Revolution, photos and videos accompanied those verbal accounts. The level of brutality was so horrific that many who participated in the Revolution said they would have preferred to be shot than to be arrested and tortured by the regime.

Long-term grievances contribute to explaining how a society reaches its boiling point, though a triggering event or events, along with active framing and mobilization of grievances, is still necessary to push people over the edge. Speaking about the torture and killing of Khaled Said and the regime's actions in general, one man said with rage and hurt in his voice, "Thirty years of being wronged, treating us like . . . Khaled Said represents the humiliation in the country." The economic hardships, the police brutality and abuse, and the corruption were all ways that the Mubarak regime robbed citizens of their dignity. People do not start revolutions because they are happy with their governments. A contributing factor to why people protest is that they are unhappy with their situation and attribute that dissatisfaction to actions taken by the regime in power. Many Egyptians reported that "people were fed up." When people have had enough and their grievances can be mobilized into actions, mass protests may ensue.

In June and July 2009, Mohammad Adel from the April 6th Youth Movement, along with blogger Dalia Ziada of the American Islamic Congress and other human rights activists who later joined Egyptian political groups such as the Egyptian Movement for Change (Kefaya), traveled to Belgrade to train in nonviolent protest tactics with Srdja Popovic of the Centre for Applied Nonviolent Action and Strategies (CANVAS). During workshops, Popovic had the trainees brainstorm on the social grievances that would arouse Egyptians' responses. In order to determine the social and political concerns that would mobilize the masses, organizers would have to return to Egypt, listen to everyday citizens, and then list their grievances. Knowing that a revolution could not take off without the involvement of the lower class, the April 6th Youth Movement focused on social justice issues and economic grievances that would incite the lower classes to protest. When mobilizing support for the Revolution, activists walked through poor areas such as Abbasseya, shouting up to the balconies, "Come on down. Anyone who comes with us will have a better life" (Egypt: Seeds of Change 2011), as well as the chant "Bread, freedom, social justice" (Egypt: Seeds of Change 2011). In a Frontline video an April 6th Youth Movement activist said, "Our mission is to get people to join up in peaceful marches and converge on Tahrir Square. We're going to a working-class district where poor people live, who are suffering from dire economic conditions" (Frontline 2011). A musician who participated in mobilizing efforts in the days leading up to January 25th recalled that he and his friends walked through the streets playing music, passing out flyers, and calling out to people, "Yella, Egyptians, come take your rights." On January 28th, once the Revolution was underway, a teacher observed others going from house to house cheering, "Don't be afraid. Come out of your house and protest."

Beyond the facts and statistics, the stories in this chapter tell us why people reached a point of frustration and what they were trying to reclaim when they demanded dignity and social justice as they protested in Tahrir Square. Now that we have evaluated some of the reasons why people were dissatisfied with the political situation, in the next chapter we will observe the mechanics of how they were mobilized online to protest against the regime.

3

Political Participation Online

From Facebook to the Streets

A young woman sporting a beige hijab and a bright smile stood in the center of Tahrir Square. Surrounded by thousands of protesters waving Egyptian flags and chanting "Down with Mubarak" and "Freedom," she gave an interview to Al Jazeera. Yelling enthusiastically to make her voice heard above the crowd, she proclaimed, "I heard about April 6th from Facebook. I'm not into politics. I just wanted to do something for my country, something positive. That's the happiest day of my life" (Egypt: Seeds of Change 2011). It was one of the first days of the 2011 Revolution and Egyptians were pouring into the streets of downtown Cairo to demand bread, freedom, and social justice. Weeks earlier, the idea of such a large number of protesters turning out to contest the Mubarak regime would have been unfathomable. However, following the successful removal of Zine El-Abidine Ben Ali in Tunisia, the Police Day protests organized by political groups and promoted by individuals on Facebook brought unprecedented numbers into the streets.

There has been much debate surrounding the role of social media in the 2011 Egyptian Revolution (Tapscott 2011). Although the movement that led to the ousting of President Hosni Mubarak has been dubbed the "Facebook Revolution," it is not the first time that foreign media has been quick to connect a social networking site with a popular uprising. The 2009 Iranian protests were labeled the "Twitter Revolution," and ever since there have been those who are adamant that social media is a vital instrument for mobilizing the masses, while others argue that social media is just a new means of communication in a history of popular uprisings that fared quite well without these new technological innovations (Tarrow 2013).

This chapter explores the role of social media, particularly Facebook, in the 2011 Egyptian Revolution, investigating how sources of information affected mobilization of individuals who were not members of political groups or movements prior to the revolutionary protests. The two main questions posed in the chapter are: (1) Does social media serve as an intermediary step between private preferences and the expression of public preferences, lowering the threshold for political participation, and (2) are there two political thresholds to be overcome, a lower one for going online and a higher one for going into the streets for political protest?

An increase in research on the role of social media in political mobilization occurred after the 2008 U.S. presidential elections when Barack Obama was able to garner the support of American youth through social media campaigns (Cogburn and Espinoza-Vasquez 2011). In 2009, Twitter served as a crucial tool in protest organization and information dissemination during the Green Movement in Iran (Karagiannopoulos 2012). However, it was the 2011 Arab Spring uprisings that sparked a surge in scholarship on the relationship between social media and political action.

While a few skeptics argued that social media platforms were built on weak ties and not conducive to high-risk activism (Gladwell 2010; Gladwell and Shirky 2011; Dajani 2012) or that authoritarian regimes' ability to monitor social media limited the utility of organizing on such platforms (He and Warren 2011; Morozov 2011), others turned to examining information flows and dissemination of news on Twitter during the 2011 Tunisian and Egyptian Revolutions (Lotan, Graeff, and Ananny 2011) or how social media benefited social movements (Howard 2011; Shirky 2011; Wolfsfeld, Segev, and Sheafer 2013). Eventually, scholarly conversations began to transition from whether social media was an effective tool for collective action (Alterman 2011) to how social media functioned in the protest mobilization process (el-Nawawy and Khamis 2013; Faris 2013).

My research revisits Mancur Olson's (1965) collective action problem and examines the relationship between social media usage and individual decisions to protest or not protest. While many works have focused on personalized social networking and the organizational processes of social media in relation to political action (Lupia and Sin 2003; Bennett and Sergerberg 2012), my research differs by outlining a multistep process in which I identify the triggering mechanisms, particularly emotional mechanisms, that lead individuals to participate politically online and later how online participation translates into protesting in the streets. Through my explanation of revolutionary bandwagoning online I also address the elusive issue of why the first protesters take to the streets, and I outline face-to-face interaction as a reinforcing mechanism for online mobilization.

Throughout my research, I found that the vast majority of individuals who protested on the first day of the uprising learned about the planned January 25th protests from Facebook. Non-protesters were more likely to learn about the protests from people in the streets or from a friend, colleague, or family member than on Facebook. I also found that on January 25th and throughout the 18 days the majority of both protesters and non-protesters reported television as a source of information on the uprising. However, because this chapter focuses on mobilization leading up to the January 25, 2011, protests, rather than mobilization during the 18 days, I explore the role of social media, which is more pertinent to the discussion than various forms of traditional media.

In this chapter, I argue that social media served the following four important functions in the few years leading up to the 2011 Egyptian Revolution:

(1) it facilitated the building of a politically conscious civil society online over the course of a number of years,

(2) it contributed to reinforcing grievances and mobilizing opposition to the regime through exposing corruption and human rights abuses,
(3) it allowed people to realize that they were not alone in their opposition to the regime, and
(4) it lowered the threshold for engaging in political participation and dissent by providing a relatively safe, easily accessible space for political expression in a country that outlawed gatherings of five or more people that could threaten public order or security.

In the few weeks leading up to January 25th, social media provided the information about when and where the protests would take place and allowed users to observe who would be attending and a potential number of how many people were planning to protest.

Theoretically, the chapter adds an intervening step to Timur Kuran's (1991) concept of transitioning from private preference to public preference and a reformulation of Roger Petersen's (2001) model of individual roles during rebellion. I argue that online spaces such as Facebook offer a third option somewhere between engaging in preference falsification and openly joining the opposition. While the revolutionary threshold, where the external cost of joining the opposition falls below the internal cost of preference falsification, may be very high for individuals joining the public opposition in the streets, the threshold for participating in the online opposition or simply professing one's true political opinion online is much lower. The significance of this chapter is that it investigates whether or not social media acts as a stepping stone to on-the-ground political action. While social media may allow for more people to express their actual political views online, it is important to examine whether and how that online participation translates to protest participation in the streets.

The chapter is divided as follows: First, I provide an overview of the way in which the Internet and social media offered a new space for the development of civil society under the restrictive Mubarak regime. Next, Internet and social media use in Egypt are viewed through the lens of political opportunity structures, following which I present my model on how individuals move from nonparticipants to online participants to protesters on the street. Finally, the chapter concludes with a discussion of the role of social media in the revolutionary process.

SOCIAL MEDIA: ORGANIZING AND MOBILIZING

For most of the twentieth and twenty-first centuries, Egyptian civil society has not enjoyed large degrees of autonomy from the state, and while state tolerance for intellectual and political dissent has varied, acceptance of opposing views has been very low (al-Sayyid 1995; Norton 2005). However, the advent of social media created new spaces for the development of civil society that were more independent of state oversight. In order to contrast the new online spaces, which fostered civil society and political dialogue in more open settings, with the more restrictive environment that traditional, on-the-ground civil society groups faced, I will begin with a few examples of the types of restrictions that various on-the-ground civil society groups and political organizations faced in Egypt.

One of the earlier laws enacted by the Egyptian government to impede political dissent was the May 30, 1944, Universities Law, as amended by the People's Assembly, which stated that professors could not elect deans of faculty. Instead, those positions would be determined by rectors of universities who were appointed by the Egyptian president on recommendation of the Minister of Education (al-Sayyid 1995, 287). The purpose of the law was to curb the political activism of academics. The state extended its control over larger segments of civil society in 1945 when Law 49 placed all charities under the supervision of the state (Abdelrahman 2004, 126). Under Law 66 of 1951, religious Nongovernmental Organizations (NGOs) found themselves overseen by the Ministry of the Interior (Abdelrahman 2004, 128).

Another significant change in the relationship between the Egyptian state and civil society came about with Law 32 of 1964, where all activities of civil society were placed under the control of the central authority (Ismael 2001, 442). The law, issued under Nasser, legalized the Ministry of Social Affairs' (MOSA) control over NGOs in Egypt. This new law gave MOSA the authority to determine whether an NGO had the right to exist, to dissolve organizations without authorization from the courts, and to participate in the internal dynamics of organizations. Violating Law 32 could result in penalties of up to six months in prison (Clark 2000, 171). According to Article 8 of Law 32, an NGO was not permitted to be established if the community did not need its services or if there were other organizations providing similar services in the area. However, the state, not the community, determined whether the service was needed. An example of an organization that fell victim to Article 8 was the religious organization Hizb al-Wasat. The state determined that other organizations were already providing similar services in the area; thus, Hizb al-Wasat was not given official authorization by MOSA to operate (Norton 2005).

Without listing all of the many laws enacted by the Egyptian government to limit the autonomy of civil society, a few others to be noted are Law 348 of 1956, which allowed for the dissolution of any NGO considered to be posing a threat to the security of the republic or republican form of the state (Abdelrahman 2004, 129), the Political Parties Law 40 of 1977, the main motive of which was to control and limit the efficacy and power of any political party (Ismael 2001, 439), Law 153 of 1999, which restricted activities that were political or related to syndicates (Fouad, Ref'at, and Murcos 2005, 116), and the 1993 law on Guarantees of Democracy in Elections of Professional Syndicates that gave the judiciary the authority to supervise syndicate elections rather than allowing each syndicate to be fully responsible for its own electoral process. The government used this law to "curb the increasing Islamic influence within professional syndicates" (Ismael 2001, 441). Government authorities were also able to limit the activities of professional associations, trade unions, and political parties, and prior authorization had to be obtained for public meetings.

Given strict government controls over political parties and civil society organizations (Ismael 2001; Fouad, Ref'at, and Murcos 2005) and the threat of imprisonment and torture for those who countered the regime (Clark 2000), I argue that social media sites such as Facebook aided in building a politically conscious civil society online in a space that was relatively safe and free from government oversight. It was more difficult for the government to identify and apprehend political activists operating online than at brick and mortar locations. Philip Howard defines "cyber-activism" as "the act of using the Internet to advance a political cause that is difficult to advance offline" (Howard 2011, 145). In the case of Egypt, this online community was built over a number of years leading up to the 2011 Egyptian Revolution.

Prior to the Revolution, social media was used as a forum for political discussion and expression and a tool for political organizing. Despite the apprehension of some Egyptians about speaking openly in their homes and on the street concerning their disenchantment with the regime, online the political discussion became quite intense and lively. One might even say that under repressive rule the Internet became the new site for de Tocqueville's town hall meetings. Political discussions and opinion sharing took place on the walls of Facebook group pages such as the April 6th Youth Movement and We are all Khaled Said (April 6 Youth Movement 2009a; Khamis and Vaughn 2012). Even those who were not so bold as actually to post on the wall took the lesser step of "liking" a political statement posted by another member of the group.

In order to understand how civil society is fostered online, it is important to outline the relationship between the core social movement organizations (SMOs) and the self-defined non-SMO members who politically participate on the SMO Facebook group pages. These non-SMO members may "like" a group page, engage in political dialogue on the page's wall, and "share" the page's posts, but because they are not involved in face-to-face organizing and do not attend physical meetings, they often do not consider themselves to be members of the SMO. While these individuals do not perceive themselves as being part of the SMO, they do participate in the group within the realm of social media. Thus, for the sake of conceptual simplicity, I define SMO "members" as those in the smaller organizational group and the loosely organized (or disorganized) individuals who participate in the SMO Facebook pages as part of the larger, extended group.

Olson (1965) contends that small groups are more effective at organizing for collective action than large groups. I would argue that when examining small groups versus large groups, the two do not necessarily need to be viewed as dichotomous; there can be small groups within larger groups. For example, the April 6th Youth Movement was a political group with a small organizational core. However, the April 6th Youth Movement Facebook page group was incredibly large, but was still run by the small organizational core. Thus, a group may be viewed as small on the organizational level, but may be larger on the participant level. The large group gets people talking, while the small group gets people moving.

The small group functions as core organizers, who plan events, make strategic decisions and form plans of action. They operate online as administrators of the larger Facebook group, but also offline, holding meetings in physical locations, securing sites for rallies, and organizing those who wish to protest in the streets. The large group encompasses those who "like" and/or participate on the group Facebook page, sometimes numbering in the tens of thousands, as well as the small group administrators. While the administrators of a page may post information, because the Internet is a minimally hierarchical space the Facebook group members as a whole promote political discussion. However, protests on the street, requiring greater organization, are facilitated by the small group. Thus, groups such as the April 6th Youth Movement comprise both the small group that organizes and the larger group that participates in political discussion online. The small group acts as an intermediary between online spaces and on-the-ground, physical spaces.

Two prominent Facebook groups involved in organizing the January 25, 2011, protests were the April 6th Youth Movement and We are all Khaled Said. Examples of Facebook use for political purposes prior to January 25th are provided by Wael Ghonim in his book *Revolution 2.0*, which offers a personal account of the author's work as an administrator for the National Association for Change and the We are all Khaled Said Facebook pages. On the National Association for Change page, Ghonim initiated opinion polls, as well as an online petition (Ghonim 2012, 45). The fact that over 15,000 participants completed Ghonim's first questionnaire (Ghonim

2012, 51) demonstrated that while there may have been only a few political activists protesting in the streets prior to the 2011 Revolution, there were thousands who were willing to engage in politics online. Ghonim also used his page to organize silent stand protests in Alexandria and other cities democratically, allowing page members to engage in discussion and make decisions on which protest tactics would be used. Other campaigns that took place fully online included one encouraging individuals to change their Facebook profile pictures to a banner of Khaled Said, a symbolic gesture in which thousands participated (Ghonim 2012, 67). Similar to We are all Khaled Said, the April 6th Youth Movement used its Facebook page to facilitate political discussion, posted political profile pictures, and created invites to on-the-ground protests. The April 6th Youth Movement and We are all Khaled Said's use of Facebook illustrates the broader environment of Egyptian small groups (SMOs) mobilizing larger groups (non-SMO members) both online and in the streets.

While I identify social media's function in helping to build civil society under restrictive regimes, it is also important to point out its limitations. Domestically, there is always a "digital divide," where some will have greater access to the Internet than others. I found that the digital divide in Cairo was based on social class, education level, and age. In my interviews, protesters who did not have access to the Internet were all from the lower socioeconomic class. Regarding non-protesters without access to the Internet, the vast majority were from the lower class. Thus, I found a correlation between social class and Internet access. While some lower-class interviewees did not have access to the Internet because of the financial cost, many were also unable to use the Internet because they were illiterate. Additionally, it was found that the vast majority of members of the We are all Khaled Said Facebook page were youth (Ghonim 2012, 113).

We have now observed the ways by which social media served as a facilitator and space for the development of civil society online, specifically under a restrictive regime. In the following section, online civil society and social media use will be situated within the social movements literature. Viewing social media use within the context of political opportunity structures will offer an initial framework for theorizing about how online civil society operates in the face of particular international and domestic constraints and opportunities, thus contributing to the formation of social movements and revolution.

POLITICAL OPPORTUNITY STRUCTURES

Identifying political opportunity structures allows us to understand the environment in which social movements and protest action take place. Political opportunity structures are the particular sets of variables that explain the variations in how movements pursue strategy. These structures are composed of "specific configurations of resources, institutional arrangements and historical precedents for social mobilization, which facilitate the development of protest movements in some instances and constrain them in others" (Kitschelt 1986, 58). Gadi Wolfsfeld et al. (2013) argue that in order to understand the role of social media in collective action one must take into account the political environment in which political dissenters operate. One important aspect of this principle is the "extent to which people have free and uncensored access to social media" (Wolfsfeld, Segev, and Sheafer 2013, 119). In this section, I place the Internet within the context of political opportunity structures in social movements theory to understand the constraints and opportunities for using social media as a tool for opposition in Egypt.

In my research, I outline political opportunity structures created within both international and domestic contexts and the interplay between the two. On the international level, the Internet is a completely free, non-regulated realm in which people are able to express any idea they wish with little fear of retribution. On the domestic level, political opportunities are determined by (a) the desire of domestic governments to control the Internet and go after those who subvert domestic Internet rules, (b) the ability of domestic governments to control the Internet and go after those who subvert domestic Internet rules, and (c) the ability of the opposition to remain technologically ahead of the government. The three regimes of Internet regulation are exemplified by the United States, Egypt, and China.

In the United States, Internet restrictions are limited to those who violate federal or state laws, such as viewing or distributing child pornography. Even local law enforcement agencies have the ability to track down violators by tracing Internal Protocol (IP) addresses. In 1994, Congress enacted the Communications Assistance for Law Enforcement Act of 1994 (CALEA), which further defined the existing statutory obligation of telecommunications carriers to assist law enforcement in executing electronic surveillance, as long as there existed a court order or other lawful authorization (Federal Communications Commission 2017). Arguing that the increased threat of terrorism called for expanding the authority of law enforcement to monitor the Internet, in 2010 federal law enforcement and security officials asked Congress to require all services that enable communications, including encrypted email transmitters like BlackBerry, social networking websites such as Facebook, and software that allows direct "peer to peer" messaging, such as Skype, to be technically capable of complying if served with a wiretap order (Salvage 2010). Despite increasing questions about law enforcement's encroachment on individuals' right to privacy, online freedom of speech is respected and Internet content remains free.

In Egypt, Internet content remains uncensored, but because free speech is limited, law enforcement attempts to track down those who voice opposition to the government online, considered a form of criminal activity. The Egyptian government's methods of curbing online political opposition have traditionally been technologically rudimentary. There is "no evidence of internet filtering in Egypt" (OpenNet Initiative 2009), and authorities "typically employ 'low-tech' methods such as intimidation, legal harassment, detentions, and real-world surveillance of online dissidents" (Freedom House 2011, 1). In 2005, the Arabic Network for Human Rights Information criticized the Egyptian Ministry of the Interior for putting into effect new rules that required Internet cafe managers and owners to record their customers' names and ID numbers (Arabic Network for Human Rights Information 2005). This policy was taken a step further in 2008 with a requirement that Internet cafes provide the names, email addresses, and phone numbers of clients before they were permitted to use the Internet. Following the provision of such information, customers would receive a text message on their mobile phone along with a pin number allowing them access to the Internet (AFP 2008). However, in practice, many Internet cafes did not implement the more stringent procedures and individuals were able to walk into establishments and use the Internet without providing identification.

While no one knows for sure to what extent the Egyptian security services monitored the Internet prior to the Revolution, all Internet users within Egypt were required to register their personal information with the ISP operator. "Those who buy a USB modem have to fill out a registration form and submit a copy of their national identification card" (Freedom House 2011, 6). These types of regulations also applied to home Internet subscribers. Additionally, the Egyptian security services used both legal and extralegal means to collect users' Internet and mobile phone records from ISPs, Internet cafes, and phone companies when investigating cases (Freedom House 2011, 7). One interviewee recalled visiting a friend's father at Amn al-Dawla (State Security) in 2010. He happened to walk into a room filled with approximately 40 to 50 people on computers tracking Facebook and blogs. He was not sure whether State Security created fake accounts or had the ability to hack into accounts. However, from two other interviews the picture became clearer that the government was able to do both.

A middle-aged man from Amn al-Dawla told me that he had gained political information from Facebook, but when I followed up with the question of whether he had obtained the information from friends on Facebook, he told me that he did not have any friends on Facebook. In a not-so-subtle fashion, he indicated to me that he was watching other people's political activity on Facebook as an agent of the state. The Egyptian government's use of fake online accounts for policing purposes is not new. Following the 2001 Queen Boat raid, when 52 men were arrested at the gay-friendly nightclub, gay hangouts began to disappear and people turned to the Internet. Consequently, members of Egyptian law enforcement began to pose as gay men online, persuade contacts to meet in a public place, and then arrest the contacts when they showed up at the agreed-upon spot (Kershaw 2003).

A second young man who participated in storming the Amn al-Dawla offices during the Revolution recounted how revolutionaries took mobile phone video of their findings, posting them on YouTube, and removed government documents from the offices, uploading them to the Amn Dawla Leaks website. Amn Dawla Leaks can be thought of as the Wikileaks of the Egyptian Revolution. One of the documents found by this particular interviewee contained information about the Egyptian government's purchase of software from a German company to spy on online users and extract their passwords. A list of activists and their passwords was also discovered. Thus, while the Egyptian government did not appear to have the manpower and technological know-how to run a sophisticated online law enforcement operation to track down dissidents, from the limited information I was able to acquire, it seems that they were attempting to increase their capabilities.

China's highly restrictive policy helps to situate the Egyptian strategy for Internet monitoring in the middle of the range between open and closed approaches. The Chinese policy is very different from that of both the United States and Egypt. In addition to tracking down those who engage in criminal activity and those who oppose the government, they take preventative measures by regulating Internet content. In 2005, while the Egyptians were asking Internet cafe owners to record customers' names and ID numbers, China's authorities were recruiting an Internet police force, estimated at 30,000, to work as censors and monitors (Watts 2005), prowling websites, blogs, and chat rooms to seek out offensive content. They also began using new monitoring software and issued a warning that all bloggers and bulletin board operators must register with the government or be closed down and fined (Watts 2005).

In addition to its Internet policing force, China has become infamous for its Great Firewall of China. The main contact points connecting China's Internet with the worldwide web consist of nine Internet access providers that control the physical lines to the outside world. Through the use of

Internet filters, traffic over the Internet lines can be restricted, and software is used to deny access to specific Internet sites and addresses (Hermida 2002). When passing through government-controlled gateways, emails containing offending words, such as "democracy," can be pulled aside and trashed (Einhorn and Elgin 2006). Finally, for companies that host their sites on servers in China, the rules are even tougher. Companies are pressured to sign the government's Public Pledge on Self-Discipline for the Chinese Internet Industry, "agreeing not to disseminate information that breaks the law or spreads superstition or obscenity or that may jeopardize state security and disrupt social stability" (Einhorn and Elgin 2006).

In the cases of the United States, Egypt, and China, the Internet as an international structure offers boundless opportunities for dissent, but domestic regimes restrict such opportunities based on desire and ability (table 3.1).

There is another factor to examine, however, which is the ability of the opposition to remain technologically ahead of the government. William Gamson and David Meyer state, "Opportunities open the way for political action, but movements also make opportunities" (Gamson and Meyer 1996, 276). These types of opportunities, created both domestically and internationally, allow opposition groups to circumvent government restraints. On the international level, groups such as Anonymous, an international decentralized online community of hackers, engage in

TABLE 3.1 INTERNET RESTRICTIONS IN CHINA, EGYPT, AND THE UNITED STATES

	China	Egypt	United States
Freedom of speech	Restricted	Restricted	Open
Social media for political discussion	Yes	Yes	Yes
Internet content regulation	Yes	No	No
Law enforcement tracks down online criminals	Yes	Yes	Yes
State enforcement capabilities	High	Low	High

international hacktivism in order to promote Internet freedom and freedom of speech. In addition to hacking Arab government websites during the Arab Spring, hacktivists set up a website during the 2009 protests in Iran that allowed information exchange between Iran and the rest of the world, despite Iranian government attempts to restrict news on protest events (Duncan 2009). They also provided support and resources to protesters, including guidance on how to circumvent government online restrictions (Hawke 2009). On the national level, domestic groups and individuals also share information concerning how to protect oneself from online identification by the government and how to go around government Internet restrictions (Mokhtari 2012). These tactics demonstrate the ability of movements to create opportunities.

THE MODEL: SPECTRUM OF INDIVIDUAL ROLES DURING UPRISING

Rather than looking only at how people mobilize, I also seek to explain the factors that determine whether or not people choose to mobilize and engage in online collective action under autocratic rule. The purpose of my model is to answer the questions posed at the beginning of this chapter: Does social media serve as an intermediary step between holding private preferences and the expression of these preferences in public, lowering the threshold for political participation? Are there two political thresholds to be overcome, a lower one for going online and a higher one for going into the streets for political protest? In order to answer these questions, I turn to Kuran's model as a starting point.

In "Now Out of Never," Timur Kuran distinguishes between an individual's private and public preferences, where private preference is effectively fixed at any given instant and public preference is a variable under an individual's control (Kuran 1991). Particularly under authoritarian regimes, people will engage in preference falsification, where the preference an individual expresses in public differs from the preference he or she holds privately. An individual's choice between joining the opposition or engaging in preference falsification will depend on a trade-off between external and internal payoffs (Kuran 1991, 17). The external payoffs of supporting the opposition are personal rewards and punishments. The net payoff becomes more favorable the larger the size of the public opposition. The internal payoff is founded in the psychological cost of preference falsification.

Given the very real threat of retribution for expressing one's preferences publicly under authoritarian regimes, different people will hold varying revolutionary thresholds, which are the particular points at which a person is willing to publicly engage in political action. As public opposition grows and private preferences remain constant, the revolutionary threshold is the point at which the external cost of joining the opposition falls below the internal cost of preference falsification (Kuran 1991). Anything that changes the relationship between the size of the public opposition and an individual's external payoff for supporting the opposition will change his revolutionary threshold. A fall in thresholds and a rise in public opposition are mutually reinforcing trends that may produce a revolutionary bandwagon (Kuran 1991).

Kuran presents a dichotomy between private preference, where people do not let others know their actual political preferences, and public preference, where people publicly join a social movement and engage in collective action. I propose adding an intervening step between private and public preference, which I will call "online preference." In this scenario, people subscribe to political Facebook pages, post comments on Facebook walls, and openly profess their political preferences online. However, they do not necessarily physically attend political meetings or protests, engage in political organization or mobilization, or take any type of political action on the ground. In such a case, people no longer engage in preference falsification, but they do not protest in the streets. They may adopt pseudonyms online, use high privacy settings on Facebook so that people cannot gain information about them, or simply assume that the government will not be confronting them in the same way that might occur if they were protesting in the streets, for which they might be arrested and possibly even tortured.

While Kuran infers that the distribution of thresholds is unknowable, Roger Petersen (2001) claims that the distribution of thresholds can be determined from a knowledge of community subsets. Petersen's thresholds are not viewed as static, but may be affected by "the operation of normative mechanisms emanating from one's own community" (Petersen 2001, 47). Individuals may alter their thresholds over the sequence of a course of events in a rebellion or resistance situation based on these mechanisms. While Kuran hypothesizes how small alterations in the distribution of thresholds may produce large differences in outcomes, Petersen's work attempts to offer more direction as to how one can understand overall tipping dynamics. Rather than modeling individuals as moving from private preference to public preference, Petersen views thresholds as a multiple step process. In the zero position, individuals are neutral, neither for nor against the regime. When individuals move from 0 to +1, the +1 level represents unarmed and unorganized opposition to the regime, such as attending a mass rally or writing anti-regime graffiti. The +2 position represents support of, or participation in, a locally based, armed organization, and the +3 position stands for mobile and armed organizations (Petersen 2001, 9). Petersen's model is richer than that of Kuran, since he identifies multiple mechanisms that cause individuals to move from each position to the next.

The triggering mechanisms in Petersen's stage one, moving from 0 to +1, are resentment formation, threshold-based safety calculations with society-wide referents, status considerations linked to local community, and focal points. In stage two, moving from +1 to +2, the triggering mechanisms are threshold-based safety calculations based on community referents and community-based norms of reciprocity. Finally, sustaining mechanisms, or those mechanisms that allow an individual to remain at +2, are threats and irrational psychological mechanisms (Petersen 2001, 14).

The mechanisms driving individuals from 0 to the +1 position are not community-based, but those leading an individual from +1 to +2 are. Moving from 0 to +1 represents unorganized, lower-risk, one-shot actions such as graffiti writing or showing up at demonstrations. The frequency of such actions reveals how many others are opposed to the regime and how many others are willing to engage in some form of resistance. "Thus, for the movement from 0 to +1, the reference group is society at large or the larger corporate groups in which the individual is embedded" (Petersen 2001, 24). In the move from +1 to +2, the battle must be fought in the village or workplace, at the community level, as the powerful regime controls much of the outside world but cannot easily infiltrate communities. Petersen places a high value on the importance of community because of the high levels of face-to-face contact and because the community allows potential rebels to cope with the high risk involved with recruitment. In the community scenario, an "individual's decision is dependent on the expected choices and actions of others" (Petersen 2001, 18).

By introducing online preference as an intermediate step between private preference and public preference, my model begins to look more like a fusion between that of Kuran and the one of Petersen, though the assumptions and mechanisms may differ. Thus, in my model, the 0 position is private preference, the +1 position is online preference, and the +2 position is public preference. While Petersen sees the move from 0 to +1 as unarmed and unorganized opposition in various on-the-ground forms, I see the move from private preference to online preference as unarmed, but not necessarily unorganized, and I limit the various forms of opposition to those conducted on the Internet. In my model, the move from +1 to +2 does not entail support for an armed organization. Instead, it indicates physical participation in a mass demonstration or protest in the street. I do not include a +3 position (figure 3.1).

Stage 1

The contribution that Petersen provides to this area of research is his determination of particular mechanisms that cause the jump from 0 to +1 and +1 to +2. Given that my case rests on the assumption of nonviolent rather than violent opposition to the regime and that I am examining

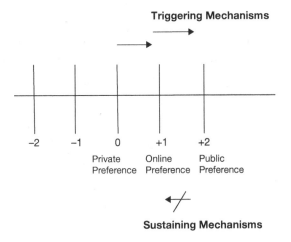

Figure 3.1 The spectrum of individual roles during uprising

online communities rather than village communities, my mechanisms are slightly different from Petersen's. Similar to Petersen's triggering mechanism in stage one, moving from 0 to +1, the triggering mechanisms in my model are resentment formation, threshold-based safety calculations with Facebook-wide referents, and status considerations linked to Facebook community. The mechanisms presented in this model are emotional mechanisms that constitute the process by which individuals decide to participate politically online and in the streets.

Beginning with the 0 position, I concur with Olson (1965) in assuming that individuals are not naturally inclined to join associations or groups. However, in his work, Olson focused on individuals residing in a democracy. Because this model looks at individuals living under repressive rule, we must go beyond the idea that people are not inclined to join groups to the idea that there is a disincentive to join or that joining does not even enter the minds of the average citizen. John Gaventa (1980) argues that in situations of inequality, the responses of deprived groups may be viewed as functions of power relationships in a way that power serves to maintain and develop non-elite quiescence. He poses the question: Why, in a social relationship involving the domination of a non-elite by an elite, does challenge to that domination not occur?

In outlining the nature of power and roots of quiescence, Gaventa presents three dimensional approaches to power, arguing that each carries with it differing assumptions about the nature and roots of participation and nonparticipation. In the One-Dimensional Approach to power, which is that of pluralists, participation is assumed to occur within decision-making arenas, grievances are recognized and acted upon, and leaders are representatives of the masses. Thus, political silence is a sign of consensus. In the Two-Dimensional Approach to power, nonparticipation is attributed to ignorance and indifference, but also, according to Elmer Eric Schattschneider (1960), the suppression of options, where power can exclude certain participants and issues altogether. If issues are prevented from arising, then actors may be prevented from acting. In the Three-Dimensional Approach, the government's ideological hegemony creates consensus and prevents conflict. Occurring in the absence of observable conflict, the situation allows for consideration of the ways that potential issues are kept out of politics "whether through the operation of social forces and institutional practices or through individuals' decisions" (Gaventa 1980, 12).

Gaventa's third dimension provides a useful model for understanding quiescence in Egypt and the state of individuals in the 0 position. The third dimension specifies the means by which power influences, shapes, or determines conceptions of the necessities, possibilities, and strategies of challenge in situations of latent conflict. An analysis of the factors at work can be approached through the study of language, symbols, and myths and how they are shaped or manipulated in power processes (Gramsci 1957; Lukes 1974). "It may involve a focus upon the means by which social legitimations are developed around the dominant, and instilled as beliefs or roles in the dominated" (Gaventa 1980, 15).

In Egypt, the Mubarak regime shaped the power process (third dimension) by promoting the concept of the "Islamist threat." This idea of the Islamist threat was that the only alternative to the Mubarak regime was the takeover of the country by Islamist extremists. Thus, it was better to have an authoritarian secular government than the terrifying "other option." The regime's argument was reinforced by incidents such as the Luxor massacre, when in 1997, 58 foreigners and 4 Egyptians were killed at the Deir al-Bahri archeological site in Luxor (Cowell and Jehl 1997) by members of al-Gama'a al-Islamiyya. Other incidents included the April 7, 2005, suicide bombing in the tourist area of Khan el Khalili in Cairo (Audi and Slackman 2009), the April 30, 2005, Cairo bus station attack by a man with a nail bomb, and another attack on tourists on the same day by two gunwomen near the Cairo citadel (Stack 2005). These attacks reinforced the regime's argument that without authoritarian rule the country would fall into the hands of extremists. As one woman with whom I spoke in 2005 told me, "The devil you know is better than the one you don't." Failure to engage in politics because of fear of extremism was articulated in depth by one recent graduate of the American University in Cairo. "I guess I was convinced by the regime of the Islamist threat, so while I knew there was a lot of clamping down on civil liberties, I was, selfishly so, kind of happy that they were clamping down on what I perceived to be a threat to my life and a threat to Egypt as well." He continued on, saying, "I was indoctrinated into thinking that any change meant Islamists, just like Mubarak convinced the West it was either him or the Islamists . . . so he convinced his own country."

There was also a second dimension of power that took place under Mubarak, when power dimensions prevented certain issues from arising. While Egyptians were known to complain about problems in the country, such as education and the economy, many were careful not to directly and publicly attribute those problems to the regime. Phrases such as "the walls have ears" were repeated, and many parents taught their children not to become involved in anything political but instead to mind their own business. One day when I was sitting in a home in Sayaida Zaineb a few years prior to the Revolution, I attempted to engage in a political conversation. I was immediately shut down and told to be careful about speaking of such things. There was a strong fear of State Security, particularly from the older generations who remembered the repression of the 1950s and 1960s. As one aspiring journalist stated, "I didn't feel safe thinking . . . torture." Thus, many were raised in a way that politics was suppressed from their consciousness.

The first triggering mechanism that leads individuals to move from 0 to +1 is resentment formation. Many of the political Facebook pages aimed to foment dissent through inciting resentment and even anger in the hearts of their followers. They did this by posting images of Khaled Said's tortured body, YouTube videos of torture and police corruption, and statements about the poor economy. These postings, along with those put up by individuals, were widely circulated on Facebook and angered individuals who viewed them. Gaventa finds that powerlessness caused by the third dimension is overcome when individuals go through the process of *issue and action formulation* where people develop a consciousness of the needs, possibilities, and strategies of challenge (Gaventa 1980, 28). Many interviewees said they were particularly shocked by what had happened to Khaled Said, as the same thing could have happened to them. Khaled Said was a young man from Alexandria who was arrested at a cybercafe and tortured to death by Egyptian police. Photos of a clean-cut, middle-class youth alongside those of his post-mortem disfigured body went viral. The event made many middle- and upper-class Egyptians realize that police brutality was not limited to the lower classes and that anyone could be affected. "It was this process of 'self-identification' with this victim, coupled by the wide circulation of his pre- and post-beating photos that have gone viral on the Internet, that made people extremely furious and outraged to the extent that they decided to take action against this brutality" (Khamis and Vaughn 2012, 149). One computer analyst went so far as to say Khaled Said "was our Mohamed Bouazizi," referring to the man who had engaged in self-immolation in Tunisia, sparking the Tunisian Revolution. It was the constant exposure to story after story of police abuse and corruption that began to make the political pot simmer, eventually reaching a boiling point. As individuals became increasingly outraged, they moved from simply viewing political stories to "liking," sharing, and commenting on them.

Regarding threshold-based safety calculations with Facebook-wide referents, Olson (1965) claims that people join secondary groups based on a cost-benefit analysis. In the case of Egypt, when an individual chose whether to post politically on Facebook or on a blog, the cost was very low because the Egyptian authorities did not have the technical know-how or resources available in countries such as China (Watts 2005) to track dissidents. Additionally, it seems that the Egyptian government focused more on the creators of blog and Facebook sites than on those who read the blogs or commented on them (Hill 2010). When interviewees who used Facebook were asked if they felt safe sharing or commenting on political Facebook posts prior to the 2011 uprising, the majority of protesters and non-protesters responded that they felt safe, they did not care, or they did not think about safety issues. One young man reported that he knew the government was monitoring Facebook, but he was not afraid because his political activities online were marginal compared to others. Another said he felt safe because "they can't arrest all the people." An even more blunt response was, "No one cared because Facebook was full of political shit. Everyone was speaking about politics. People you wouldn't imagine would talk about politics were speaking about it." The perspective for many was that only committed activists and organizers would be pursued by the authorities, while an everyday student or worker making an occasional political comment or post would not be given much attention.

Kuran's concept of revolutionary thresholds may be useful when examining online preference. As the number of individuals expressing preferences online grows, more people are likely to feel comfortable expressing opposition online. Facebook users can easily gauge how many others feel the same way they do by looking at the number of "likes" on a Facebook page. These "likes" embolden individuals to participate online due to threshold-based safety calculations that the government will not single them out if many others online express similar opinions. However, one must take into account distortions of the numbers resulting from international, non-Egyptian participation, which may also have a positive effect on Egyptians' expressing online preference. Thus, both the visible count of "likes" on a Facebook page and reinforcing participation from non-Egyptian, international individuals lower the threshold for political participation.

Other factors to be examined are how people come to participate online and how they initially gain political information on Facebook, as well as the mechanism of status considerations linked to Facebook community. Most people do not join Facebook for political purposes. They join for social reasons, to interact with their friends. A friend may post a political article on his page, whereupon another friend may comment on it for all their friends to see. Maybe someone posts a comment and a usually non-political person decides to add in his two cents, not intending to make some great political statement, but to respond to a friend's opinion. Maybe someone sees that a friend "liked" the page April 6th Youth Movement, so he goes and checks out the page to see what it is all about. The fact that Facebook is not a defined political space but is primarily a space for social interaction greatly lowers one's threshold for political participation in terms of openly expressing one's political beliefs. If one physically attends a political meeting, he is going with the intention of being political. If someone logs on to Facebook, he is not necessarily doing so to be political. Thus, Facebook captures those who are not necessarily politically inclined from the outset but who are, in the process of social networking, exposed to "political" messages. While the recipient's eventual participation in political discussion may be an unintended consequence of going online, the sender's message may be considered intended, as he posts political comments or articles with the intention that others will read them and possibly react to them.

When interviewees were asked whether they had read any political Facebook pages, specifically those contesting the Mubarak regime, prior to the Revolution, a sizeable number of individuals who protested in the 2011 Revolution (though fewer than half), but very few non-protesters, responded in the affirmative. Many more non-protesters than protesters did not have a Facebook account. Individuals without a Facebook account were more likely to be illiterate, socioeconomically disadvantaged, or older. What we can observe here is that protesters were more likely to have had a Facebook account than non-protesters and were more likely to gain political information from that Facebook account. The most popular political Facebook page for both protesters and non-protesters was We are all Khaled Said. A young upper middle-class singer explained, "Khaled Said was very emotional for me. It could have happened to any one of us."

Many protesters also followed the April 6th Youth Movement, while fewer followed Kefaya.

When interviewees who read political Facebook pages were asked how they became aware of them, a very few reported learning about them from the news, Internet searching, or face-to-face interaction, whereas a large majority of protesters and non-protesters responded that they knew from friends who either shared or sent invites on Facebook. A student from Nasr City disclosed the source of his knowledge of political Facebook pages, saying, "I followed We are all Khaled Said. My friend would send me blogs and pages about police brutality." However, it should be noted that only 12 non-protesters interviewed read political Facebook pages before the Revolution, which may indicate that exposure to political Facebook pages had an effect on the decision to protest. When those who were exposed to political Facebook postings shared by friends were asked if they themselves "shared" these postings (or news about events), posted comments, and/or "liked" comments on the postings, most protesters and non-protesters cited some combination of sharing, commenting, and/or liking political postings. "I was trying to educate people because people before the revolution were politically ignorant. They didn't know anything about politics. They were so passive," a young doctor from Maadi recalled. However, many more protesters were exposed to political posts shared by friends than were non-protesters. It should be noted that not everyone who read political Facebook pages actually "liked" the page, so the popularity of some of the group pages was underrepresented in the number of "likes" they received. What we can observe from these findings is that individuals on Facebook were most likely to learn about political Facebook pages and gain political information from friends' sharing, even if they were not on Facebook for political purposes to begin with, and that those who protested in the Revolution were more likely to have engaged in active political participation on Facebook than non-protesters. Thus, there is an indication that Facebook served as a stepping stone to on-the-street protesting.

The status considerations linked to the Facebook community mechanism are related to a key finding in Olson's research that incentives are not necessarily economic; they can be social sanctions and rewards. Olson recognizes that in addition to economic incentives there are alternative incentives such as personal prestige, social status, and self-esteem (Olson 1965, 61). The incentive in the case of Facebook may not be directly connected to politics. The incentive may be the personal prestige, self-esteem, or social status connected to the reading of one's post by others, their "liking" it, commenting on it, or agreeing with it (Tanner 2011). Therefore, what we can observe in a cost-benefit analysis of individuals' expressing online preferences in Egypt is that the costs may be political while the benefits may be social. When one performs a cost-benefit analysis, both the costs and benefits do not have to fall within the same category, whether that classification is economic, political, or social. In my research, the realm of perceived costs of openly expressing one's preferences online may be very different from the realm of perceived benefits of such participation.

Stage 2

In stage two of the model we examine how, and if, individuals move from +1 to +2, meaning whether individuals intensify their political participation by taking their online grievances into the streets. In this stage, the triggering mechanisms are belief in the possibility of success based on the success in Tunisia, status considerations linked to Facebook community, and threshold-based safety calculations with Facebook-wide referents, enhanced by community encouragement linked to work, family, and friend communities.

The first way in which Facebook brought individuals into the streets was simply to inform them that a protest was going to take place. Of the individuals who knew in advance that protests would take place on January 25th, most knew about them from Facebook. "Right before January 25th I saw that the group pages I 'liked,' We are all Khaled Said and April 6th Youth Movement, were advertising the protests and talking about it," a film editor from Faisal recalled. Even for those who knew about the protests from face-to-face interaction with colleagues or word on the street, the information circulating by word of mouth most likely originated from Facebook, as that was the place where the protests were announced and promoted. Linking back to stage one mechanisms, the majority of individuals who protested for the first time on January 25th or before who learned about the planned January 25th uprising on Facebook cited previous grievances, mainly economic issues, police brutality, and corruption, as the reason for protesting. Thus, for many, the grievances that had been enhanced by information circulated online led them to political participation on Facebook, where their grievances were further articulated and from where they were eventually propelled into the streets. A young finance trader from Zamalek emotionally explained that he was inspired to protest after continuously "seeing the brutality of the regime online and in videos." All he needed was a date and time.

The second way that Facebook caused individuals to move from +1 to +2 was through discussions and promotion of the success of Tunisia. Following Ben Ali's resignation speech, the We are all Khaled Said Facebook page added the word "revolution" to the advertisement for the January 25th protests, calling it "January 25: Revolution Against Torture, Poverty, Corruption, and Unemployment" and changed the page's profile picture to an Egyptian flag with a Tunisian symbol in the red section of the flag (Ghonim 2012, 136–137). References to the Tunisian uprising began to appear on the April 6th Youth Movement Facebook page on December 28, 2010, and on January 11, 2011, a picture of the Tunisian flag was posted on the page's wall (April 6 Youth Movement 2011).

When asked if the success of Tunisia had any effect on their view of the protests, almost every interviewee replied in the affirmative. The repeated line was, "If they could do it, we could do it," or "Because change happened in Tunisia, it could happen in Egypt." The responses of interviewees did not reflect pan-Arabism. The Egyptians interviewed in this study did not refer to a common identity with Tunisia. Instead individuals explained, "I didn't like when the foreign minister said Egypt isn't Tunisia. It was a bit provoking. Tunisia is smaller," and "Tunisia did it. As Egyptians we think we're stronger." Another student from Shubra compared Egypt to Tunisia, saying, "Egyptians are the bravest fighters in the world. It says this in the Qur'an." Thus, it was an Egyptian sense of pride and feelings of superiority to Tunisia that made them believe that they could, or at least empowered them to attempt to, overthrow Mubarak. Wael Ghonim was on point about Egyptian pride for being cultural and scientific leaders when he wrote, "Our pride had now been challenged: Tunisia had taken the lead in the quest for liberty.... The psychology of the proud and courageous Egyptian played a major role in enabling our country to follow in Tunisia's footsteps" (Ghonim 2012, 133).

The door that Tunisia opened represents the importance of perceived opportunities. From the time of the Tunisian Revolution, nothing about the situation in Egypt had really changed. However, the fact that the Tunisians had been successful in overthrowing Ben Ali caused a transformation in Egyptians' perception of what was possible. Beyond the issue of competition, a better way to understand the effect of Tunisia outside of the Arab nationalism context is represented by two quotes from individuals who protested: "It felt like another country in the region close to us. It was a different context, but something familiar. Similar socioeconomic conditions," and "Tunisia gave us inspiration. It was the same dictator with the same regime. It broke the barrier of silence." The success of Tunisia, which was promoted and discussed on Facebook, contributed to a breaking of the fear barrier and a belief in the possibility of success as Egyptians made their decision about whether or not to go out into the streets. "Tunisia was the spark that triggered Egypt."

The third way in which Facebook caused individuals to move from +1 to +2 was through the observation of the number of others declaring that they would protest on January 25th. This mechanism may be called "threshold-based safety calculations with Facebook-wide referents." Facebook groups such as the April 6th Youth Movement and We are all Khaled Said had sent out invitations on Facebook for people to attend the January 25th protests. Some of these invitations, such as the one from the April 6th Youth Movement, used the term *intifada* (uprising/rebellion). As the invitations were circulated, individuals would click the "join" button, indicating that they would attend.

As many who use Facebook know, the number of individuals who click the "join" or "going" button does not indicate the actual number of individuals who will attend an event. Some people will not reply to the invitation but will attend anyway, and some will say they are attending but will not show up. Thus, as many interviewees reported, it was difficult to gauge from invitation acceptances how many people would actually participate in the January 25th protests. However, they did know that more people would show up than at any other protest before. How did they know this?

On April 6, 2009, the April 6th Youth Movement organized A General Protest in Egypt, also dubbed "The Day of Anger in Egypt." Only 70 people accepted the online invitation to participate (Facebook), although 454 people did end up attending the event (April 6 Youth Movement 2009b). Given the large number of individuals who had liked the April 6th Youth Movement Facebook page, the number of actual participants for the event was very low. With turnout for many political events often in the low hundreds, despite hundreds, and sometimes thousands, of members of Facebook pages, it appears that prior to the Revolution social media was more effective in raising political awareness and facilitating political discussion than bringing people into the streets. While many were willing to take the risk of speaking out online, fewer were willing to take the greater risk of protesting in the street. During the 2008 Day of Anger, police were instructed to arrest anyone participating in pro-democracy demonstrations (AFP 2009).

The difference in the January 25th protests was that for the first time it was not 70 people who accepted the invitation but over 80,000 (Sutter 2011). While no one knew how many would actually attend, the drastic increase in the number of invitation acceptances indicated that the number of participants would be unprecedented, even if only 25% of those who accepted actually showed up. A computer programmer in his forties explained, "One hundred thousand accepted on Facebook. We knew it was going to be big. The build-up was huge." Thus, individuals were able to make threshold-based safety calculations with Facebook-wide referents through observing the number of acceptances to the protest invitation. In sum, if individuals were concerned about safety in numbers, they were relatively assured that there would be enough protest participants to reduce the likelihood of their being arrested.

Kuran's proposed explanation for why the first few individuals choose to leave their private preferences and expose such preferences publicly, by protesting despite the enormous risk to their personal safety, is that if an individual's "private opposition to the existing order is intense and/or his need for integrity is quite strong, the suffering he incurs for dissent may be outweighed by the satisfaction he derives from being true to himself" (Kuran 1991, 18-19). In this study, I found that social media allows individuals to make predictions of how many people will attend a protest, thus altering the reasons why the first protesters go out into the streets. Many individuals who are potential bandwagoners, i.e., people who only protest after they see others out in the streets but would not be the first ones out based on Kuran's explanations, protest on the first day because bandwagoning has already taken place online before protest in the streets has even begun. Thus, a new explanation for why the first individuals go out is that by going online they are able to estimate in advance how many others will participate.

However, it is not only the number of individuals attending but also who is attending. When one views acceptances to an event on Facebook, the screen displays the names of Facebook friends who have accepted the invitation. Petersen points to the mechanism of "status considerations linked to local community," where individuals gain status through participation and may be sanctioned for nonparticipation. While I would not argue that individuals can be sanctioned for nonparticipation on Facebook or that the community pressure on Facebook is equivalent to that which can be achieved through face-to-face interaction, there is something to be said for what I would call profile pic-to-profile pic interaction. Returning to the stage one mechanism of status considerations linked to Facebook community, it appears that by not only seeing the number of individuals attending but also that one's friends are attending, individuals are encouraged to participate because of the positive status attained through "joining."

My findings on status considerations and participation are not limited to the Egyptian case. In 2010 and 2014 an experiment was conducted on Facebook using an "I Voted" button. The treatment group had an "I Voted" button that they could click on to demonstrate to their friends that they had voted in the United States national elections. Similar to the January 25th invite, individuals were able to see how many others in the United States had voted and also how many of their Facebook friends had voted. The findings for 2010 were that 340,000 more people voted because of the "I Voted" button (Peralta 2014). Those notified that their friends had voted were more likely to vote than the control group who did not receive a notification, and the decision to vote seemed to be tied to the behavior of Facebook friends.

The final mechanism that we will observe in stage two is community encouragement linked to work, family, and friend communities. This is a mechanism that functions offline but reinforces the online mechanisms. Many interviewees who cited learning about the January 25th protests from Facebook prior to January 25th also heard about them from friends, family, and/or colleagues. After discussing the invitation that they had seen on Facebook and the number of people who were talking about the protests and saying that they would go, many friends, family, and/or colleagues decided to attend the protests together. Thus, the face-to-face interaction that Petersen describes was key to reinforcing the mechanisms that occurred online. After individuals found out from Facebook that there would be a protest, were aware that protests had succeeded in toppling a regime in another country, and knew that many others, including Facebook friends, would be attending the protests, their decision to participate was reinforced through face-to-face interaction with people they knew and through feeling assured that there would not only be many others in the streets when they arrived at the protests but also that they would have friendly faces going along with them. One must keep in mind that for the majority of participants, January 25th was the first protest they had ever attended. Thus, knowing that there would be someone who would attend with them and being encouraged to attend in face-to-face conversation by those close to them was just as important as knowing that they would not be part of a perilously small number when they arrived at the protest site.

CONCLUSION

The importance of this chapter is that it not only tests existing theories but also contributes to theory building by adding new dimensions to existing theories. It also investigates the mechanisms that lead individuals from being nonparticipants to active political participants. Taking into consideration the advent of social media, it also reconceptualizes Timur Kuran's work on nonviolent protest in Eastern Europe by including a new level of analysis, "online preference," and reconfigures Roger Petersen's model of individual participation in rebellion.

I argue here that social media, particularly Facebook, was the most important tool for disseminating information and mobilizing individuals to protest in the weeks leading up to the 2011 Revolution and on January 25th. I also find that while social media is not a necessary element of the revolutionary process nor does it always accelerate the rate of mobilization, in the Egyptian case, Facebook facilitated the building of a politically conscious civil society online over the course of a number of years prior to the Revolution. The majority of the population was hesitant to protest in the streets in the years leading up to the Revolution because of the harsh crackdowns on demonstrations by state security. However, a large number of individuals gradually became increasingly comfortable being involved in political discussion on Facebook and engaging in online political actions such as using political Facebook profile pictures. While many were unwilling to participate in public political discussions on the street, Facebook provided a safe environment with a greater level of anonymity where individuals were able to observe that they were not alone in their political ideas. The possibility to observe large numbers of people expressing their political views had the effect of lowering the threshold for political participation, as political discussion online became normalized.

I have demonstrated that Facebook mobilized the opposition through reinforcing grievances against the regime. As Facebook users were constantly bombarded with posts and videos exposing regime corruption and police brutality, they became more and more dissatisfied with the regime and its practices. Fomenting emotions of anger and resentment is the foundation of anti-regime mobilization.

Theoretically, the chapter tests Kuran's concept of transitioning from private preference to public preference and adds the intervening step of online preference. As technology progresses, we witness not only new mobilizing tools but also new mobilizing and protest spaces. Whereas at the time of the Eastern European revolutions the only possibility of mass gathering in opposition to the regime was through street protests, in the era of social media a new and safer space for political protest has been created through Facebook. Those who may not be ready to risk their safety and confront authorities on the ground now have the option of voicing dissent online for others to see and making a stand through political posts and the adoption of political profile pictures.

I also investigate here whether social media serves as a stepping stone to on-the-ground protest or whether individuals who protest online will remain in their safe space as an alternative to street protests. As we have seen, many who protested on the first day of the Revolution protested because of grievances that had been amplified by negative information about the regime on Facebook. Additionally, promotion of the success of Tunisia on Facebook had the effect of moving people offline and into the streets.

Reinforcing theories of information cascades and bandwagoning, I have also demonstrated how an individual's ability to see how many others plan to attend a protest, along with how many Facebook friends say they will be attending, affects the decision to protest and how these factors drew out many protesters for the first day of the Revolution. While Kuran's explanation for first protesters out centers on their being selfless individuals who possibly have a higher moral standard than the rest of the population, I demonstrate that individuals are able to break the barrier of fear quite early by estimating how many people will attend a protest based on the number of people who accept the Facebook invitation to a protest event and by the number of groups that publicly proclaim that they will participate. Thus, revolutionary bandwagoning takes place online before anyone even starts protesting in the streets. I find that Facebook not only mobilized individuals online but also served as a stepping stone to on-the-ground protests.

The importance of profile pic-to-profile pic interaction adds a new dimension to Petersen's theories of community-based and face-to-face interaction. While not everyone who participated politically online decided to protest in the streets during the 18 days, we are able to see how Facebook affected those who did. Thus, there are two thresholds to overcome, a lower one for going online and a higher one for going into the streets for political protest.

Investigation of the mechanisms, particularly emotional mechanisms, that lead individuals from being nonparticipants to active political participants is also done here. However, if we are to examine the Revolution in phases, the chapter only tells the story of political mobilization leading up to January 25th and the motivations of those who protested on the first day of the Revolution. In the next chapter, we will observe how the emotional mechanisms of moral shock and national collective identity led people to protest because of government violence against protesters during the 18 days.

4

The January 25th Uprising

Government Violence and Moral Shock

Jehan was a young receptionist from Haram. She had spent her entire life being apolitical, "minding her business and surviving." When the Revolution began in 2011, she could not imagine that protesters could successfully challenge the powerful Mubarak regime. Jehan was surprised and impressed with the large number of Egyptians taking to the streets, but protesting was not for her. By the fourth day of the uprising, January 28th, Jehan could no longer bear to sit in front of the television from the comfort of her home watching the extreme police violence against her people. Government forces were shooting live rounds at protesters, firing tear gas and water cannons, and running people over with police vehicles. She had to do something; she had to "help others." When asked why she decided to protest, Jehan replied succinctly, "The blood. The violence against protesters."

This chapter examines rational altruistic decisions to protest and the emotional mechanisms that produce such decisions. In rational choice approaches, altruism, "the motivational state with the ultimate goal of increasing another's welfare" (Baston and Shaw 1991, 108), entails costs for one individual and benefits for another. In a collective, political approach, political altruism can be defined as "all actions (a) performed collectively, (b) that have a political aim and (c) an altruistic orientation" (Passy 2001, 6).

During the 2011 Egyptian Revolution, many people decided to protest because of the violence against protesters committed by the Mubarak regime. This decision to protest was altruistic and based on the moral shock of viewing fellow Egyptians being shot at by security forces for demanding their rights. Thus, the decision of whether or not to protest because of violence against protesters entailed a cost of being injured or killed. In this chapter, I find that individuals' desire to come to the aid of those already protesting in the streets was a result of empathetic emotions based on collective identity and a newly formed vision of national identity born out of opposition to the Mubarak regime and its failure to meet the needs of its people.

The chapter begins with an outline of instances of violence during the 18 days and people's personal stories about their decision to protest in reaction to that violence. The following section discusses moral shock as a protest-driving mechanism and individuals' descriptions of experiencing moral shock. Next, I examine concepts of collective identity and nationalism, followed by an exploration of expressions of nationalism in twentieth-century Egypt. Subsequently, I look at the new form of nationalism that developed in Egypt in the decade leading up to the 2011 Revolution and how this articulation of collective identity based on victimization and a rejection of the Mubarak regime mobilized individuals to protest. Finally, I briefly identify cases where components of the moral shock emotional process are absent and explain decisions not to protest. I conclude with a discussion of the place of emotions in rational decisions to protest.

GOVERNMENT VIOLENCE AGAINST PROTESTERS

Findings on the relationship between government repression and protest are mixed, with some results showing that repression encourages protest

(Gurr 1970; Opp and Roehl 1990; Khawaja 1993) and others demonstrating the contrary (Gupta, Singh, and Sprague 1993), particularly in the short run (Rasler 1996). Rather than examining whether government violence accelerates protest, this study explores the process by which government violence activates a particular emotional mechanism that leads to the decision to protest. It also demonstrates that when key elements of that process are missing, people choose not to protest. In my research, I found that regime violence against protesters was one of the most common explanations that people gave for why they took to the streets against Mubarak on January 26th and the following days. When a high school student from Maadi was asked why he decided to protest, he responded, "Violence against protesters. That's why most people were against the regime. The regime tried to use power to get out of trouble."

In the years leading up to the Revolution, the Egyptian police were known to beat and arrest activists in the streets, and videos of police brutality were increasingly circulated on the Internet, but the Revolution was the first time that citizens observed the police take the additional step of shooting at, and even killing, protesters in public spaces. The extent of regime violence was unprecedented and disturbed many Egyptians who watched the reports on television or witnessed the brutality live in the streets.

On January 25th, as protests flared up in Cairo, Alexandria, Suez, Mansura, Beni Suef, and other areas of the country, the media reported that three protesters had been killed by regime forces in Suez (Fahim and El-Naggar 2011). These first three deaths had a shock effect on the psyche of the Egyptian population. The regime had actually shot its own people. That day, demonstrators in Cairo were injured in clashes with police; security forces in riot gear confronted protesters with water cannon trucks, and rock-throwing battles between the police and protesters ensued (Fahim and El-Naggar 2011). By nightfall, the police escalated the violence against protesters by attacking the Tahrir Square sit-in with shotguns and live rounds (El Hakim 2012). When asked why he protested, a salesman from El-Marg stated, "What I saw on the 25th; the violence. People I saw die in front of me. People were getting killed inside the Ministry of Interior vehicles." A student from Saad Zaghloul described watching from his balcony on the 25th as the police blocked protesters from marching down his street. When two protesters approached the police to negotiate, they were hit by volleys of tear gas unleashed by security forces. Witnessing the injustice of peaceful protesters' being subjected to the suffocating effects of tear gas and the reality of his own apartment filling with the gas, this young man felt encouraged to protest against the regime. In fact, there were many accounts of individuals near the Square but not initially protesting who were angered when they observed plainclothes police beating and arresting protesters.

By Wednesday the 26th, the police were firing rubber bullets, tear gas, and concussion grenades at protesters in Cairo in an attempt to drive demonstrators out of Tahrir Square. Television images displayed plainclothes police officers beating demonstrators, and the Ministry of Interior released a statement warning that it would "not allow any provocative movement or a protest or rallies or demonstrations" (CNN 2011a). A teacher from Imbaba recalled, "The police were there in the morning to protect the people, but at night they were beating them, also spraying people with water and tear gas. I saw a lot of people on TV where the police ran over them with cars." In addition to using water cannons and batons to disperse protesters, police fired live ammunition into the air, and both a protester and police officer were killed in central Cairo (Al Jazeera 2011b). The Committee to Protect Journalists claimed that ten journalists were beaten that day by Egyptian security personnel while covering protests (CNN 2011a). The attack on journalists only served to fuel the fire. When journalists are attacked, the media is often moved to increase its coverage of protest violence, allowing journalists to share their own stories of injury at the hands of the police.

The scene in Suez on the 26th was even more tumultuous than on the 25th. Medical personnel in the city reported that 55 protesters and 15 police officers had been injured (Al Jazeera 2011b). In Suez, police fired rubber-coated steel bullets, tear gas, and water cannons at protesters, and in Ismailiya the police wielded batons and used tear gas to disperse demonstrators (BBC News 2011a). In the northern Sinai area of Sheikh Zuweid, hundreds of Bedouin and police exchanged live gunfire, leading to the death of a 17-year-old man and bringing the national death toll to seven by the end of Thursday the 27th (Al Jazeera 2011b). The significance of the ongoing violence was not only that it was an unprecedented use of force by the police but also that the footage was broadcast on television for the whole country to see. Hour by hour, Egyptians sat in their homes watching their compatriots being shot, beaten, and brutalized by their own government, the most horrific images being played over and over again for maximum effect.

If Egyptians thought the violence that took place up to the 27th was shocking, government actions on the 28th were beyond any form of repression they could have imagined. In the early hours of January 28th, which activists dubbed the "Day of Rage", the government took the extreme, repressive step of shutting down the country's Internet and blocking text messages. Fearful of the potential size of the day's protests and the Muslim Brotherhood's call for its members to take to the streets, the regime attempted to stifle mobilization by cutting off communications. The act only intensified anger, and tens of thousands poured into the streets. A student from the affluent Zamalek area claimed that cutting off the Internet and phones "sent me into a rage. They cut off people's ability to communicate."

When the masses take to the streets posing demands, the government may address protesters with concessions, repression, or by minimally acknowledging protesters while facilitating their right to demonstrate, as occurred during certain periods of Occupy Wall Street. By opting for a repressive Internet shutdown that targeted the entire population, rather than solely those already protesting, the Egyptian government's response may have inadvertently accelerated protest rather than diffused it. A young man from Faisal related that he had protested on January 25th but then decided to end his venture into public activism. Later, on January 27th, there were rumors about an information blackout, but he did not believe that the government would take such aggressive action. Suddenly, while at Cairo Jazz Club, he experienced the blackout. He became "angry" that the government was demonstrating "full power" against its people. He recalled:

> Really I couldn't imagine how hard [the government] thinks about us, like this silly thing. "We'll do this to stop you." But it's not going to help if I just say, "OK they cut the Internet," and I stay at home.... The way that [the regime] is still treating these people who are speaking, who just want to be heard, and [the regime] is doing this ... because they have the control, they have the power. They used to stop people from talking before, but with this obvious way it was ...

He believed that the communications blackout demonstrated the government's fear of protesters and convinced him that protesters were gaining ground. Hence, after the shutdown, he returned to the streets, remaining camped in Tahrir Square for the rest of the 18 days. When a government responds firmly to protests, the aim is to deter others from joining and encourage those in the streets to return home. However, these actions may also signal to protesters that the government is unleashing its full authority because protesters have demonstrated that they pose a significant threat. Thus, government repression may serve to provide recognition to the power of protesters rather than the power of the government.

On January 28th, clashes took place throughout the country, leaving 11 dead and 170 injured in Suez. At least 1,030 were injured nationwide. Live television broadcast riot police responding to protesters with rubber bullets, tear gas, and water cannons, and BBC Arabic reporter Assad Sawey described his arrest and beating by plainclothes policemen in Cairo (BBC News 2011b). In a CNN running timeline of events, there were reports of a police truck driving on the 6 October Bridge randomly firing tear gas at point blank range. At 9:45 a.m. there were eruptions of automatic and single-shot gunfire in Alexandria, and at 9:49 a.m. Al-Masry Al-Youm newspaper reported on Twitter that one woman had been killed in the Cairo clashes. At 11:34 a.m. a Cairo protester was shot when he picked up a rock to throw at police (CNN 2011c). As protesters began to burn government buildings, a ship captain from Sayaida Zaineb recalled, "I didn't believe the Sayaida Zaineb police station was on fire until a friend woke me up and told me. I saw with my own eyes a police car running over people and police shooting people." After viewing the horror firsthand, the captain made his decision to protest "because the police were so hard with the people and took them to jail."

Stories of regime brutality and death continued throughout the day. A 25-year-old man from Mansheyat Nasr claimed that he had sympathized with the protesters from the beginning. "When I saw the hungry . . . a lot of people with good education and don't work. I'm not educated, but thank god I have work." However, "After seeing violence on the Friday of Anger, I went out."

On Saturday the 29th, reports from the day before continued to pour in and new incidents of regime repression were exposed to the Egyptian public (Bhatty and Hirst 2011). In Beni Suef, 17 people attempting to attack two police stations were shot dead by police. At 5:38 p.m. witnesses claimed that there were snipers on the roof of the Ministry of Interior building in Cairo firing live rounds at anyone attempting to approach the building. A middle-aged man who worked in the tourism industry described the violence he experienced firsthand: "There were gunshots out of nowhere. You would be standing next to someone and the person would fall. We didn't know where the shots were coming from." The severe violence against protesters had a profound effect on those sitting at home. A young circus performer, citing the killing of protesters as the reason he decided to protest, remembered, "One of my friends got injured." For some it was watching the images of unknown citizens being assaulted that caused them to go out into the streets; for others it was knowing people who had been hurt or killed personally.

One alleged regime action that infuriated the public was the release of prisoners onto the streets. While Nile TV reported that hundreds of prisoners had escaped from a Fayoum prison (Ahmed, Abdoun, and Elyan 2011), many did not see the event as an "escape" but instead as a "release" orchestrated by the government to wreak havoc on the population. Police had virtually disappeared from the streets, and men with metal bars and knives were roaming the city of Cairo. A development analyst from Nasr City described her experience with the lack of security:

> It was the first time I felt scared in Cairo. . . . I was on a train going back from Alexandria and there wasn't anyone collecting the tickets. It was the day when the prisoners escaped. There were prisoners on the train. I never felt so scared, and then they had all these army men come with guns, searching for prisoners.

The news covered the widespread looting in Cairo, and citizens, armed with machetes and hockey sticks, set up popular committees to protect their residences and local streets. People barred themselves in their homes and were terrified by rumors of rape and armed robbery. Laila's account describes the fear and anger that the residents of Maadi endured.

Laila had never been so scared in her life. "There was no police, no army, no control over anything. . . . It was the hardest night ever." On January 29th, Laila and her mother were alone in their home in Maadi. Rumors were spreading that people were being kidnapped, houses were being robbed, women were being raped, and cars were being vandalized. Everyone was talking about the threats in the street, but no one could confirm which stories were true and which were not.

The police had abandoned their posts in response to the anti-police protests, leaving the Cairo population unprotected and afraid. "We had no one; we had no protection." Laila's mother gathered together knives, sticks, and anything else in the house that could be used as a weapon. "It wasn't a comedy show, it was real." When Laila went to her balcony and looked down on the street below, she saw neighbors who had formed a popular committee to protect the neighborhood. There were three men around 60 years old, two boys around 15 years old, and the *baweb* (doorman). "These were the protectors of the realm. These were the only responsible men out there." If they saw a suspicious car coming or thieves approaching, the popular committee would loudly bang on building walls or clang with iron and yell "asha asha," which means wake up, wake up. Sometimes women would descend from the buildings to carry food to the men standing guard outside.

Laila and her mother were unable to sleep the whole night and were left isolated from friends and family because the government had cut the phone lines. When the landlines resumed operation, Laila phoned a friend in Nasr City who related stories she had heard about thugs and thieves raping women, breaking into houses, killing people, and stealing cars. "What kind of jungle are we living in? What kind of regime just lets the thieves and the thugs out to kidnap and rape people? There was no protection." Laila explained:

> We were so scared. I got angry. I don't care what happened in the protests; you shouldn't just let the thieves and thugs out to scare the people off. And I was also angry first because of the people dying and then the reaction. . . . It's like we're going to punish you, we're going to show you who the big guy is here. You can't just live without us. We are everything. The regime, the police, the Ministry of the Interior, we are the big boss here. But they're not. That got me so pissed off, the whole police thing . . . and they let a lot of thieves and thugs out. That was a big thing. Five hundred prisoners escaped from I don't know which prison and they're now on the streets killing and raping women and the police are not doing anything because they have orders. Ten-year-old boys and twelve-year-old boys were actually the ones keeping the peace. It was crazy. But they did a good job actually.

By 11:18 p.m. on January 29, 2011, AFP news agency reported that the death toll from the first five days of protesting had reached 102 and that thousands were wounded (Bhatty and Hirst 2011).

Battle of the Camel

In addition to the government violence in the first week of the Revolution, particularly on the days of the 25th, 28th, and 29th, another frequently cited incident that impacted decisions to protest was the "Battle of the Camel." Leaving 11 dead and over 600 injured, this move to end the protests only provided the Revolution with more momentum.

Around noon on February 2nd, pro-Mubarak demonstrators began to approach Tahrir Square from the Abdel Moneim Riyad opening, led by Abdel Nasser El-Gabry and Youssef Khattab, who were members of parliament (Kortam 2013). Then, as the world looked on, men on horseback and camels rode into the Square carrying whips and clubs, viciously attacking protesters. It was one of the most shocking and horrifying incidents of the Revolution. Later, there were reports that the two members of parliament had hired the thugs from the Nazlet El-Saman district of Cairo (Fathi 2012). During the Battle of the Camel, a middle-aged father from Maadi was whipped twice by a horseman. In response, the man pulled one of the riders off of his horse. It was "like the old Egyptian movies of people in the time before Islam where people rode horses and made war." Protesters determined that the riders had been paid by the Mubarak regime when they uncovered E£1,000 in the pocket of one of the horsemen.

Pro-regime marches continued to approach the Square from all directions and one witness reported, "In a matter of minutes, we were outnumbered. We were about 20,000 and they were at least 70,000" (Fathi 2012). The pro-regime demonstrators raided protesters' tents and ripped down banners, but anti-regime protesters fought back. As busloads of regime supporters continued to be unloaded near the Square and assailants threw Molotov cocktails at protesters, anti-regime protesters began to break the pavement in Tahrir Square, hurling stones back at their attackers. Toward the evening, as police persistently fired live ammunition at anti-regime protesters, anti-regime protesters were able to push the pro-regime attackers out of the Square.

On the previous evening, February 1, 2011, President Mubarak had given a speech promising that he would not run for office when his presidential term ended and had spoken of his love for Egypt, vowing that he would remain in the country until his death. The speech touched the hearts of many Egyptians, and protesters began to leave the Square. One protester from Shubra explained that after the Mubarak speech, he changed his mind about protesting because he felt sorry for Mubarak, "but then the Battle of the Camel happened the next day and I changed my mind back to being against Mubarak." An engineer from Mounira initially decided to protest "because I saw people killed.... After the speech some friends said that they won't go out and protest again. I told them, 'You said this because you didn't lose anyone. If one of your friends were killed, you wouldn't say this.'" The next day, following the Battle of the Camel, his friends decided to return to the Square.

It is clear that violence against protesters was a major factor in individual decisions to protest. As one protester put it:

> I didn't think [the protests] were going to be big enough, and actually they wouldn't have been big enough unless the brutal killing and brutality started. So it wasn't going to be that big unless the police started to be very aggressive against the protesters. That's when people started to go, started to take actions, and the numbers went down to the streets.

However, the response "violence against protesters," to describe why individuals decided to take to the streets only explains why they protested. The aim of this chapter is not only to understand an aspect of why they made the decision but also what mechanisms were involved in the decision-making process. Thus, the next section of the chapter examines *how* violence against protesters led individuals to abandon the safety of their homes and protest, knowing that the government was shooting at demonstrators.

MORAL SHOCK

Jasper (1998) divides emotions in social movements into two categories: affective, which are usually based on stable bonds and loyalty (sentiment), and reactive, which are transitory, context-specific emotions, usually in reaction to information and events. The power of affect emotions may be understood by Affect Control theory, which describes the effectiveness of persuasion in appealing to an individual's fundamental sentiment about things in society (Berbrier 1998, 440). In contrast, reactive emotions are shorter-term responses to events and are "evoked by external stimuli" (Sin 2009, 92). Rather than a binary, "affects and reactive emotions are two ends of a continuum with a grey area in the middle" (Jasper 1998, 402). Two emotions that are seen as primarily reactive are anger and outrage. Shock, anger, and outrage are emotions that may develop outside of a movement or even before individuals join a movement.

When an event evokes such a strong sense of outrage that an individual becomes inclined toward political action, the emotional mechanism at play is termed "moral shock" (Jasper and Poulsen 1995, 498). In Egypt, moral shock was the emotional mechanism triggered by government violence against protesters that led non-activist individuals to make the initial decision to protest. The types of events that produce moral shock are usually public, highly publicized, and unexpected. Emotions are tied to moral values; therefore, shock and/or outrage may arise when there is a perceived infraction of moral rules. Emotions may be conditioned by a person's expectations, which derive from knowledge about appropriate conditions in the world (Hochschild 1983, 219-221; Jasper 1998, 401). In the case of the Egyptian Revolution, moral shock is the emotional mechanism that best explains why violence against protesters led others to take to the streets. The emotion encompasses not only the "shock" people experienced when presented with unexpected images of violence against their protesting compatriots but also the assault on moral values felt by those who perceived what was taking place as an injustice.

Moral shock leads to protest when there is someone to blame for the events that elicit the emotion. During the 18 days, citizens blamed Mubarak and his regime for the slaughter in the streets. "Protesters were peaceful and didn't do anything wrong," a student from Heliopolis declared, implicating Mubarak as responsible for violence committed against protesters and absolving protesters as innocent victims of the brutal regime. When a particular institution or government is assigned blame for violating moral standards, a common response is moral outrage (Reed 2004). Similar to moral shock, moral outrage is a specific type of anger that is ignited in individuals and acts as an emotional mechanism, one that orders preferences in a manner that impels people to end these moral transgressions against others whom they might not even personally know. From the first few days of the 2011 protests, when citizens fell at the hands of the regime, the Egyptian people began to experience this outrage. "What happened in Suez . . . seven people died in the first three days. That made all Egyptians angry."

Injustice is the unacceptable condition most closely associated with "the righteous anger that puts fire in the belly and iron in the soul" (Gamson 1992, 32). The outrage felt by Egyptians, as they looked on in horror, sprang from the sense of injustice associated with the killing of protesters who were only demanding their rights. These were rights to which many Egyptians believed all citizens were entitled. "What really made me go was the amount of brutality and amount of torture that I saw. I couldn't stay at home while other people were getting killed for just asking for their rights." According to this young woman, it was "the emotional . . . even if the number wasn't that great and I saw the same thing, I would have protested." Thus, a common perception was that protesters were justified in demanding "bread, freedom, and social justice" while the Mubarak regime was unjust for shooting protesters asking the state to fulfill these basic needs. This sense of injustice underpinned moral shock and moral outrage.

The mobilizing effects of moral shock founded on a perception of injustice were anticipated by anti-regime activists prior to the Revolution. In June 2009, Mohammad Adel from the April 6th Youth Movement traveled to Belgrade to train in nonviolent protest tactics with Srdja Popovic of the Centre for Applied Nonviolent Action and Strategies (CANVAS). In workshop discussions on possible framing tactics for the April 6th Youth Movement, Popovic pushed Adel to think about frames that would be effective in mobilizing the Egyptian population. They concluded that frames using bread-and-butter issues would be more potent than political frames and the Mubarak regime would have trouble repressing protesters demanding social benefits such as economic resources or better health care. Popovic claimed that in theory, when the government cracks down on people asking for social benefits, protesters become angrier and larger numbers may take to the streets in solidarity. However, if protesters demand democracy, at the slightest threat of force from the regime they may return to their homes. Popovic anticipated that, applying this theory to Egypt, there would be different reactions based on the two frames: economic resources would be viewed as a basic right, while the meaning of democracy would not be clear in the minds of many. Thus, the continuation of protest, despite the government's violent response to the demands for what people considered their basic rights, confirmed Popovic's theory.

Moral outrage is a powerful motivator and mobilizer. Moral outrage "plays a significant role in the delegitimation of the polity and the engendering of collective action whenever state conduct is perceived as arbitrary, as violating willy-nilly what is socially accepted as 'just,' 'allowable' punishment, and 'bearable' suffering" (Reed 2004, 667). A 21-year-old media company manager proclaimed, "I protested because of the violence against the protesters, and it wasn't right. [The regime] was using guns, tear gas, and rubber bullets. It was really horrible and I felt bad about that. So I decided to go into the streets." When asked about her analysis of the costs and benefits of protesting, a student from Maadi responded:

> The injustice you feel, you wouldn't think of the benefits. You just need to help. Like when you are in the street seeing some guy beating down a woman and harassing her and raping her. You don't think OK if I go defend her I will have any benefit because you know he may take you also. He may harass you and you might not be able to stand up to him, but you can't just stand there and watch.

Verhulst and Walgrave (2009) argue that protest participation barriers are more difficult to overcome for "first-timers." In order to motivate first-time protesters, extra incentive is needed. The emotional reaction of being scandalized by what they may deem immoral actions drives first-time protesters to make the decision to protest. Moral outrage may be placed in Pearlman's (2013) emboldening, rather than dispiriting, cluster of emotions, where moral shock/outrage encourages individuals to protest.

What follows is an excerpt from an interview with an upper-middle-class oncologist who outlined the experiences that led to her decision to protest. Prior to the Revolution she was apolitical. She described the shock and horror of the violence she witnessed and how the sense of injustice led her to protest against the regime and care for victims in Tahrir Square.

Mariam worked in the oncology department at El-Demerdash public hospital. On the night of the 28th, she was in the middle of working a 24-hour shift and decided to follow the news on television late in the evening when her department was inactive. Word began to spread on television and throughout the hospital that there was gunfire in Tahrir Square and that the situation was serious. Those who were able began to make their way to the Square, but Mariam had to remain at the hospital. El-Demerdash is in the Abasaya district of Cairo, but from the hospital it was also possible to see the 6th of October Bridge and Ramses. As Mariam looked out, she observed people running while government tanks rolled down the streets.

Suddenly, the government cut the phone lines and Internet, and the doctors' only access to the outside world was Al Jazeera. The patients, nurses, and doctors panicked as they attempted to contact their homes and were unable to do so. Mariam abandoned her post to see what was happening in the ER and surgery rooms. She found friends who worked in intensive care standing on the street outside the hospital. They told her, "We have many, many gunshot wounds and people are dying inside." There were ambulances everywhere. Ambulances would rush to the doors of the ER and five or six people would be thrown from the ambulance. Then the vehicle would speed back toward the Square to retrieve more of the injured.

El-Demerdash hospital had a reputation for treating the lower class. As Mariam stood in front of the ER, a very expensive car pulled up to the curb. The car window rolled down and the woman inside called out, 'They told me my son got shot." The distraught mother continued to scream, "My baby's shot; my son is shot. They told me they brought him to Demerdash. Where can I find him?" While the woman cried in panic, a young boy, presumably her son, sat crying beside her. Mariam replied, "Everyone who has been wounded is rushed to the ER." The woman sprinted out of the car toward the hospital doors.

Mariam entered the ER and there were patients everywhere, both upper and lower class, mostly men. She had never seen anything like the scene in front of her. There were not enough beds to accommodate all the patients and some were sitting on the floor. "There was every kind of wound there, people with their eyes blown, people with bullets . . . and a lot of injuries just from the gas."

By the next morning, the blood bank was running out of blood because there were not enough donors to meet the demands of the large number of wounded. Around 7:00 a.m., Mariam returned to the ER and encountered a friend who worked as an anesthesiologist in the operating room of general surgery. Her friend recounted the events of the night before when the onslaught of wounded protesters prevented physicians from conducting anything more than exploratory surgery and there was little time to clean wounds. The body count was so overwhelming that doctors were unable to issue death certificates for all the deceased. "I remember them saying that the count was 31 dead people at Demerdash, but this wasn't official. I don't think there was ever an official number and most of them didn't have death certificates with a real cause."

Mariam made her decision to protest after the events on the 28th, the Friday of Rage. It was the first time in her life that she "found an interest in politics." As she put it, "On the 28th I started to be political. I decided I would go," though she did not actually protest until two days later on the 30th. "The reason that triggered the protest for me was seeing all these people dying and bleeding in front of me and the women crying and screaming. People were dying for no reason. They were young people, they looked like normal people. I got very pissed. I'm a doctor. I've seen many people dying every day, but not like that. It was so, so cruel. They got shot, they got beat up, and they were dying, and they did nothing wrong." Demerdash was the third hospital from Tahrir Square, not the first, and still her hospital was engulfed in chaos. "So, this is when I decided that I can't believe this is happening in my country. I've never seen anything like that before, and I decided that there has to be something done."

Reed (2004) finds that morally shocking events not only focus a potential participant's attention on a particular problem but also offer a "cognitive space" for re-evaluating an existing political order based on moral standards or the urgency of the social climate (Reed 2004, 662). In Mariam's story, we observe how the morally shocking nature of the events on the 28th led her to re-evaluate her approach, or lack of approach, to the regime, propelling her into the streets to protest. Following the recognizable pattern of moral shock, Mariam indicated her empathy for protesters and sense that an injustice was occurring when she referred to the protesters as "normal people" who "did nothing wrong."

As revolutionary violence moved past the first few days, the division between the just and unjust became more solidified in people's minds. A swimming instructor from Sayaida Zaineb who described being "angry about government violence" as the reason for his decision to protest used the term "martyrs" to describe protesters who had been killed. His use of the word "martyr" implied that he viewed protesters as dying not only for a just cause but also for a sacred one. Putting dead protesters on a pedestal, making them infallible martyrs, exemplified people's distinction between those who were justified in their actions and those who represented injustice.

Moral outrage can also serve as a revolutionary accelerator (Reed 2004, 656) and sustainer. A 24-year-old woman who worked as a designer recounted, "On TV I saw a guy killed who I saw in Tahrir Square the day before. I could tell by his shirt. That's what kept me protesting." While many people attributed their initial decision to protest to violence against people they did not know, as the Revolution continued they experienced additional shocks when friends and/or family were killed in the protests. These additional shocks had a sustaining effect and caused them to return to the streets day after day. "Once you start spilling blood, there is no stopping it. If I'm a parent and my child got killed, I'd move mountains. Same if I'm a child with parents who got killed." A young graphic designer said, "Before I was happy with my career and salary. My family and I didn't get into trouble. No problems with anyone. My father and uncle had good conversations with Suzanne Mubarak. Two friends got killed at Qasr El-Nil. That's why I kept going out." While some works (Verhulst and Walgrave 2009) point to moral shock as a mechanism for instigating first-time protest, I argue that, in addition, a sequence of additional shocks incurred while protesting may serve as a sustaining mechanism. Many protesters demonstrated during the day and returned home at night. Thus, each day, or on many days, they were faced with a new decision of whether or not to protest. The news that a friend or family member had been killed would produce additional shocks, which would sustain and accelerate their drive to protest. However, the death of a friend or a family member was not the only type of moral shock that occurred once individuals began to protest. When people protest they tend to create bonds of community and solidarity with those around them (Oliner and Oliner 1992). Thus, the shock of seeing a fellow protester killed may produce an effect similar to that of facing the brutally unjust violation of a relative or close friend and may impel a protester toward a sustained response.

COLLECTIVE IDENTITY AND NATIONALISM

In the previous section of the chapter, we examined how the moral shock and outrage of viewing violence against protesters caused many individuals to protest. In order to experience moral shock, an individual must believe that an injustice has occurred, meaning that one group perpetrated the injustice while another group was victimized. If an individual views one group as victims of injustice, then it is likely that she either sympathizes or empathizes with them, a condition necessary to the emotional dimension of moral shock. Sympathy is "an emotional response stemming from the apprehension of another's emotional state or condition, which is not the same as the other's state or condition, but consists of feelings of sorrow or concern for the other" (Eisenberg and Eggum 2008, 54), while empathy means "understanding others' thoughts and feelings and feeling with them" (Oliner and Oliner 1992, 380). In the following pages, I propose that the emotional content of moral shock was engendered by empathy with the victims of violence based on nationalist collective identity, normally a mostly affective emotional sentiment. I also demonstrate that the form of nationalism that created empathy was not the top-down Egyptian nationalism constructed by a series of regimes but was instead a new type of nationalism whose elements were introduced into the national consciousness in the years leading up to the Revolution. These new facets of nationalist discourse were founded on feelings of shared grievances and victimization by the regime. The shared victimization as a component of national collective identity was publicly proclaimed in the chants heard in Tahrir Square. Thus, the Egyptian people modeled a new national collective identity based on countering the regime, rather than a nationalism constructed by it. This type of collective identity, articulated by those in the Square, caused individuals sitting at home to develop empathy for the protesters. Some studies have shown that high levels of collective identity make individuals more likely to protest under repression (Fireman and Gamson 1979; Gupta, Singh, and Sprague 1993). Chants about previous injustices committed by the regime, injustices to which those sitting at home could relate, coupled with the morally shocking injustice of the attacks on protesters, led many to go out into the streets to protest.

Egyptian Nationalism in the Twentieth Century

In order to understand the new national collective identity that developed in the years leading up to the 2011 Revolution, it is helpful to begin with an outline of other forms of Egyptian nationalism that arose during the twentieth century. Nationalism can be viewed as a "consciousness of belonging to the nation, together with sentiments and aspirations for its security and prosperity" or "a social and political movement to achieve the goals of the nation and realize its national will" (Smith 1991, 72). Nationalism, which is also defined as "a political principle, which holds that the political and the national unit should be congruent" (Gellner 2008, 1), is a type of collective identity. The term "collective identity" sometimes refers to a feeling of solidarity among members of a social movement, and at other times it may refer to a type of social categorization in whose name a movement claims to speak (Jasper 1998, 415). More generally, identities may be founded on ascribed traits such as race, class, or nationality. Jasper (1998) argues that collective identity is not simply a way of drawing cognitive boundaries. Collective identity is an emotion, "a positive affect toward other group members on the grounds of that common membership. Defining oneself through the help of a collective label entails an affective as well as cognitive mapping of the social world" (Jasper 1998, 415). Thus, participating in a social movement can be a pleasurable act, independent of the movement's goals and achievements, because protesting allows an individual to articulate something about himself and his morals, finding happiness and pride in them (Jasper 1998, 415).

Over the years, views of nationalism in Egypt have fluctuated between Pharaonism, Egyptian particularist nationalism, Orientalism, and Pan-Islamism (Tibi 1997, 184). National identity has reflected the relationship between the people and the state, as well as the regime's manipulation of national ideology in order to maintain authoritarian rule.

While the emergence of modern Egyptian nationalism can be traced back to the late nineteenth century, when nationalism emphasized territorial factors and external loyalties to the Ottoman Empire (Jankowski 1991, 244), the present discussion begins with the nationalist movement against British domination of Egypt and Sudan, led by Saad Zaghlul. The movement against British colonialism culminated in the Egyptian Revolution of 1919. From March through April 1919, peasants, urban workers, and many others staged a revolt against 30 years of British domination. The revolt was triggered when four leaders of the Egyptian national movement were arrested on March 9, 1919, and exiled to Malta because they had insisted on recognition of the Egyptian delegation at the Paris Peace Conference in order that they might demand acknowledgment of Egypt as an independent state (Goldberg 1992, 261). Adopting slogans of Egyptian nationalism (Goldberg 1992, 262), Egyptians revolted against British rule. The 1919 Revolution was a grassroots movement that saw the emergence of Egyptian liberalism. All walks of Egyptian society were represented in the movement, which expressed nationalism as a refutation of foreign domination and exploitation by a colonial oppressor. According to Tignor (1976), the 1919 Egyptian Revolution marked "a peak period in the growth of Egyptian nationalism and saw the emergence of Egypt's most important political party. The Wafd was to remain at the centre of political life until the military coup d'etat of 1952" (Tignor 1976, 41).

On July 23, 1952, military officers, led by Mohammad Naguib and Gamal Abdel Nasser, staged a military coup. The aim of this Free Officers Movement was to overthrow King Faruq and end the British occupation of Egypt. The Egyptian Revolution of 1952 led to the eventual rule of Gamal Abdel Nasser and the introduction of a new type of nationalism defined by his regime. Musekamp (2010) argues that rather than being static, Egyptian nationalism as a state ideology "has been modified and rearticulated based on challenges the state has faced. The authoritarian regimes in Egypt since 1952 have maintained power as much through ideology as bureaucracy" (Musekamp 2010, 25).

Nasser was an Egyptian nationalist who allowed for the coexistence of Egyptian and Arab identities. The initial form of nationalism to which Nasser subscribed was a national identity that grew out of opposition to British occupation. Nasser transformed this anti-British nationalism into one that rejected Egypt's domination by any foreign power. The reasoning behind Nasser's Arab nationalism became clear on July 26, 1957, when he gave a speech celebrating the nationalization of the Suez Canal and emphasizing the link between Arab nationalism and Egyptian national interests:

> Our policy is based on Arab nationalism because Arab nationalism is a weapon for every Arab state. Arab nationalism is a weapon employed against aggression. It is necessary for the aggressor to know that, if he aggresses against any Arab country, he will endanger his interests. This is the way, brotherly compatriots, that we must advance for the sake of Egypt, glorious Egypt, independent Egypt. (Jankowski 2002, 33-34)

In Nasser's speech, the purpose of focusing on the unity of all Arabs was to demonstrate strength against any potential foreign aggressor. Thus, Arab nationalism served the purposes of Egyptian nationalism and the safekeeping of Egyptian independence, a cause for which Nasser had fought through the Free Officers Movement. Discussing Egyptian sovereignty and independence in another speech at Al-Azhar, Nasser emphasized the Egyptian "homeland" (*watan*) and "the people of Egypt" (*sha'b misr*) as important factors in his view of Arab nationalism (Jankowski 2002, 30). At no point did Arab nationalism overtake Egyptian nationalism as a dominant ideology (Dawisha 2003, 136). Nasser's Arab nationalism also did not take on a religious tone. In fact, Arab nationalism was a secular ideology rejecting religion as a foundation for national identity. As discussed in chapter 2, one of Nasser's most fundamental domestic challenges was the threat from the Muslim Brotherhood. The secular nature of Nasser's nationalism aimed to marginalize the Brotherhood.

The integration of Islam into the nationalist discourse took place under the rule of Anwar Sadat and continued during the Mubarak regime as a counter to the Islamist militancy and extremist ideology that emerged in Egypt during the 1970s. Responding to a movement that challenged the secular state by claiming that the regime was apostate, Sadat attempted to co-opt Islamic discourse in order to endow the state with religious legitimacy. Through a popular referendum in 1979/1980, Sadat amended the Egyptian constitution to include Islam as the state religion and made Islamic law the guiding force in state legislation (Musekamp 2010, 30). Musekamp (2010) argues that the state thus altered the way that it articulated Egyptian nationalism. "However, the state has tried to alter the nationalist discourse only to the extent that Egyptian nationalism both retains credible unifying characteristics and reinforces the legitimacy of the ruling authority, especially in the face of significant domestic opposition from Islamist groups" (Musekamp 2010, 27).

Mubarak continued Sadat's incorporation of Islam into his nationalist ideology as a means of maintaining and consolidating his power. While attempting to preserve a secular state, Mubarak paid lip service to Islam through state censorship of books and films offensive to Islam, promoting religious themes in the media, implementing prayer services in government offices, and opening up controlled public dialogue with the regime's religious opposition (Musekamp 2010, 32). Both Mubarak and Sadat turned their backs on Nasser's nationalist ideology. Sadat implemented his *infitah* (open door) economic policies, reinforced the state's Islamic status, linked Egypt to the West, and signed a peace treaty with Israel, and Mubarak continued with the coexistence rather than confrontation approach to Israel (Hatina 2004, 100). Thus, under Sadat and Mubarak, state policy reflected de-Nasserization.

Ideologies and norms are not simply inherited from history and tradition but are selectively chosen in modern times to suit the needs of the state or movement. Fred Halliday finds, for example, that "it is contemporary forces which make use of the past: they select and use those elements of the past, national, regional or religious, which suit their present purposes" (Halliday 2005, 322). Halliday (1997) presents the idea of changing national identities depending on the economic, political, or cultural climate. In his *The Formation of Yemeni Nationalism*, Halliday discusses the way in which Yemeni leaders used history selectively, based on the type of nationalism that they wanted to create or the circumstances they faced. The national identity alternated: sometimes they were Arab, sometimes Islamic, and sometimes they derived from the pre-Islamic period as the descendants of Saba and Himyar. In a similar fashion, Sadat and Mubarak constructed a national identity that aimed to maintain the secular nature of the state while simultaneously promoting the state's Islamic legitimacy as a counter to its Islamist opponents.

As we have observed so far, national identity can be created in a bottom-up manner, such as during the 1919 Egyptian Revolution with its expression of nationalism as opposition to colonialism, or in a top-down manner, such as in the attempts of Sadat and Mubarak to construct a national ideology that aided in the maintenance of authoritarian rule in the face of opponents. According to Bourdieu, "The state molds *mental structures* and imposes common principles of vision and division . . . and it thereby contributes to the construction of what is commonly designated as national identity" (Bourdieu 1991, 61). The state engages in a construction and consolidation of a particular vision of the state consistent with the values and interests of those producing them (Bourdieu 1991, 55). In the second half of the twentieth century and the beginning of the twenty-first century, the Egyptian government made a concerted effort to construct a narrative of national identity that assisted in legitimizing its authority and repelling challengers. However, a "regime's domination over political authority is only as far-reaching as a plausible nationalist ideology permits it to be" (Musekamp 2010, 27).

Nationalism by the People

Calhoun (1997) argues that the concept of nationalism partially grew out of popular challenges to the authority and legitimacy of those leading the country (Calhoun 1997, 69). An important part of the development of nationalism was the idea that "political power could only be legitimate when it reflected the will, or at least served the interests, of the people subjected to it" (Calhoun 1997, 69). In the decade leading up to the 2011 Egyptian Revolution, the Mubarak regime began to lose its legitimacy as it failed to serve the interests of the Egyptian people.

In the mid-2000s, political opposition began to grow against the Mubarak regime. As movements such as Kefaya formed, a new component of nationhood was put forth by activists based on a collective identity of victimization by the regime. This new identity that was constructed and framed by opposition groups in the years leading up to the Revolution challenged the regime's legitimacy by faulting the Mubarak government for failing to serve the interests of its people. Early attempts at reappropriating the narrative of Egyptian nationhood for the people were made by the Kefaya movement in 2005. Movement organizers changed the words to the national anthem to include demands for freedom of speech and human rights, singing, "I need revolution to reform my country." The new words to the national anthem emphasized the denial of people's rights by the regime, and the use of the word "my" indicated that the country belonged to the people, not the regime.

In 2010, when the We are all Khaled Said movement emerged as a response to the death of the young Alexandrian man who had been tortured and killed at the hands of police, Wael Ghonim, a founder of the movement, established a Facebook page challenging police brutality under the banner of "We are all Khaled Said." The significance of the name was that it engendered a collective identity where everyone was, or could be, Khaled Said. As discussed in chapter 2, a large percentage of Egyptians had either endured violation by the state police themselves or knew someone else who had been subjected to it. Thus, the phrase "we are all" emphasized Egyptians' collective feelings of victimization. According to Taylor and Dyke (2004):

> Acting collectively requires the development of solidarity and an oppositional consciousness that allows a challenging group to identify common injustices, to oppose those injustices, and to define a shared interest in opposing the dominant group or resisting the system of authority responsible for those injustices. (Taylor and Dyke 2004, 270)

The fact that We are all Khaled Said was the most popular anti-regime movement demonstrated that a large number of individuals dissatisfied with the Mubarak regime were ready to cloak themselves in the garments of Khaled Said and say, "I identify with this man; I identify with the collective that feels abused by the police, and the opponent of this collective is the regime." Emotions such as victimization become a resource for social movements when they can be strategically framed to encourage action against the perpetrators of the injustices that cause the emotion.

In Egypt, the term *al-sha'b* is traditionally used to refer to the Egyptian people, but *sha'bi* as an adjective is more often used to mean "popular" in terms of popular quarters (*sha'bi* neighborhoods) or popular music (*sha'bi* music), often implying lower class or from the streets. In 2008, opposition activists such as those from the April 6th Youth Movement used the term *al-sha'b* (the people) when referring to those who were stripped of their basic rights and suffered poor conditions due to the regime's failed policies (Onodera 2009, 55). Throughout the 18 days of the 2011 Egyptian Revolution, the most popular chant was "*Al-sha'b yurid isqaat al-nidham*" (The people want the downfall of the regime). In this chant, *al-sh'ab* meant all Egyptians who were not associated with the regime. According to

Eyerman, "Demonstrations are processes of identity and empathy formation re-enacting narrative dramas, as public practices, a form of ritual theatre" (Eyerman 2005, 50). Through collective acts, including singing and shouting slogans such as "the people" wanting the "downfall of the regime," protesters separated the regime from the rest of the nation. The implication was that protesters did not include the regime in their conceptualization of what it meant to be Egyptian. The separation of the regime from the national collective was also articulated in protest signs declaring, "Mubarak. The people have spoken. Take your regime & get out," and "For the sake of Egypt. Go away." This type of collective identity in opposition to the regime was exemplified by people's claims that the benefit of protesting in the Revolution was "contributing to the regime's downfall" and speaking of "changing the regime; showing people what Egypt is." Gribbon and Hawas (2012) argue, "So far removed from the needs and aspirations of the majority of Egyptians was the prevailing government that a thorough rebirth of the concept of popular, collective will was in order" (Gribbon and Hawas 2012, 16).

Symbols and ceremonies possess and produce emotive collective qualities. "In many ways national symbols, customs and ceremonies are the most potent and durable aspects of nationalism. They embody its basic concepts, making them visible and distinct for every member, communicating the tenets of an abstract ideology in palpable, concrete terms that evoke instant emotional responses from all strata of the community" (Smith 1991, 77). During the 18 days, Egyptians reappropriated the signs and ceremonies used by the government to reinforce its hegemonic nationalist discourse. Protesters waved Egyptian flags en masse and sang the national anthem to emphasize their relationship with the collective "self" in opposition to the Mubarak regime. The words of the national anthem, which begins "My country, my country, my country, you have my love and my heart," held significant meaning in the context of anti-regime protest. In addition to proclaiming devotion to one's country, the lyrics discuss keeping the homeland "safe from every enemy," which now included Mubarak, and peoples' willingness to "sacrifice ourselves for you, my country." A national anthem that professes a collective willingness for self-sacrifice becomes particularly poignant during a time when citizens are being shot by the government for demanding improvements to their country.

When asked about their cost-benefit analysis during the decision-making process to protest or not protest, many individuals offered similar explanations, saying that the benefit was "not about us; we love this country" and "I would have felt ashamed if I didn't protest. This time Egyptians really cared for their country, not personal benefit." Many people discussed the need to protest in order to "complete the goals of people who died on the 25th" and "support the youth generation who died there." A few even listed the possibility of becoming a *shaheeda* (martyr) as a potential benefit of protesting, which is a viewpoint that is interesting to consider on its own because social scientists often categorize death as a cost of protesting, not a benefit.

The common theme running through many discussions was that the benefit to protesting was not personal advantage but rather the improvement of the nation as a whole. When someone says, "If I go out, I could change the country, not for myself, for my country as a whole," the statement implies a sense of nationalism. However, this nationalism was not characterized by the nationalist discourse constructed by the state; it was a new type that contested the state. It "places the nation at the centre of its concerns, and its description of the world and its prescriptions for collective action are concerned only with the nation and its members" (Smith 1991, 74). This new nationalism began to take shape in the anti-regime movements leading up to the Revolution and then took off once protests began.

During times of revolutionary protest, shifts in political opportunities provide a space for challenging dominant national identity frames put forth by the government. The new frames, articulated by protesters, function as a means of mobilizing dissent against the power to which grievances are attributed. In 2011 Egypt, this new national identity was founded on a national collective victimization and a plight inflicted by what was perceived as an outside institution.

If we reflect back to the different articulations of collective identity in Egypt in the twentieth century, the new form of nationalism that took hold during the 2011 Revolution is reminiscent of the 1919 Revolution against British occupation, when the movement defined nationalism as an expression of opposition to foreign domination and a government that collaborated with the exploitative power. However, in 2011, it was not a foreign power but rather a domestic regime that the people rejected. Following 1952, various regimes, rather than the people, had defined Egyptian nationalism as a means of consolidating power. In 2011, the Egyptian people reclaimed the right to determine what it meant to be Egyptian. The resulting new concept of collective identity, based on victimization by the Mubarak regime and the regime's failure to meet the people's needs, resonated with those sitting at home.

Peoples' decisions to protest were partially founded on a desire to join anti-regime protesters who were reclaiming the narrative of Egyptian identity. Rather than submitting to state definitions of Egyptian nationhood that emphasized the country's, and more particularly the regime's, distinct place in regional politics, Egyptians were taking back the country for its people, saying, "It's our country and time for people to hear our voices." The perception of many was that the Mubarak regime had hijacked the country, so it was "Egyptians' dream to return Egypt to her real people." "By taking back the streets, protesters—al-sha'b—took back their rights, and with that, reappropriated an entire lexicon that had been abused by the regime" (Gribbon and Hawas 2012, 17).

When social identity predominates over personal identity, individuals define themselves based on what makes them similar to others (Turner 1999). "The redefinition from an 'I' into a 'we' as a locus of self-definition makes people think, feel and act as members of their group and transforms individual into collective behavior" (van Stekelenberg and Klandermans 2013, 4). When those at home heard the protesters' chants in Tahrir Square, they experienced an emotion of collective national identity that propelled them into the streets. A middle-class business owner claimed, "I wanted a better leader, not for me, but for my country," while a film director related, "I was thinking who was there and how many we were. I was looking to see what I could add or share in supporting this. Nobody before this day said anything about Mubarak in a loud voice." People wanted to join in the "beautiful experience of Egyptian solidarity." Jasper (1997) claims, "The 'nation' is a powerful collective identity capable of inspiring massive mobilization" (Jasper 1997, 361). What we have observed is that a sense of collective identity based on national victimization stimulated the empathetic emotions of potential protesters, causing them to go out and protest in the streets.

WHY NOT PROTEST?

The previous section explored how government repression of protesters activated the moral shock/outrage emotional mechanism, driving individuals into the streets to protest. However, such an explanation does not contribute to an understanding of why individuals might be unhappy with government violence but decide not to protest. In this section, I briefly investigate instances where elements of empathy or feelings of injustice are absent from the emotional process, thus deterring protest.

Inherent in the manner in which moral shock functions as a causal mechanism is its ordering of an individual's preferences in a way that leads her to protest. Thus, part of the emotional process entails a drive to take action to correct the injustice that the individual perceives as occurring. However, there may also be scenarios where individuals experience anger about government violence against protesters but where the emotion does not meet the level of moral shock that compels one to join in protest. In my research, I found that many individuals who claimed to be angry about violence against protesters but who held a favorable view of the Mubarak regime failed to protest because they lacked the key component of empathy.

While this book has so far focused predominantly on individuals who had grievances against Mubarak and his regime prior to the Revolution, there were also many Egyptians who liked Mubarak. Members of both the lower and upper class who were content with Mubarak cited security, stability, Mubarak's patriotism, economic prosperity, and having had no other president with whom to draw a comparison as reasons for their satisfaction with the regime.

Many pointed to stability and Mubarak's protecting the country from war as significant reasons for their allegiance to the president. Giving praise to the former leader, one housewife from Imbaba said, "He is from the military, so he loves this country. Maybe he stole money, but he was faithful to the country." Some segments of the population were willing to excuse Mubarak's indiscretions because they believed emphatically that he was a committed patriot. Others in the upper class expressed satisfaction with Mubarak based on economic factors and the benefits they had enjoyed under the corrupt system. A wealthy car importer and advertising executive from Zamalek recalled life under Mubarak, saying, "Personally, I had nothing to complain about at that time." From his perspective, the economy was thriving and his business had profited. When asked if he disliked any aspect of the Mubarak regime, the executive replied, "No, on the contrary. I was loved by the Mubarak regime, especially by Suzanne." Having produced ad campaigns for Suzanne Mubarak, which required their meeting on a weekly basis, he believed that Mubarak, Suzanne, and their older son, Alaa, were "nice people"; he just did not like Gamal, Mubarak's son who was being groomed for the presidency. A young student who attended the American University in Cairo reminisced on the Mubarak era. Being a member of the upper class, she loved Mubarak because she was "taken care of." He "provided us with an easy life to go out and have fun." One of her friends chimed in, "I liked how easy I could get things done with one phone call," referring to *wastaa* (connections).

There were also members of the lower class who, before the Revolution, had believed they were doing well financially. In retrospect, one unemployed man from el Nasrya explained his former satisfaction with Mubarak, saying, "We were blind. We never saw what was happening. We had food. Didn't know the conditions of our life." His poor financial position was normalized through being surrounded by others living under similar conditions. However, some members of the lower class had been more than financially comfortable. One cabaret worker claimed that during the time of Mubarak "there was money." This particular woman had brought home E£8,000 per month before the Revolution, and many other cabaret workers cited similar amounts. Thus, some members of the lower class who worked in areas such as cabaret entertainment, shipping, and drug dealing enjoyed relative economic prosperity under Mubarak.

Another reason for contentment with the Mubarak regime was ignorance of other possibilities. As one 31-year-old lower-class man claimed, "Mubarak was good. I didn't like him as a person, but I liked him as a president. There was no one else." Those in their early thirties or younger had never experienced a time when Mubarak was not president of Egypt. They had spent their entire lives surrounded by billboards and posters of Hosni Mubarak's face and were indoctrinated to the point where a different president was not even conceivable. A young woman from Shubra said about Mubarak, "I was born and he was there. I lived 20 years and he was still there. . . . Unchangeable." One day during the Revolution a little girl had said to her, "Oh, are we going to change Mubarak? I thought there was a Mubarak in every country in the world." Thus, many citizens, particularly those who were too young to have seen another president, accepted the regime and its system as a given.

Finally, some people expressed displeasure with police actions, but did not equate the police with the Mubarak regime. A wealthy dentist said that for her, Mubarak and the police were separate. She thought Mubarak was "brainwashed" by people around him, but that he was good. She was angry at the police for the killing of Khaled Said and brutality, but opined, "That wasn't Mubarak; that was the police." This idea of a good leader in his ivory tower who is ignorant of, rather than a participant in, the corruption and abuse in his country was portrayed in a 2008 Egyptian film titled *The President's Chef* (Hamed 2008).

Empathy is a key component of the moral shock emotional process. While many Mubarak sympathizers expressed being disturbed by government violence against protesters, when asked about the potential benefits of protesting they replied, "Nothing," or "I wouldn't get anything." A sea transportation logistics coordinator from Qala'a explained that he had no problem with the regime. "I had work and I was married. I didn't have troubles to protest about." Like many other people who did not share in the identity of victimization because they either benefited from the regime or were satisfied with it, he was content with the trajectory of his life. Thus, while violence against protesters may have evoked the emotions of anger or discomfort in these people, lack of empathy prevented them from experiencing moral shock.

Another element of moral shock is injustice. In order to experience moral shock a person must identify that there is an injustice occurring against one group and directly attribute the cause of the injustice to another group. Some individuals who were unhappy with government violence against protesters experienced conflicting emotions about whom they should view as unjust. Demonstrating her sympathy for her leader of 30 years, a housewife from Imbaba explained that she did not like the Revolution. "I wanted Mubarak out, but not in this way. What happened to Mubarak was more than he deserved." Although she was dissatisfied with Mubarak, she was not in favor of the undignified way that protesters had attempted to remove him. Thus, she believed that injustices were being perpetrated by both sides. Mubarak was unjust by using violence against protesters, but the protesters were unjust by disrespecting Mubarak. Ambiguity about the attribution of injustice disrupts the process of moral shock. When individuals are equivocal about the blame for injustice or do not experience empathy, they will not risk their lives to protest in the face of government violence.

In addition to cases where elements of the moral shock process were missing, there were also instances of people who were incensed by government violence against protesters, identified the Mubarak regime as the perpetrator of the injustice, empathized with the protesters based on the national collective identity of victimization, but decided not to protest. The most common explanations for not protesting under these conditions were fear of violence, family pressure not to protest, or need to join popular committees to protect their neighborhoods. The reason these individuals did not protest is because a different emotion took precedence over moral shock. This chapter looks at how the moral shock emotion is activated and how, when particular elements of the process are absent, the moral shock emotion does not completely form, leading people not to protest. How another emotion takes precedence over moral shock is beyond the scope of this study. However, from a preliminary assessment, it appears that not protesting because of fear of violence may be related to primal survival instincts, while joining popular committees to protect one's family or obeying orders from family not to protest may be connected to what Jasper (1998) calls complex secondary emotions or "affective" emotions. Affective emotions are based on stable bonds and loyalty. In cases of not protesting because of family bonds, it appears that purely affective emotions prevail over those that include reactive sentiments.

People often experience multiple emotions simultaneously and react to the emotion that is most salient at the time. Studies in psychobiography that examine how a person's developmental history affects decision-making may help to explain in more depth why, depending on a person's experiences, personality type, and the emotional memory from which she draws, one emotion takes precedence over another.

CONCLUSION

This chapter demonstrated that when individuals were deciding whether or not to protest, one of the reasons why they made the choice to protest was violence committed by the regime against protesters. Protesting because of an injustice inflicted on someone else is an altruistic decision. Knowing that the cost of protesting could be injury or death, some people still chose to protest because they found a benefit in coming to the aid of fellow citizens. The emotional mechanisms that produce the decision to protest because of violence inflicted on protesters are moral shock and moral outrage. Uncovering these mechanisms is important to understanding how individuals come to protest and not just why. Thoroughly examining these processes on the individual level provides a more nuanced analysis of decision-making. Many people protested because of the moral shock of seeing protesters brutalized, feeling a sense of injustice that their fellow Egyptians would be killed for demanding their rights. That moral shock arose from the emotion of empathy with protesters already in the streets.

The empathy felt by those deciding to protest was due to feelings of a collective "self" based on new elements of national identity introduced by the Egyptian people rather than those that had been promulgated by the regime. The new nationalism was founded on feelings of collective victimization resulting from the regime's persecution of its people and failure to meet their needs. Citizens sitting at home observed expressions of this national identity in the chants and songs of protesters in the streets, and this particular form of collective identity resonated with them, thus producing empathy for protesters and impelling those sitting at home to join their compatriots. However, when crucial elements of moral shock, such as empathy or unambiguous attribution of injustice to the regime, are absent, individuals do not protest.

In the previous chapters, we examined a number of factors that affected individual decisions to protest. In chapter 2, we looked at popular dissatisfaction with the Mubarak regime and how the upper and lower classes shared many grievances due to similar experiences and encounters with the state. Chapter 3 explored how social media affected mobilization. It demonstrated that social media served as an intermediary step between private preferences and public preferences, lowering the threshold for political participation. It also showed that there were two political thresholds to be overcome, a lower one for going online and a higher one for going into the streets for political protest. Now that I have provided examples of the relationship between structure and emotional mechanisms in decisions to protest or not protest leading up to and during the 2011 Egyptian Revolution, in the next chapter I examine political opportunities, mobilization, and cycles of protest under the rule of the Supreme Council of the Armed Forces (SCAF) transitional government.

PART II

The Transition and Downfall of Morsi

5

Protest Dynamics under the Supreme Council of the Armed Forces Transitional Government

Mona stepped out of the metro station into the sweltering June heat and headed toward the south side of Tahrir Square in the direction of the Mugamaa, the government complex notorious for long lines and thick bureaucracy. As she approached the office building, Mona observed a number of tents pitched near the entranceway. The temporary structures were part of the ongoing sit-in to pressure the Supreme Council of the Armed Forces (SCAF) into going ahead with the presidential elections, which were set for later that month. A large poster hanging from one of the tents with a photo of former presidential candidate Hazem Salah Abou Ismail read "Courage doesn't bring death closer, and being a coward doesn't slow down death. Either I live with dignity in this life or I live with it with my lord." The words inscribed next to the picture of the Salafi Islamist were a reminder that for some people, when nothing less than freedom and social justice would suffice, liberty in death was preferable to the shackles of oppression on earth.

The walls of the Mugamaa were covered in a rainbow of graffiti: "No SCAF," "Fuck the police," and "Get out military rule." A year and a half before, it would have been inconceivable to write such obscenities about the government in a public space, but then again, it would have also been unimaginable that protesters would take to the streets and remove Mubarak, their president of 30 years.

As Mona neared Mohammed Mahmoud Street, the martyr murals painted on the walls in front of the old American University in Cairo campus came into view. Most striking was an enormous portrait of a martyr's mother holding a sign that read "The young revolutionaries will avenge my son," and another of a mourning mother in black, weeping. The walls of Mohammed Mahmoud Street encapsulated the more than one year of battles for justice and change: the martyrs who had died for their country's freedom and the pain of those they had left behind, the fury directed at SCAF due to its brutal repression of protesters and its obstruction of the transition process, and the people's determination to see the Revolution to its completion. Interspersed between the pharaonic revolutionary art and phrases such as "No to a new pharaoh" were stencil paintings of martyrs' faces in photo frames with the words "R.I.P. Khaled" and "R.I.P. Osama" below.

Mohammed Mahmoud Street had become a public, open-air display of political art that documented every twist and turn of the political process and cycles of protest. Graffiti artists would paint subversive images such as a head with half the face of President Mubarak and half the face of Field Marshall Tantawi, implying that there was no difference between the government of the former dictator and that of SCAF. In response, SCAF would order the walls of Mohammed Mahmoud whitewashed to erase any trace of politically challenging imagery. Each time the government whitewashed the walls, artists took the action as an opportunity to paint new depictions of updated political realities. The battle between graffiti artists and whitewashers mirrored the cycles of contention between protesters and security forces in the streets.

The previous chapters explored protest mobilization leading up to and during the 2011 Egyptian Revolution. This chapter examines how changes in political opportunity structures following the revolutionary protests affected subsequent anti-regime mobilization and the dynamics between the SCAF government and those who contested it. I argue that changes in political opportunities created during the 18-day uprising altered repertoires of contention and reconfigured the power relationship between the regime and its opponents.

I also propose that particular elements of protest dynamics under SCAF led to a relatively quick transition to civilian rule. The key factors that characterized the interaction between protesters and the government were their interests, concepts of how to achieve goals, strategies, reactions, learning, strengths and weaknesses of each side, concepts of legitimacy, and the changes in political opportunities. The cycles of contention between the regime and its opponents were also permeated by tensions between the attempts of protesters to maintain and further open political opportunities and the efforts of the regime to close them. The interaction of all these factors eventually served to push SCAF toward facilitating parliamentary and presidential elections. Additionally, I find that there are ways to view protester perceptions of the regime that are not limited to a weak/strong binary. Protesters did not construe the regime as weak but instead saw SCAF as strong but challengeable. The emotional mechanism that motivated protest in this scenario was the post-revolutionary emboldening effect.

CHANGES IN POLITICAL OPPORTUNITY STRUCTURES

According to Charles Tilly, "The outcome of any particular struggle alters the positions of the participants" (Tilly 2006, 57). Following the 18 days of the 2011 Egyptian Revolution, the positions of both the regime and its opponents had changed significantly. Protesters were empowered by their success in overthrowing Mubarak, which had opened fresh political opportunities. The position of the new government, run by SCAF, had been weakened by these opportunities created by protesters. Protesters had proposed a new legitimacy principle according to which any person or group claiming power would have to be supported by the people. However, it should be noted that, in this case, "the people" refers to those who were active in the streets and not the entire Egyptian population.[1] This new definition of legitimacy was particularly relevant for the ruling military government, as the military had always prided itself on being a military of the people.

Regimes create environments of political opportunities and threats. Any change to the environment produces alterations in contention, particularly in the way that regimes repress or facilitate collective action (Tilly 2006, 43–44). Spirals of contention may ensue, which provide new opportunities for claim-making (Tilly 2006, 44). By overthrowing the Mubarak regime, protesters forged new opportunities for dissent and altered repertoires of contention in Egypt. No longer was opposition to the regime limited to Facebook protests and silent stands. If the people were dissatisfied with their government, the nascent avenue to express that displeasure and demand change was mass protest.

On January 25, 2011, protesters opened up political opportunities by staging the first mass protest against the Mubarak regime. These opportunities were opened a bit more on January 28, 2011, when tens of thousands more took to the streets to oppose Mubarak, despite the risk posed by the regime's violent repression. Opportunities were further opened on February 11, 2011, when Mubarak stepped down in response to 18 days of mass protests against him. One of the purposes of protest under SCAF was to open these opportunities further and continue to challenge the regime in power until the demands of the Revolution were met. In contrast, the aim of SCAF's violent repression of protesters was to try to close the political opportunities that had been opened during the Revolution, thus giving SCAF control of the political process.

Doug McAdam et al. argue that repertoires of contention are shaped by the regime that the opposition confronts (McAdam, Tarrow, and Tilly 2001). However, when the opposition's repertoires change, the regime's repertoires of response may also be altered under the impact of the opposition it confronts, as occurred during the 18 days. In the year following the 2011 Revolution, SCAF's answer to mass protests was to alternate between violent repression and concession. While SCAF continued to rely on old repertoires of violence against protesters, it also employed a new tactic of concession because it feared losing whatever legitimacy it held in the eyes of the people. SCAF's inability to close political opportunities through violent tactics without losing its legitimacy eventually led it to acquiesce to opposition demands for quick parliamentary and presidential elections. In the following pages, I examine SCAF's ascent to power, along with its political and economic interests.

THE MILITARY DURING THE 2011 REVOLUTION

The role the military played in the transitional period following the 18 days of the 2011 Revolution had its beginning during the protests, when the institution made the choice not to back the Mubarak regime. According to Zoltan Barany (2011), autocratic regimes depend on the loyalty of their soldiers and police. While there are multiple security apparatuses that work to preserve a regime, such as intelligence agencies, police, and the armed forces, during a revolution "regime survival turns on the military (primarily the army) and its willingness and capacity to bring in the tanks, the heavy weapons, and the men in numbers large enough to contain a mass uprising" (Bellin 2012, 131). Eva Bellin (2012) argues that the two factors that determine whether the military will repress an uprising are the institutional character of the military and the level of social mobilization.

The military's purpose is to defend the country, maintain security, and protect its own institutional interests. These institutional interests include preserving internal cohesion and morale within the corps, protecting the image and legitimacy of the military, and securing the military's economic position (Bellin 2012, 131). A military's decision about whether to repress an uprising is shaped by perceptions of the legitimacy of the regime by soldiers, security officials, and the general public; the relationship between the military and the state, as well as civil society; whether the soldiers called upon to suppress an uprising are ethnically divided; the extent to which the military relies on the state; and the military's relationship with foreign powers (Barany 2011, 29).

The Egyptian military chose not to intervene in the 2011 Revolution and protect the Mubarak regime for a number of reasons. First, conscripts felt a degree of kinship with the protesters, many of whom were their friends and family; it would, therefore, have been difficult to maintain internal cohesion and morale if soldiers were ordered to shoot at protesters. Second, the military prided itself on being a military of, and for, the Egyptian people. Thus, firing on protesters would undermine the institution's legitimacy. It would also be difficult to argue that the army was serving the maintenance of order and security if it killed peaceful protesters (Bellin 2012, 132). Third, the military's economic interests had been diverging from those of the state in recent years as Gamal Mubarak's cronies impinged on the military's economic territory. Hence, the long-standing, tacit agreement giving the military its own profitable sphere of economic activity was being threatened. Fourth, the army was unhappy with the regime for increasing privileges to police and security apparatuses that employed as many as 1.4 million people (Barany 2011, 32). Finally, while the United States government initially supported the Mubarak regime during the Revolution, as time progressed and more protesters were killed, the U.S. began to put pressure on Mubarak to leave and on the military not to intervene on the side of the Egyptian government.

Under a special relationship, the U.S. government was providing the Egyptian military with a large amount of annual aid, including approximately $2 billion in 2010. At the beginning of the 2011 Revolution, many senior Egyptian military officials were being hosted at the Pentagon for the annual bilateral defense talks of the Military Cooperation Committee, which was jointly chaired by Assistant Secretary of Defense, Sandy Vershbow, and Lieutenant General Sami Anan, the chief of staff of the Egyptian armed forces (Rozen 2011). During the Revolution, President Obama had direct conversations with President Mubarak urging him to step down (Nicholas 2011) and also placed steady pressure on the Egyptian army to deliver on protester demands (Dreyfuss 2011). The U.S.'s announcement that it had assurances from the Egyptian military that it would not fire on protesters (Macey 2011) indicated that the military was circumventing regime authority by engaging in political discussions and decision-making independently of the Mubarak government and that it believed that its interests coincided with the demands of the U.S. government not to repress protesters.

The Mubarak regime lost its legitimacy with the military when it used extensive violence against protesters. "The generals concluded that Mubarak's mix of concessions (agreeing not to seek reelection or have his son succeed him) and repression (the February 2 attacks) had failed, and that rising violence and disorder would only hurt the military's legitimacy and influence" (Barany 2011, 31-32). Military leaders realized that they could play a novel and important role under a new regime (Gause 2011, 82), and "with Gamal's crony capitalist allies out of the way, there [was] no longer any competitor whose ambitions [were] a counterweight to the army's appetite for economic expansion" (Marshall and Stacher 2012).

SCAF TAKES OVER

In an attempt to demonstrate efforts at political reform, on January 29, 2011, Mubarak appointed former spy chief Omar Suleiman as vice-president, and in a televised address on February 10th, Mubarak handed over "the functions of the president" to Suleiman while retaining the title of president. However, on February 11, 2011, Suleiman made a statement on television that Mubarak was stepping down and authority would be transferred to the military's Supreme Council of the Armed Forces, led by Field Marshall Mohamed Hussein Tantawi, Mubarak's veteran defense minister. In a statement on the 11th, the military announced that it would lift the emergency law in force as soon as the precarious atmosphere ended and that it would guarantee changes to the constitution, as well as free and fair elections. SCAF's stated objective was to restore stability (Karawan 2011, 43). Its first cabinet included Ahmed Shafiq as prime minister, Samir Radwan as minister of finance, Ahmed Abul Gheit as minister of foreign affairs, Counselor Mamdou Mohyiddin Marie as minister of justice, and Lieutenant General Mahmoud Wagdy Mohamed Mahmoud as minister of interior. Ahmed Shafiq was a former senior commander in the Egyptian Air Force and had been appointed prime minister by Mubarak on January 31, 2011, during the 18 days of the uprising. Ahmed Abul Gheit had been the foreign minister of Egypt under Mubarak since 2004 and retained his post under SCAF. Lieutenant General Mahmoud Wagdy Mohamed Mahmoud had been appointed minister of interior by Mubarak on January 31, 2011, and had participated in the repression of protesters during the 18 days. Thus, SCAF's initial cabinet comprised many members of the old regime, including some of those who had taken action against the Revolution. Not all the newly-appointed ministers were figures from the former regime. Ahmed El-Borai, a prominent law professor and member of the United Nations Committee on Migrant Workers, was appointed minister of manpower and immigration, and Samir Radwan had previously worked for the International Labor Organization (ILO). However, some of the most prominent and politically influential ministries were allocated to Mubarak-era figures.

MILITARY INTERESTS

In order to understand SCAF's decision-making during its year in power, it is necessary to examine the military's interests, which were predominantly economic. The Egyptian military has had a strong presence in the economy since the 1952 Revolution, also known as the coup of the Free Officers, and eventual assumption of the presidency by Gamal Abdel Nasser. During Nasser's presidency, the state used nationalization programs to take hold of the country's economic assets and means of production. The new ruling elite of military officers took charge of managing state-owned enterprises, a task they were unprepared to fulfill (Abul-Magd 2011). In the 1970s, when President Anwar al-Sadat rerouted the Egyptian economy from socialism to a market economy, the military's economic monopoly began to wane. As the state embarked on a path of privatization of state-owned sectors that the military controlled, the military was forced to share economic influence with crony capitalists who were close to Sadat (Abul-Magd 2011).

The military regained its power after the 1979 peace treaty with Israel. Rather than laying off thousands of army officials who were no longer needed, the state decided to establish the National Services Projects Organization (NSPO), an economic body that founded commercial enterprises run by retired generals and colonels (Abul-Magd 2011). The NSPO managed factories that only produced civilian goods (Joudeh 2014). The military enjoyed subsidies and tax exemptions for these enterprises, it was not accountable to any government body, it was above the laws and regulations applied to other companies, and it benefited from other special privileges. Even after 1992, when President Hosni Mubarak implemented intensive economic liberalization plans, military companies remained untouched and high-ranking army officers profited from the government's corrupt privatization deals through prestigious positions in newly privatized enterprises (Abul-Magd 2011).

In addition to the NSPO, the military's role in the civilian economy was, and still is, also managed by another holding company, the Arab Organization for Industrialization (AOI). AOI is controlled by the ministry of state for military production and oversees nine factories that produce civilian and military goods (Joudeh 2014). The army also manages a number of subsidiaries of state-owned holding companies and has shares in public-private ventures, many of which are embedded in transnational conglomerates "that reach into several economic sectors, from construction and maritime shipping to weapons manufacturing" (Marshall and Stacher 2012). Additionally, retired officers control enterprises that fall under the category of "commanding heights," "including the Suez Canal Authority (one of the biggest sources of foreign exchange in the country), as well air and sea transport companies (including all seaports), electricity, water and sanitation projects" (Raphaeli 2013).

The Egyptian military also partners with foreign companies, such as the Chinese national oil company (Sinopec), for drilling and oil production and Italian companies Breda and ETI for petroleum services and gas stations. The army joined with Chrysler for the assembly of Jeep Wranglers, using funds from its U.S. military aid package for their production (Raphaeli 2013). In addition, the military benefits from maritime transport and foreign investment in the Egyptian energy sector through its holdings in Tharwa Petroleum, Egypt's sole state-owned oil company, which engages in exploration and development (Marshall and Stacher 2012).

Military ventures also include real estate. While Egyptian law allows the military to seize public land for the defense of the nation, in reality it has conducted land seizures for commercial purposes (Raphaeli 2013). The Armed Forces Land Projects has engaged in residential building on public lands confiscated by the military, and the army also owns real estate in Sharm el-Sheikh, a resort town (Raphaeli 2013).

According to Safa Joudeh, "Military enterprises have undercut local entrepreneurship, enhanced a deep-rooted patronage system, and led to unequal development" (Joudeh 2014). The military is able to veto business contracts that interfere with its business interests and has access to reduced-cost state resources. The military also holds a competitive advantage through free labor supplied by conscripts (Cousin 2013). In a secret cable signed by U.S. Ambassador to Egypt Margaret Scobey in September 2008, it was stated that "military-owned companies, often run by retired generals, are particularly active in the water, olive oil, cement, construction, hotel and gasoline industries." Embassy staff claimed, "We see the military's role in the economy as a force that generally stifles free market reform by increasing direct government involvement in the markets" (Simpson and Fam 2011).

It is clear that the Egyptian military can be seen as much as a business as a fighting army. Marshall states:

> The Egyptian military produces a staggering array of manufactured goods: kitchen cutlery, flat-screen televisions, agricultural and household chemicals, refrigerators, industrial machinery, railway cars, and election booths. And while many of the military's factory webpages make a concerted attempt to promote their wares, the careful observer gets the feeling that the production of air

conditioners and gas stoves has superseded the production of guns and ammo. (Marshall 2012)

With the military controlling anywhere from 5% to 40% of the Egyptian economy (Marshall and Stacher 2012), it becomes clear that one of its primary goals is securing its economic interests.

In an interview on military interests, Robert Springborg claimed that the military was in favor of Mubarak's privatization initiatives as long as it gained from them. Its reason for opposing intensified privatization efforts in 2004 under Prime Minister Ahmed Nazif and overseen by Investment Minister Mahmoud Mohie Eddin was that Gamal Mubarak's cronies, rather than the military, were benefitting from the sale of state-owned enterprises (New Sources 2011).

When SCAF assumed power in February 2011, it began by ensuring that politicians and businessmen would not infringe upon the military's economic endeavors, pushing out businessmen who challenged the military's economic position (Cousin 2013). One of its key tactics was its selective anti-corruption campaign. "By jailing big businessmen like Ahmad 'Izz, an intimate of Gamal's, and unpopular officials like the former housing minister, Ibrahim Sulayman, the SCAF channeled the public's demand for justice" (Marshall and Stacher 2012). However, civilian businessmen tied to the military were not targeted for prosecution, signaling that failure to accept the military's role in the economy would lead to marginalization in the business world. In 2011, the Assistant Minister of Defense, General Mahmud Nasr, made a statement that the military "would never surrender the military-controlled projects to any other authority because these projects are not assets owned by the state but are 'revenues from the sweat of the ministry of defense and its own special projects'" (Raphaeli 2013).

According to Marshall and Stacher (2012), SCAF created new electoral laws that benefitted supporters of the status quo, with one-third of seats in the lower house of Parliament allotted to single-member districts, giving an advantage to those who profited from the patronage of Mubarak's National Democratic Party (NDP). SCAF also went further with a provision that half the seats in the lower house be reserved for workers and peasants, slots that were usually filled by retired military and police. The retired military and police members of parliament "then take up membership in the parliament's defense and national security committee, the only body with even nominal responsibility for overseeing the military" (Marshall and Stacher 2012). Another attempt by the military to secure its position through legislative channels was SCAF's March 30, 2011, constitutional declaration that established new rules for the formation of the Constituent Assembly, giving a privileged role to SCAF. The declaration infringed on the constitutional document that had passed in the national referendum.

It was never clear whether SCAF desired to engage in direct rule when it came to power after the 18 days, and it can even be argued that SCAF did not want the responsibility of presiding over a country marred by economic troubles and a dissatisfied population with high expectations. However, it is apparent from SCAF's actions during its time in power that its primary aim was to entrench the economic position and institutional independence of the military in a manner that would secure it from challenges by any future regime.

CYCLES OF CONTENTION

SCAF's year in power was characterized by cycles of contention, with SCAF taking actions to secure its position and protesters challenging these attempts at power-grabbing. In the following pages, I outline how both violent repression and tactics of accommodation failed to quell dissent, eventually forcing SCAF to facilitate a transition to civilian rule.

On February 25, 2011, protesters returned to Tahrir Square and the Parliament Building to demand the dismissal of Prime Minister Shafiq, the release of political prisoners, and the prosecution of those responsible for killing and torturing protesters. Opposition to Shafiq stemmed from his ties to the Mubarak regime. In response, the military violently dispersed the protests, using soldiers and masked plainclothes police to beat demonstrators and attack them with Tasers (Khawly 2012). Later, on March 3, 2011, Shafiq resigned from office, days before a planned sit-in demanding that he step down and after he was shamed on television by writer Alaa Al Aswany for being a member of the Mubarak regime. Essam Sharaf, who had been minister of transportation from 2004 to 2005 under Mubarak, was appointed prime minister in Shafiq's place, based on the recommendation of opposition activists. In addition to Shafiq, the foreign, justice, interior, and oil ministers also stepped down. The former governor of Minya, Mansour El Essawi, became interior minister, Mohamed Abdel Azi Al-Guindy took on the role of justice minister, and Nabil Elaraby became foreign minister. "The prompt acceptance by the military of Shafiq's resignation shows the sensitivity of the ruling generals to the demands of the uprising's leaders" (Associated Press in Cairo 2011).

However, on March 9, 2011, Egyptian soldiers and thugs again attacked anti-SCAF protesters. Witnesses claimed that hundreds of men in civilian clothes, armed with wooden sticks, metal pipes, and paving stones, beat demonstrators in Tahrir Square. Then the attackers and a few army officers forced protesters into the Egyptian Museum, handcuffed them, and beat them with electric cables, sticks, and metal pipes (Human Rights Watch 2011a). It was also reported that female demonstrators were beaten, subjected to electric shock, strip-searched, and forced to submit to virginity checks (Amin 2011). Attempting to suppress challenges to its rule, on March 23, 2011, SCAF approved a cabinet decree criminalizing protests and strikes. Anyone organizing or calling for protests or strikes would face imprisonment and/or a E£500,000 fine (Egypt Independent 2011).

SCAF's anti-protest law failed to quell dissent. Explaining his decision to violate the law, one young man said, "I just wanted to say to the SCAF, fuck you. No one is going to stop us. It's our Square; it's our revolution." Protests in Tahrir Square continued, and on April 8, 2011, dubbed "Cleansing Friday," tens of thousands of protesters, including 15–21 army officers, demonstrated in the Square against the military government, demanding full dismantling of the Mubarak regime and transition to civilian rule (Watson and Fahmy 2011). Protesters chanted, "The army and people are not one hand." Ten protesting officers were arrested and sentenced to ten years in prison, and at least one protester was killed (Ibrahim 2012a). In order to break up the protests, police fired shots, beat protesters with batons, and tasered them (Reuters 2011). Following the incident, SCAF released a statement saying that the attacks had targeted thugs and members of Mubarak's National Democratic Party who were conducting sabotage in the Square (Ibrahim 2012a). In another statement they said that anyone participating in sit-ins in the Square past the military-imposed curfew was an outlaw (Ibrahim 2012a). Few heeded the military's warning.

Following April 8th, other instances where the military used live ammunition, rubber bullets, and tear gas to disperse protesters included the May 15, 2011, protests at the Israeli embassy in Cairo commemorating the Palestinian catastrophe and June 28-29, 2011, when, outside of Cairo's Balloon Theater in the Agouza district and later in front of the Interior Ministry, police clashed with demonstrators who were led by relatives of martyrs of the Revolution demanding justice.

On July 8, 2011, tens of thousands demonstrated in Alexandria, Suez, and Cairo, where a month-long sit-in in Tahrir Square was begun with at least 26 political parties and movements taking part. Protesters called for all politicians linked to the Mubarak regime to be removed from the prime minister's cabinet and, accusing SCAF of intentionally slowing revolutionary progress, for the executive power of SCAF to be reduced. Many protesters chanted, "Down with the Marshall," referring to Field Marshall Tantawi. Additional demands included terminating military trials for civilians, suspending police officers accused of killing protesters, restructuring the Interior Ministry, holding public trials for former members of the Mubarak regime accused of crimes, and creating a better budget that would respond to the needs of the poor (Abdel Kouddous and Slazar 2011). By July 11th, hundreds of university professors were holding simultaneous sit-ins across the country calling for the replacement of university administrators appointed under Mubarak with elected representatives (Abdel Kouddous 2011).

On July 17th, the tenth day of the sit-in, Prime Minister Essam Sharaf unveiled a cabinet shake-up in an effort to appease protesters. Sharaf, who was being pressured to resign by his former supporters protesting in Tahrir Square, had been negotiating for days with SCAF over the firing of ministers. According to some reports, there was a power struggle taking place between SCAF and the weak civilian government, and a senior military official reminded the local media that "Sharaf was not entitled to appoint or dismiss ministers under the interim constitution" (Shenker 2011). Major General Hassan al-Ruweiny claimed that SCAF was the only body with authority over the cabinet, "a statement likely to infuriate protesters, who have already drawn comparisons between recent public statements by SCAF and the rhetoric deployed by Mubarak's regime" (Shenker 2011).

At least 14 of the 27 cabinet members were eventually replaced. Hazem el Beblawy, who had previously worked for the United Nations, was named the new deputy prime minister and finance minister, and Mohamed Kamel Amr, a former Egyptian representative to the World Bank and former Egyptian ambassador to Saudi Arabia, was appointed foreign minister. Another significant change was the replacement of Zahi Hawass by Abdelfattah al-Banna as minister of antiquities. Hawass, a well-known figure in Egypt, had come under criticism for his praise of Mubarak during the Revolution. Other measures taken by the prime minister to address the demands of the sit-in included the firing of over 600 senior police officers accused of violence against protesters during the Revolution. However, the positions of justice minister and interior minister did not change. Although Interior Minister Mansour el-Essawy and Justice Minister Mohamed al-Guindy were unpopular with protesters, they were well-liked by SCAF.

Despite SCAF's efforts to address protesters' grievances, the sit-in continued until August 1, 2011, the first day of Ramadan, when security forces cleared Tahrir Square by force. Both army soldiers and police participated in shredding tents, as well as arresting and beating protesters. The military deployed over a dozen tanks in the Square to prevent protesters from returning, but by the evening hundreds were back, chanting, "Down with military rule." It was also reported that soldiers and police officers stormed the Omar Makram Mosque, where 500 people were praying, and beat suspected protesters (Afify and Audi 2011). Later, on September 9, 2011, the military government extended the emergency law in response to the storming of the Israeli Embassy in Cairo by anti-SCAF protesters.

One of the most horrifying incidents of SCAF violence against protesters took place on October 9, 2011, in the Maspero district of Cairo. The protests had been organized in response to the attack on a church in Aswan by Islamist radicals. Protesters claimed that the government was too lenient on perpetrators of anti-Christian violence and demanded that the governor of Aswan be sacked. They also called for Field Marshall Tantawi to step down. Protesters felt that state television was fanning the flames of sectarianism. As thousands of Christians, and some Muslims, marched from the Shubra district of Cairo toward the state television building in Maspero Square, demonstrators were attacked by plainclothes police, and clashes with security forces ensued. At least 24 were killed and 212 injured, as protesters were hit with live ammunition and run over and crushed by military armored vehicles. Army soldiers were also reported to have thrown dead bodies of protesters into the Nile (Ibrahim 2012a).

The most deadly clashes under SCAF rule took place in November 2011 on Mohammed Mahmoud Street off Tahrir Square. There, on Friday, November 18, 2011, tens of thousands participated in "The Friday of One Demand" protest, calling for SCAF to cede power to civilian rule. Protesters were attacked by military and security forces that fired rubber bullets and tear gas into the crowd. Clashes continued when security forces attacked a sit-in in Tahrir Square on the morning of November 19, 2011. The sit-in had been organized by families of those killed or injured during the 18 days of the Revolution and was a continuation of the protests that had been violently dispersed on June 28–29, 2011. News of what had happened to the families spread and demonstrators began to return to the Square. The protests extended beyond the issue of martyrs. "The military is stealing our revolution," said protester Ihab Farouk. "When we started our revolution in January, we had hope. Now there's no elections, no security, no money, no jobs. So we don't trust anyone but ourselves. Now we're starting a new revolution" (Chick 2011b). On November 19th alone, almost 50 people were killed and over 1,500 injured by security forces that attacked protesters with tear gas, rubber bullets, and batons (Taha and Kortam 2013).

The intensity of violence perpetrated by the police, Central Security Forces, and the military against demonstrators during the Mohammed Mahmoud clashes was shocking. Protesters claimed that the tear gas used against them was stronger than ever before. Symptoms from inhaling it included epileptic fits, coughing up blood, and collapsing. Tear gas canisters were also used as weapons, when the security forces aimed them at protesters. The most horrific aspect of the clashes was the use by security forces of snipers whose aim was intentionally to shoot out the eyes of some protesters. Following the violent events, the Muslim Brotherhood and its Freedom and Justice Party came under criticism by opposition activists for not having officially participated in the Mohammed Mahmoud battles and supporting protesters (Ibrahim 2012c). The Freedom and Justice Party was gearing up for parliamentary elections set to begin on November 28th, and many felt that the party wanted to avoid coming into direct conflict with the military.

In response to the violent events, SCAF called for crisis talks with the major political parties and movements, and on November 21st, the interim civilian cabinet, including Prime Minister Essam Sharaf, submitted its resignation, which Field Marshall Tantawi accepted. Later, on November 25, 2011, Sharaf was replaced with Kamal El-Ganzouri, who had been prime minister under Mubarak from 1996 to 1999. Describing the relationship between regime violence and concessions, one young woman observed that if one day there was violence, "the next day, the military would come out with a speech and start meeting our demands because people died. The military could not just sleep on it and not say anything." Thus, when the military used violent tactics, it then felt compelled to pull back and offer some type of concession.

On November 22, 2011, Tantawi made a televised statement that a new government with a proper mandate would be formed, parliamentary elections would be held on November 28th as scheduled, and presidential elections would take place by June 2012. Tantawi attempted to reassure the public that a transition to civilian rule would occur by stating that

SCAF did not intend to remain in power and that the military had been restrained when attacked with insults and accusations that tarnished its image. According to Tantawi, the transition process was difficult, and, "We do not care who runs for elections and who is elected president and yet we are accused of being biased" (Abdoun and Rabie 2011). He even offered that SCAF would give up power through a national referendum if it became necessary. In addition to claiming that the military "has not fired a single shot at any Egyptian" (Abdoun and Rabie 2011), Tantawi offered his regrets over the recent clashes and condolences to the families of the victims. He also said that military trials for civilians had been limited and that investigations into the Maspero and Mohammed Mahmoud clashes would be transferred from the military to public prosecution. Despite attempts to appease demonstrators, chants of "leave, leave" continued from protesters demanding civilian rule from a packed Tahrir Square. "Many likened the speech to ousted president Hosni Mubarak's first televised appearance during the January uprising that eventually toppled him" (Abdoun and Rabie 2011). They saw the speech as political theater rather than an offer of real concessions.

On December 16, 2011, army soldiers attacked an anti-SCAF protest camp outside of the Cabinet Building near Tahrir Square. Protesters, who had been staging a sit-in calling for a transition to civilian rule, were beaten with clubs and electric prods. In response, thousands took to the streets. Protesters threw stones at security forces that were building a concrete wall and setting up barbed wire to create a barrier between Tahrir Square and the parliament building. In response, soldiers on rooftops hurled stones back at the protesters. Soldiers in riot gear proceeded to chase protesters through the streets into Tahrir Square and set fire to tents in the Square (Michael 2011). By the end of the clashes, at least three people were dead and 257 wounded (Dahan and Elyan 2011).

Addressing the incident, the prime minister denied that military and police had shot at protesters, instead claiming that the attacks and killing of protesters were committed by third parties and unknown assailants. In a press conference on state television the prime minister said, "I stress here that the armed forces didn't engage with protesters and didn't leave the building." He argued that the government was for "the salvation of the revolution" and that protesters outside the Cabinet Building were "anti-revolution" (Michael 2011).

The Port Said Massacre took place on February 1, 2012, when 74 people were killed and over 1,000 injured during violence at the Port Said stadium following a football match between Al Masry, the home team, and Cairo-based Al Ahly. When the match was finished, Al Masry fans ran across the pitch to attack Al Ahly fans, who were unable to escape because the steel doors of the stadium were bolted shut. Dozens were crushed to death. The police stood by and watched, refusing to open the stadium gates as fans attacked one another with rocks, chairs, knives and swords (Fahmy 2012a). Armed thugs were also reported to have arrived at the stadium in cars during the second half of the game (The Guardian 2012c), indicating that the attacks may have been planned in advance.

The next day, in response to the massacre, Al Ahly fans gathered at the team's headquarters in Zamalek, Cairo, and were joined by fans from the rival Zamalek football club who came out in support. Anti-regime protesters and football fans chanted against military rule, blaming SCAF for the deaths in Port Said. A 10,000-strong march began from Al Ahly headquarters to the Interior Ministry near Tahrir Square. The police responded with tear gas, rubber bullets, and birdshot, leaving three dead. The health ministry reported 1,500 injured in the clashes. Protests continued for days, with thousands in the streets demanding that SCAF hand over power to civilian rule.

The Port Said Massacre was not a sports issue but rather a political one. A particular group of Al Ahly fans, the Ultras, were known to chant anti-SCAF slogans at football matches. The Ultras from both Al Ahly and Zamalek clubs had played a prominent role in the Revolution against Mubarak, particularly during the Battle of the Camel, and had challenged state authority. Many believed that the chaos created by the riots in Port Said was used by SCAF to justify further repression, including cracking down on dissenters such as the Ultras. It was also seen as a pretext to reimpose the emergency law that had been recently canceled. Field Marshall Tantawi had earlier stated that the emergency law would be reinstated if the regime needed to combat "thuggery" (Maass and Petkov 2012). In response to the events, Tantawi declared that the massacre had been caused by violent conspirators who wanted to destabilize Egypt (Maass and Petkov 2012), using a common regime tactic of blaming an unknown third party.

Protests continued on a smaller scale for the rest of SCAF's rule, but on June 16-17, 2012, Egyptians were finally permitted to vote for a new president, which resulted in the election of Mohamed Morsi. Prior to the election, the Supreme Court dissolved the Islamist-dominated parliament on June 14, 2012. This action would have benefited secular candidate Ahmed Shafiq, had he won, and could have served as a blow to Islamist candidate Mohamed Morsi. Later, SCAF made a few power grabs in the final hours. While the presidential elections were taking place, SCAF issued a "complementary constitutional declaration" giving it control of the constitutional drafting process and immunity from oversight, in particular of military activities. The decree also granted the military body broad powers over military affairs, the national budget, and legislation under the new government (Aboulenien 2012). Thus, Morsi began his presidency in a relatively weak position.

UNDERSTANDING REGIME-PROTESTER DYNAMICS UNDER SCAF

When SCAF initially took control of the country, many Egyptians were elated. They held the military in high esteem and "were over the moon with SCAF." A general practitioner observed, "Right after the 18 days I don't think we were protesting against SCAF. It was nothing personal between us and Tantawi." The purpose of the protests was to encourage SCAF to complete the goals of the Revolution and prevent remnants of the Mubarak regime from remaining in power. However, as time went on, many lost their trust in SCAF and believed it was trying to retain control of the country. "They have been controlling the country since 1952. It would be a disaster for them to lose control of the country now," one university student claimed. Another young woman explained, "We really had high expectations of them, but because of how slowly they met the needs of protesters, the nation's needs, and how they overreacted in terms of violence and violations of human rights, that's when we thought, we held them in a really high position but they're not actually as good as we thought they were."

Similar to the effects of violence on protest participation during the 18 days, military and police violence against protesters became a motivator in itself for Egyptians to protest against SCAF. Repression may not be a useful way to quell opposition because it can cause the opposition to protest more (Khawaja 1993; Francisco 1995; Carey 2006, 8). SCAF's use of violence against protesters, either by itself or in combination with concessions, angered protesters, based on perceptions of injustice described in the previous chapter. To review, moral shock is the emotional mechanism whereby an individual perceives that a moral injustice, such as the killing of protesters, has occurred. The individual attributes blame for the injustice to a particular party (the government) and, in this case, empathizes with the victims of the injustice, driving the individual to protest. During the 18 days, individuals sitting at home were outraged by government violence against protesters and empathized with them based on a national collective identity founded on victimization by the Mubarak regime. Thus, moral shock became a motivator for protest. Similarly, under SCAF both police and military violence against protesters infuriated members of the Egyptian public, driving them to protest. "Right after the 18 days it was not personal. After it started getting violent, then people started being furious," one young woman observed.

Rather than being a deterrent to protest, SCAF-sanctioned violence only served to fuel protests, particularly during the Mohammed Mahmoud clashes. One young man described how on the first day of Mohammed Mahmoud, the number of people protesting was moderate in size. However, because of the government's sheer brutality in confronting protesters, each day the numbers taking to the streets grew. Expressing his feelings of collective national identity, the young man said, "I was seeing a lot of people getting injured and a lot of people killed. It was my feeling that I'm Egyptian, that I should do something for those people because they are my brothers and sisters." An upper-middle-class father in his forties who participated in the Mohammed Mahmoud clashes with his wife by his side explained: "We show that we don't care about our lives anymore. We don't care about our safety. We are in an anger situation. They will not take my country; they will not take my freedom; they will not take my rights. . . . One of my greatest fears is that my kids feel that there is no hope because the Revolution is failing." The anger that protesters felt stemmed not only from the violence against protesters but also from the belief that SCAF was trying to rob Egyptians of the Revolution that they had been sacrificing so much to complete.

Throughout the year of SCAF's rule, the response by many youths to police and military police violence was typified by one student who said, "I don't give a shit anymore. I'm going to go there, open my shirt, and take all the bullets. You see this kind of behavior not because we think SCAF cannot [hurt us]. We just don't give a fuck." The abandon with which protesters put their lives on the line, disregarding the consequences for themselves and their families, reflected immense anger about government violence but also an intense, almost primal, need to fulfill the demands of the Revolution. There were also many who wished either to avenge their loved ones who had been killed in protest violence or to ensure that there had been a purpose in their deaths.

During the cycles of contention under SCAF, the regime employed tactics of both violent repression and concession in order to deal with protesters in the streets. In the theoretical literature on the relationship between government responses to protest and protesters' perceptions and reactions to those responses, Karen Rasler (1996) finds that when a regime offers concessions, it further spurs protests. If protesters obtain their desired public good, they are more likely to view protest as the best way to achieve their goals (Muller and Opp 1986; Ondetti 2006, 85); thus, they continue to protest. Additionally, offering concessions signals that the government is unable to maintain power with repressive methods (Ginkel and Smith 1999, 304). Policies of accommodation under restrictive regimes lead to perceptions that the government is weak and that the weakness can be exploited by protesters. Not only accommodation but also policies of "inconsistent signaling" create views of the regime as inept (Ferrara 2003, 306). Thus, actual or perceived weakness increases the opposition's belief that it has a higher probability of achieving its goals. Mark Lichbach claims, "Dissidents' beliefs and expectations about their potential successes and failures are crucial to collective dissent. Rational dissidents do not participate in losing causes" (Lichbach 1995, 62).

Two problems with the literature on government concessions and protest are: (1) most works assume that concessions offered to protesters by the government are perceived as concessions by the protesters themselves, and (2) these works propose a simple binary where protesters can only understand the regime as either weak or strong. Protesters at the July 2011 sit-in made a number of demands, including the removal of Mubarak-era officials. Sharaf's response was to ignore the numerous concerns put forth by protesters and focus solely on the issue of ministers who had held office under the Mubarak regime. However, the Mubarak-era officials that Sharaf removed were strategically unimportant to SCAF. Thus, the institutional concessions that the prime minister offered were aimed at making sacrificial lambs out of unpopular ministers to whom he was not committed. At the same time, ministers such as the ministers of interior and justice were viewed as politically and strategically important. These positions required that the individuals who encumbered them demonstrate unwavering support for SCAF policies. The minister of interior was required to oversee and initiate repressive acts against protesters and opponents of the regime on behalf of the SCAF government. SCAF needed the minister of justice not to oppose constitutional decrees and laws put forth by it to ensure its long-term independence and power. SCAF was unwilling to risk changing the ministers of interior and justice, who had demonstrated their allegiance to the interim government. Thus, for SCAF and Sharaf the concessions offered to protesters were not really concessions at all, even though there was an attempt to frame them as such.

Possibly more important than the fact that Sharaf's cabinet shuffle was not really a concession from the regime's standpoint was the protesters' view that the move was political theater. Protesters did not perceive the removal of these non-strategic ministers as concessions; instead, when the regime played on pre-existing grievances to offer cosmetic concessions, they felt that their intelligence had been insulted and were even more motivated to continue to protest. Protesters described concessions as "not real." One man from Shubra explained, "Of course [the concessions] were fake, for sure. They just wanted to make the people shut up and stay at home." However, the insincere attempts at appeasement made him want to protest more "because they think they can cheat us, and no one can cheat us." It is because protesters did not take the concessions seriously that after Sharaf changed the composition of his cabinet the sit-in did not end.

SCAF's use of violence against protesters and its meaningless offer of concessions both further motivated protest. Egyptians were unwilling to settle for anything less than a swift transition to civilian rule through parliamentary and presidential elections, as well as a referendum on a new constitution. Previous literature argues that concessions will lead protesters to perceive the regime as weak. I propose that when protesters perceive the concessions offered by the regime as superficial, when the regime's gesture towards compromise fails to demonstrate any significant sacrifice on its part, protesters do not view such offers as acts of weakness but instead see them as a further affront to protesters and their demands.

I contend that when Sharaf, under the directive of SCAF, offered concessions to protesters, such acts did not make protesters see the military government as weak. "We all know that the army has the power. They have everything. They control everything. They are not weak; they are so strong, the strongest group in Egypt. There is no one stronger," claimed one protester. On the other hand, the success of protesters in removing the 30-year Mubarak regime in only 18 days signaled to them that even SCAF was challengeable. One young woman declared, "They are in power and we don't like that. We're going to challenge the SCAF." Hence, a distinction must be drawn between perceptions of a regime as weak or strong versus challengeable.[2]

Implied in the view of a regime as weak is that the regime will inevitably be overthrown or that protesters are almost guaranteed to achieve their goals if they persist in their protest because the regime is too fragile to continue to resist. Inherent in the perception of a government as strong is the assumption that protesters view a regime as too powerful for acts of protest to be capable of achieving change. In contrast, to see a regime as challengeable means that protesters are unsure if their demands will be met through protest. However, there is a space open for the possibility of achieving goals through the acts of protesting and publicly contesting the regime. Protesters' success in removing Mubarak opened the door to the possibility that a strong regime could be successfully challenged, but it did not ensure such an outcome. When asked if he thought the anti-SCAF protests would be successful, one protester explained, "You always have to think about that. If you're not thinking about that, why are you protesting?" He continued by clarifying that though he and his fellow protesters assessed the SCAF government as being extremely powerful and strong, the success of protests in removing Mubarak made Egyptians feel that they had the potential to challenge anyone. Therefore, there was a possibility that the protests against SCAF would be successful and SCAF would concede to demonstrators' demands.

Post-revolutionary Emboldening Effect

The premise that SCAF was challengeable derived from an emotion that I call *post-revolutionary emboldening effect*, an emotional mechanism that motivates protest based on the belief that the power of the people can be greater than the people in power. This belief emerges from a revolutionary victory, such as removing a president. Within the emotional process, protesters feel empowered because of triumph in a revolution that they attribute to their own act of protesting. The emboldening emotion is founded on a change in cognition based on learning.

Post-revolutionary emboldening effect reflects an individual's belief in his ability to effect change through his physical presence in a protest. The newfound recognition of self as participant in the process of social and political transformation is significant for someone who has spent the majority of his life sitting on the sidelines as an observer under an authoritarian regime. Thus, the success of everyday Egyptians in overthrowing a powerful dictator activated the post-revolutionary emboldening effect emotional mechanism and signaled to them that protest was a potentially effective vehicle for achieving their goals. In Egypt after the 18 days, the power attributed to protest versus other forms of political participation was so great that during the 2012 presidential elections, some individuals reported not voting because they did not trust the fairness of the electoral process, but they did believe that protest was an effective way to engage politically.

When individuals were asked if prior to the Revolution they had believed that political and social change was possible through protest, the majority of respondents replied "no." Egyptians had lived with the inevitability of Hosni Mubarak for 30 years and had come to see him as nearly invincible. However, when on February 11, 2011, Mubarak stepped down as president of Egypt, the post-revolutionary emboldening effect was activated; the people had made the impossible possible. One young man described his belief in his power to challenge SCAF despite his perception of the Council as strong by saying that after the Revolution, "The people can challenge anyone, every single group. We broke everything in the 18 days, we broke fear. After that we could do anything." A few protesters spoke of being "in a state of euphoria." The emboldened emotional state in which Egyptians found themselves made them believe that they could go on to challenge the authority of even the strongest power in the country, the military governing body.

When a particular action leads to a significant success, individuals absorb that information into their learning processes. Antonio Damasio (2003) ran clinical tests on patients with damaged ventromedial prefrontal cortexes to understand the relationship between emotions and decision-making on the unconscious level. Damasio found that decision-making processes involve estimating effects from past experiences and the rewards or costs that may have been incurred during such events. Individuals protesting against SCAF were able to estimate the effects of the 18 days and weigh the reward in that scenario, which was the overthrow of the leader. Such an assessment produced the emotion of post-revolutionary emboldening effect whereby protesters were emboldened to protest against SCAF. James Jasper (1998) speaks to the concept that emotions are based on cognitions that are changeable through learning. Before the Revolution, Egyptians described the possibility of change through protest as "impossible" because "Mubarak was so strong." However, the act of overthrowing Mubarak through protests altered such emotions and cognitions.

When protesters oust a leader quickly, the post-revolutionary emboldening effect not only drives individuals to continue protesting because they believe even more goals may be achieved through such actions but it also leads them to conclude that they can achieve change at a rapid pace. "Right after the 18 days we were protesting to continue demolishing the old regime. We wanted to see change really fast. We wanted all the shit that happened for 30 years to change in just one month. So we continued protesting to ensure justice would take place, and we thought this could happen because we were in a state of euphoria after being successful after throwing out Hosni Mubarak and the regime," one protester explained. One key aspect of the post-revolutionary emboldening effect is that it encourages individuals to protest based on a cost-benefit analysis based on information through learning that protest can lead to spectacular success. The flip side of the effect is that it may cause a mismatch between expectations and reality. Many protesters supposed that if Egypt's president of three decades could be removed so quickly, surely the remainder of the Revolution's demands could be fulfilled in a comparable time frame. Protesters wanted change, and they expected it expeditiously. The post-revolutionary emboldening effect led to a disconnect between protesters' assumptions about prompt systematic changes and the reality of what was possible, even if the transitional government had been committed allies. A young affluent protester described: "We thought, oh, if we got one we could get two and if we get two then we're going to get three. We thought it was going to be that easy. So after the 18 days it was mainly just to continue, because we knew if we stopped at that point, they could just replace Hosni Mubarak with another person, and corruption would continue to be at the core. People wanted to see proper and accurate change going on and they wanted this change to be really fast." Thus, the emotion of post-revolutionary emboldening effect made protesters view SCAF as challengeable, but it also encouraged unrealistic expectations for the rate of political transformation.

When we examine protest cycles under SCAF, at no point did protesters view SCAF as weak. SCAF controlled the armed forces and their weapons, and it was supported by the country's major institutions, as well as strategically important ministers. Protesters demonstrated against SCAF despite its strength because the political opportunities that were opened through the successful removal of Mubarak created a perception that the regime might be strong but it was challengeable. The emotional mechanism that characterized the view of SCAF as challengeable and motivated protest was the post-revolutionary emboldening effect.

CONCLUSION

The purpose of this chapter was to examine protest dynamics under SCAF and demonstrate how the contentious interactions between the military and protesters led to a relatively quick transition to civilian rule. These interactions were influenced by each side's interests and goals, strategies, relative strengths and weaknesses, and relevant concepts of legitimacy, as well as the changes in political opportunities.

As outlined, the primary goal of protesters was to achieve the aims of the Revolution, namely bread, freedom, and social justice. The objectives of SCAF were to secure its finances and independence in the face of an unknown future regime. A problem was that the perception of each side about how to achieve its goals led to conflicting strategies. Protesters concluded that the way to achieve the aims of the Revolution was through a swift transition to civilian rule. In contrast, SCAF believed that it needed to remain in power long enough to manipulate laws and institutions in its favor. One side's strategy to attain its goals was to protest, while the strategy of the other side was to use violent repression against its opponents. Protesting served to sustain and further open the political opportunities that had been expanded by the protests against, and overthrow of, Mubarak, while violent repression aimed to close those newly opened political opportunities. The reaction of protesters to violent repression was to become angry, mobilize more demonstrations, and delegitimize SCAF. SCAF's response was to offer concessions to protesters because it was afraid of losing legitimacy in the eyes of the population, as the army considered itself a "military of the people". However, the types of concessions offered were unsubstantial. Protesters continued to protest because their major demands were not met and they were angered by the regime's violent repression. While protesters did not view SCAF as weak, they nevertheless believed that the regime was challengeable, based on the opening of political opportunities, and thus concluded that protest was the best strategy to achieve their goals. Protesters' empowerment to contest SCAF was also based on the activation of the post-revolutionary emboldening effect, an emotional mechanism that motivates protest based on demonstrators' success in overthrowing a government, an accomplishment that they attribute to the act of protesting.

SCAF learned that it could not quell dissent through violence or concessions, so it eventually facilitated the transition to civilian rule, arguably much more quickly than would have happened without the protests. Concurring with my assessment, Ibrahim claims, "The [Mohammed Mahmoud] clashes, which led to numerous subsequent marches and rallies against military rule, ultimately forced the SCAF to provide a formal timetable for relinquishing political power" (Ibrahim 2012c).

An important aspect of the interaction between protesters and SCAF was the relative strength of each side. The protest movement held an advantage because it relied on momentum from the recent revolution. The population was on a revolutionary high. There were a large number of individuals willing to protest repeatedly and they were not afraid to die for their cause. In fact, some viewed dying as a benefit because they would be memorialized as martyrs in the struggle. Karl-Dieter Opp and Wolfgang Roehl argue, "Repression may generate or raise expectations of important others not to abstain from protest but to increase it. Moreover, informal positive sanctions (prestige, approval, or attention granted to persons who have been exposed to repressive acts) may be generated" (Opp and Roehl

1990, 524). When a movement has many people willing to protest in the face of violence and it has a relatively unified demand for transition to civilian rule, its weaknesses are few. According to Maha Azzam:

> Despite a strong sense among many Egyptians that the revolution has not attained its goals of dismantling the old order, it is clear that the barrier of fear has been broken, so much so that the SCAF is itself now threatened by the new politics of confrontation from the street. The position of the military still remains a "red line" that activists are warned not to cross, but that line is in fact constantly being crossed by activists, journalists and political groups. Never before have so many Egyptians spoken out so openly against the upper echelons of the military. (Azzam 2012, 9)

In contrast to the protesters' strength, while SCAF had a monopoly on violence, strong coercive capacity, and control of a police force willing to do its bidding, it also had a weakness which centered on its inability to maintain legitimacy. When protesters succeeded in overthrowing Mubarak, they made it clear that any new government could only maintain legitimacy through the support of the people. William Gamson and David Meyer state, "Opportunities open the way for political action, but movements also make opportunities" (Gamson and Meyer 1996, 276). By redefining the terms of legitimacy, anti-Mubarak protesters created new opportunities. SCAF was arguably susceptible to this new definition of legitimacy because the army already claimed to be legitimate as a military of the people. Thus, when the chants changed from "The people and the military are one hand" to "The people and the military are not one hand," SCAF's status diminished considerably because it could no longer claim authority based on the will and support of the people. Each subsequent protest further eroded SCAF's status as protesters publicly refuted the foundation of SCAF's claim to legitimacy. Because SCAF could not continue to use violence to close political opportunities without relinquishing its legitimacy, it was forced to facilitate democratic elections. This chapter ends with the 2012 transition to civilian rule. In the next chapter, I examine the foundations of opposition to the Morsi presidency.

6

Grievances against the Morsi Government

Amira and I lounged in our chairs, smoking hookah and sipping mango juice in our favorite Maadi hangout. It was a Friday night and the sounds of clanging dishes and booming voices filled the room. Suddenly, the chatter stopped and all heads turned to face the salt-and-pepper-haired heart surgeon-turned-comedian whose image had appeared on the TV screen. "Welcome back to *Al-Bernameg*. Last Thursday the president addressed the country, and even though the president usually leaves a lot to be desired in his speeches, this speech was unlike any before . . ." Bassem Youssef continued his set mocking the length of Mohamed Morsi's speeches, the president's convoluted answers to questions, and the circumstances surrounding the constitutional referendum. Youssef had been dubbed the Jon Stewart of Egypt. Similar to *The Daily Show*, *Al-Bernameg* mixed political soundbites with comedic commentary. The satire show went on air following the 2011 Revolution and gained mass popular appeal in 2012 during Mohamed Morsi's time in office, serving as an outlet for those distressed about the political situation. As grievances grew concerning the country's direction, Egyptians looked forward to Youssef's weekly lampoons of the president. It was the first time in memory that a prime-time television program in Egypt had openly mocked the country's leader. Christopher Fry once said, "Comedy is an escape, not from truth but from despair." The tragedy of Morsi's presidency fed the comedy, and Egyptians laughed to ease their anger and dashed hopes.

When Mohamed Morsi assumed power in June 2012, he faced a number of economic and political challenges. In addition to an economy that was failing to recover following the disruption caused by the 2011 Revolution, military decrees had robbed him of full executive powers. This chapter examines the grievances against Morsi that grew in number over the course of his presidency. Certain structural factors, actions by the military, and decisions by remnants of the Mubarak regime were outside Morsi's control. However, the president's decisions played a large part in many problems that plagued the country during his time in office. While grievances alone did not cause the 2013 uprising against Morsi, they undoubtedly contributed to it.

MORSI'S ELECTION

Understanding the role of grievances in President Morsi's downfall first entails investigating the strength of his political mandate. In June 2012, Morsi was elected president of Egypt in a tight race that saw him capture 51.7% of the vote in an election with a turnout of 51% (The Carter Center 2012). In order to assess the strength of Morsi's support, it is essential to examine the primary reasons why voters elected him. Solid backing came from members of the Muslim Brotherhood and various other Islamist groups seeking to place a candidate with similar ideological values in the presidency. He also gained votes from Islamists unaffiliated with any group or party. However, Islamist support by itself would not have been enough to secure Morsi's presidential win.

A large number of those who voted for Morsi did so because they could not stomach voting for Ahmed Shafiq, who had been minister of civil aviation under Mubarak. "I voted for Morsi because I couldn't vote for Shafiq. His hands were full of blood," said one man. Many voted against Shafiq, rather than for Morsi. A student from Attaba claimed, "I was running away from Shafiq." Others voted for Morsi because he seemed like a "good Muslim" and a "man of the people." There were also those who voted for Morsi based on the belief that because the Muslim Brotherhood had been persecuted by previous regimes, members of the organization would be more sympathetic to the cause of human rights and would not perpetrate the same abuses. Some individuals favored the Islamist organization because of its history of involvement in the community. One young man recalled, "Before the Revolution I knew people from the Muslim Brotherhood and did volunteer work with them. I liked the social services they provided to the lower class. The Muslim Brotherhood had money, so I thought they wouldn't steal." Others simply voted on hope. "I was trying to believe that they were wrong before but would be better."

Almost half of voters, i.e., 48.3%, did not support Morsi and voted for his opponent Ahmed Shafiq, who was favored by many due to his political credentials and experience in the Mubarak regime. Some were also strongly opposed to what was described as "Muslim Brotherhood rule," based on knowledge of the organization's violent history and fears that religion and politics would become interwoven. There was also a large percentage of the population that did not vote at all, because either they disliked both candidates, they did not have national identification cards, or they worked in an area of the country far away from their polling station and were therefore unable to vote. Others believed in protest as an agent for change but were not yet convinced that voting would make a difference. What these various reasons for not voting indicate is that not all non-voters were politically apathetic and that those who were not had the potential eventually to be mobilized either in favor or against Morsi. By the end of Morsi's presidency, the grievances against him were so widespread that political actors were able to frame this dissatisfaction and transform complaints into mass protests against the president. In fact, the turnout for the protests on June 30, 2013, was possibly higher than the total voter turnout for the 2012 presidential elections.

Because Morsi's election was not based solely on solid support by ideologically like-minded voters but was also founded on a mixture of deals with various political factions and on the support of those who opposed Shafiq, when Morsi did not meet the demands of the people he soon learned the limitations of his political mandate.

EXPECTATIONS AND PROMISES

The 2011 Egyptian Revolution centered on demands for bread/life, freedom, and social justice. In more specific terms, many cited the poor economic situation, police brutality, and government corruption as their main grievances against the Mubarak regime. Therefore, the expectation was that these particular grievances, along with many others, would be addressed swiftly with regime change.

Contributing to Morsi's downfall were these high expectations, fueled by great promises made by Morsi himself and the poor performance of the Morsi government. When an uprising results in the overthrow of a ruler, the population often holds unrealistic expectations that the next person in power will quickly solve all the country's woes. When these expectations are not met, citizens may become disenchanted with the new government very quickly, which was the case in Egypt post-2011.

During Morsi's election campaign he vowed to tackle the security vacuum, traffic congestion, bread scarcities, food shortages, and lack of public sanitation, all within his first 100 days in power. These promises, which originated in the Muslim Brotherhood's Renaissance Project, set very high hopes for a rapid transformation of the economy and success in dealing with problems that had plagued the country for decades. Thus, Morsi's pledges for the first 100 days reinforced the population's view that the country would turn around swiftly.

Rather than tempering these unrealistic expectations, Morsi's speech in Tahrir Square on June 29, 2012, only served to raise them. Morsi vowed to strengthen the tourism sector, achieve justice for the martyrs and wounded of the Revolution, rejuvenate the economy and "alleviate the suffering of millions of Egyptians seeking a decent, dignified life," respect the constitution and law, advance democracy, and establish the principles of freedom and social justice while removing all forms of injustice, corruption, and discrimination (IkhwanWeb 2012). Opening his jacket and pushing his security guards aside to show that he was unafraid because of his support from the people and his trust in God, he proclaimed, "I come to you, today, my beloved Egyptian people, and I wear no bullet-proof vest, because I am confident, as I trust God and I trust you, and I fear only God. And I will always be fully accountable to you" (IkhwanWeb 2012). Morsi made an array of promises, and many Egyptians who had supported him only hesitantly during the elections now felt hope for a fulfillment of the Revolution's aims.

The grumbles of a disgruntled population began to be heard soon after Morsi's first 100 days in power when there was still no security, garbage was not picked up in the streets, traffic congestion was heavy, the economy, including tourism, continued to decline, and gas shortages and power outages were rampant during the hot summer months. It did not help that Prime Minister Hisham Qandil demanded that people wear cotton clothes and gather in one room in order to save electricity (Al Arabiya 2012a). From the perspective of Morsi's critics, there was little progress in the president's first 100 days and he failed to fulfill his promises. A secretary from Saad Zaghloul had supported Morsi in the beginning "because the Muslim Brotherhood were good people and said they were going to do good things for the country. I was satisfied with the promises, but not with the results." Even Morsi admitted in an October 2012 speech that he had failed to meet all his targets.

Morsi's inability to fulfill his promises in his first one hundred days marked the onset of a long list of grievances against the Morsi presidency that accumulated over the course of his year in office. The following section examines what those grievances were.

OVERVIEW OF GRIEVANCES

The grievances against Morsi were many, too many to include in this chapter. Some of the most frequently reported reasons for dissatisfaction with the government were the unhappiness of both the lower and upper classes with Morsi's speeches and his representation of Egypt abroad; the president's mixing of religion and politics; questionable political decision-making and appointments; favoritism toward the Muslim Brotherhood and the exclusion of other groups; Muslim Brotherhood militia violence against protesters at the Ittihadiya Palace; and economic decline. Some Egyptians simply disliked the Muslim Brotherhood. The lower class was more likely to be bothered by the Morsi presidency because of negative feelings about the Muslim Brotherhood, the violence against protesters at Ittihadiya, and deteriorating economic conditions. While the upper class was also affected by the economic decline, the poor state of the economy had a greater impact on the lower class because they barely had enough money to eat. Those in the upper class were more likely to be displeased with Morsi's speeches and representation of Egypt on the international stage, the mingling of religion and politics, and Morsi's political decisions and appointments. The lower class was more comfortable with integrating religion and politics, but many of them disapproved of the Muslim Brotherhood because of its violent history. Where upper-class and lower-class grievances most coincided was in dissatisfaction with Morsi's pandering to the Muslim Brotherhood while ignoring the clamor of discontent from the rest of the country.

Other common complaints about Morsi included the absence of security and stability, electricity and gas shortages, and the fomenting of sectarianism when Islamists used anti-Shi'ite rhetoric during the June 15, 2013, Egypt-Syria Solidarity Conference, as Morsi sat in tacit approval. Some believed that months of hate speech culminating in the statements made at the conference contributed to the mob attack killing of four Shi'ite Muslims in the village of Abu Musallim in the Giza governorate on June 23, 2013 (Human Rights Watch 2013). Many also blamed the Morsi government for negligence when a train plowed into a school bus near Manfalut killing 50 people, mostly children (Blair 2012). When asked whether there were any government actions that affected their decision to protest on June 30th, many replied with answers similar to that of a middle-aged woman from Shubra: "Everything. He destroyed the country."

ECONOMIC WOES

While the Egyptian people attributed the poor state of the economy to Morsi's inadequacy as president, in reality there was plenty of blame to go around regarding the declining economic situation following the 2011 uprising. The January 25th Revolution and the political unrest that followed led to a fall in the value of the Egyptian pound. In order to prevent the pound from continuing to slide, the policy under the first transitional government of the Supreme Council of the Armed Forces (SCAF) and continued under Morsi was to prop up the pound using the country's foreign exchange reserves. Doing so allowed the value of the pound to remain artificially high. Reserves that stood at $36 billion at the time of Mubarak's ouster fell to $15 billion by November 2012. By the end of 2012, this currency policy was no longer sustainable, as Egypt's foreign reserves dropped to record low levels. Because Egypt relied heavily on foreign imports, low reserve levels caused problems on a number of levels. As the world's largest importer of wheat and a number of other food products, Egypt faced the problem of a dollar shortage for purchasing necessary food staples from abroad (Badawi 2013). Additionally, international business and transactions were disrupted because U.S. dollars became hard to come by. The Egyptian Central Bank initiated U.S. dollar auctions to prevent a run on the pound (Shahine and El-Tablawy 2012), and banks began to put restrictions on the number of dollars that could be withdrawn per day. They also charged large fees for transferring money out of the country. The black market for dollars became very active, with independent money exchanges giving much higher than official rates to individuals selling dollars and charging even higher rates for those trying to buy them.

In addition to currency issues was the reluctance of foreign investors to risk their capital in Egypt because of the political unrest that never seemed to subside. It was reported by Democracy Index that there was a 700% increase in the number of protests in the year Morsi was in power compared to Hosni Mubarak's final year as president (Taha 2013). There were, on average, 1,140 protests per month in 2013 compared to 176 protests per month in 2010 (Taha 2013). Between January and March 2013, there were over 2,400 protests or strikes. In total, there were 9,427 protests against the Morsi regime during Morsi's first and only year in power (Taha 2013). Even prior to Morsi's presidency, from January to June 2012 under SCAF, there were as many as 185 protests or strikes per month, accounting for 29% of protests in the 2012 calendar year (Aboulenein 2013). The large number of protests, combined with the ever-shifting political landscape of changes to the law and frequent government appointments and resignations did little to placate investors' concerns about the stability of the country.

Not only did political unrest scare off investors but it also made tourists hesitant to visit Egypt. Before the Revolution, in 2010, the tourism sector had generated $12.5 billion, but in 2012 that number dropped to $9.4 billion (Farouk 2012). The Central Agency for Public Mobilization and Statistics (CAPMAS) reported that the number of tourists dropped from 14.7 million in 2010 to 9.8 million in 2011. Morsi, who had initially promised to improve the tourism sector, saw the numbers climb to 11.5 million in 2012, but those numbers were nowhere near pre-revolutionary levels. While some tourists took advantage of cheap package deals to beach resorts such as Sharm El Sheikh and Hurghada, the number of foreigners visiting Cairo and its primary attractions such as the Egyptian Museum and the pyramids was reduced to historically low levels. This in turn led to an increase in harassment of tourists at the pyramids by overly aggressive and sometimes violent vendors (Sarah 2013) who were trying to make money on the few tourists left, further deterring visitors to Cairo.

Another lingering problem for the Morsi regime was the International Monetary Fund (IMF) loan that never was. Given the poor financial state of the Egyptian economy, extending from the time SCAF was in power, the Morsi government attempted to negotiate a $4.8 billion loan package from the IMF. However, the terms that the IMF set were politically difficult for Morsi, given that there were already weekly protests against his rule. The demands of the IMF for subsidy reductions and other measures that would have been an additional economic strain on the average citizen could not be implemented at a time when a large segment of the population was already voicing its displeasure with the government. Mass protests would have certainly ensued.

The economic problems in Egypt following the Revolution were exacerbated by a mixture of flawed policies by SCAF that were continued by the Morsi regime, political unrest that deterred investors and tourists, and the population's lack of confidence in, and support for, Morsi's political and economic decisions, leaving him in a weak position and unable to implement the hard measures needed to revive the economy. Thus, the poor state of the Egyptian economy could be attributed not only to Morsi but also to other forces. However, when it comes to mobilizing society against a regime, perception is more important than fact. Instead of a reduction in the unemployment rate by 5% per year, as was the aim of the Renaissance Project, Egypt's unemployment rate actually rose from its original 9% to almost 13% in two years, and during that same time economic growth slowed to 2% from approximately 5.5% (Halime 2013). A middle-aged woman from Zamalek expressed her frustration with Morsi: "His mismanagement of the economy was so severe that it affected everyday life in a very short space of time . . . petrol shortages, inflation, food prices, and power cuts. Usually it takes years for these things to come into effect." Affluent Egyptians complained of financial loss due to electricity shortages and the declining economy, and lower-class workers worried about a decrease in work opportunities and the inability to make ends meet. The Morsi period was described as being "economically the worst days I've ever lived" and as "unfair under Mubarak and more unfair under Morsi. He made living difficult." Even graffiti on a wall in downtown Cairo spelled out: "We don't want beards; we want bread."

ELECTRICITY AND GAS

Much of what takes place on the Egyptian political scene is covert, and the reasons for electricity and gas shortages during the Morsi period will never be known for sure. However, there are indications that these problems were partially due to Morsi's mismanagement, partially due to increased use of electricity and gas as the Egyptian population continued to grow, and partially due to what is known as the *ancien regime*, or those major players from the time of Mubarak.

There is no question that Egypt has an ongoing electricity problem. In Cairo and other major cities, power outages lasted on average 90 minutes on many days in summer 2012. One reason for these shortages was that peak demand for power was approximately 3,000 megawatts more than could be provided by the national grid (Sabry 2012). While the actual reason for power outages was tied to a long-term problem of a growing population and a system that could not keep up with demand, conspiracy theories, a popular pastime in Egypt, circulated that electricity shortages were due to Morsi's providing power to Gaza.

Egypt's electricity complications are also tied to its gas problem. "Around 70% of Egypt's electricity is produced via natural gas" (Esterman 2013). Egypt has had long-term fuel shortages, in part due to hoarding and black market sales of gas (Sabry 2012), along with currency crises and corruption. While Egypt has petroleum resources, it is unable to attract a satisfactory amount of investment in the oil and gas sectors to meet its energy needs. The country requires outside investment because bringing natural gas to the marketplace is both difficult and expensive. Under Mubarak, Egypt engaged in long-term contracts to spread cost risks and "in order to secure agreements between buyers and sellers, promote cost stability and assure investors that they'll have time to recoup their capital outlay" (Esterman 2014). However, such contracts locked Egypt into low export prices. From the Mubarak era to 2012, Egypt exported its surplus natural gas to Israel at below market prices. This contractual obligation to export gas at below-market rates left a shortage of gas for its own country, thus forcing Egypt to compete on the global market to import gas (Esterman

2013). The difference between Egypt's export and import prices due to the lack of uniformity in the natural gas market and the fact that there is no actual market price for gas placed a heavy burden on the economy; in addition, gas contracts signed in the early 2000s under the Mubarak regime lacked transparency and accountability and were subject to widespread corruption.

Despite the many real problems that Egypt faced regarding gas, some people suspected that those who controlled gas supplies were creating additional problems in order to damage the Morsi regime. While these reports were based on speculation, it was curious that during the week before June 30, 2013, there was a nationwide gas shortage leading to eight-hour gas lines that stoked anger against the Morsi presidency, whereas on July 4, 2013, when Morsi was ousted, gas supplies suddenly returned to normal levels.

SECURITY AND SEXUAL HARASSMENT

In addition to electricity and fuel, another immediate concern for the Egyptian public following the 2011 uprising was the lack of security. During the January 25th Revolution, the Egyptian police retreated from the streets and never seemed to return. There were reports of increased incidents of robberies, violent carjackings, and individuals being shot in the road because of minor disputes. However, the issue that continued to top the headlines was sexual harassment and gang rapes.

For many years prior to the Revolution, incidents of sexual harassment in the streets, from verbal abuse to groping, were commonplace in Egypt. This repugnant behavior was depicted in the 2010 film *678* (Diab 2010). However, after the Revolution, with police notably absent, harassment escalated to frequent instances of gang rape, particularly on the Cairo Corniche and at protest sites. The assault on the security of women took two forms: (a) harassment of women going about their daily lives and (b) violent sexual assaults on women choosing to participate in political protests.

In 2013, the United Nations Entity for Gender Equality and the Empowerment of Women published a report stating that 99.3% of Egyptian women had faced sexual harassment on the Egyptian streets. Women experienced anxiety when leaving their homes, anticipating lewd remarks at best and groping, or even rape, at worst. While these types of sexual violations affected women on a daily basis, it was the sexual assaults in Tahrir Square that continued to make headline news.

Violence against women was a tactic that had been used by the Mubarak regime during the 2005 Kefaya protests, when female protesters could be seen on television being dragged and assaulted by security forces (Slackman 2005). However, the statistics on rape at protests in Tahrir Square during the Morsi regime were truly abhorrent. At one protest in Tahrir Square, there were 18 confirmed attacks on women, with six needing hospitalization (el Sheikh and Kirkpatrick 2013). One of the women was stabbed in her genitals, while another required a hysterectomy. Women were mob attacked, had their clothes violently torn off, and were raped in the middle of the Square. There were 169 reported incidents of mob sexual assaults from June 30th through July 3rd, and particularly on July 3, 2013, as the Morsi government fell, more than 80 women reported being sexually assaulted at the anti-Morsi protests (Kingsley 2013c).

Following a protest in the Square in November 2012, a local journalist reported that when a man had tried to rip an attacker off a woman even by bashing the perpetrator's head against a metal bar, the latter had continued on as if he felt no pain. In another instance, a woman failed to stop an assault even after gouging her attacker's eyes with her nails. It seemed to some observers that the men committing these assaults showed signs of having taken the drug PCP before going to the Square so that they would be immune to pain should they be caught up in scuffles or arrested by police and tortured.

There was also speculation that the men committing these attacks had been paid by individuals or groups affiliated with the Muslim Brotherhood to scare women away from attending protests. Mohamed Abu Al Ghar, president of the Egyptian Social Democratic Party, believed that the "Muslim Brotherhood 'plotted the sexual harassment in Tahrir Square' to intimidate the demonstrators" (el Sheikh and Kirkpatrick 2013). While these speculations cannot be confirmed, the fact that some citizens blamed the government for the attacks, or at least for the failure to stop them, did not bode well for the Morsi presidency.

Although the government did not respond adequately to the growing epidemic of sexual violence, the blame for it was often placed on the women themselves. A *New York Times* article from March 2013 quoted Adel Abdel Maqsoud Afifi, a police general, lawmaker, and ultraconservative Islamist as saying, "Sometimes a girl contributes 100% to her own raping when she puts herself in these conditions," and Reda Saleh Al al-Hefnawi, a lawmaker from the Muslim Brotherhood's Freedom and Justice Party (FJP) posed the question, "How do they ask the Ministry of Interior to protect a woman when she stands among men?" (el Sheikh and Kirkpatrick 2013).

The horrific sexual assaults on women in Tahrir Square, the harassment women experienced in the streets due to reduced police presence, and the increase in violent crime made many citizens view the Morsi government as incapable of attending to their basic needs of security and stability.

SPEECHES AND INTERNATIONAL REPRESENTATION

When asked if there were any government actions or stories in the news that caused individuals to be unhappy with the Morsi regime, one of the more common responses was "Morsi's speeches." Describing Morsi, in so many words, as a buffoon, based on his reputation for rambling, incoherent speeches, an engineer from Garden City observed, "He is like a cartoon character. Every time he speaks you win if you understand one word of him. He is an idiot."

In the second half of the twentieth century and beginning of the twenty-first century, Egyptians had grown accustomed to strong military leaders who presented themselves in an authoritative manner. However, the impression that Egyptians had of Morsi was that he was weak and incompetent. Morsi's failure to project presidential power caused him to lose the respect of his people. Speaking of Morsi's unsuitability for the position of president, a young man from Sayaida Zaineb explained, "He was just like a village manager.... It was too much for him to head a village."

Critics of the regime argued that Morsi lacked presidential qualities when representing Egypt on the international stage and that he shamed his country. When a young college graduate traveled to Dubai, people in the Emirates mocked him for his country's choice of president. "Even the passport control officer made fun of me," he exclaimed.

One of the more humiliating moments of Morsi's presidency has often been referred to as the "ball-scratching incident." In September 2012, Morsi held a live television press conference with Australian Prime Minister Julia Gillard. As cameras rolled, Morsi adjusted his package on live television. In response, the Twitter scene blew up. Posts such as "I cringed watching this! No one told Morsi that it's 'frowned upon' to touch your penis in public?" appeared, along with other comments too explicit to repeat. Egyptians, including Islamists, found Morsi's actions mortifying. As one unemployed technical high school graduate put it, Morsi had "no international respect... he was scratching his balls on camera." Many felt that "Morsi made a fool out of the country" and that he was "embarrassing us in front of other presidents."

Another embarrassment for the Morsi presidency occurred on June 3, 2013, when Egyptian politicians were broadcast on television discussing ways to halt Ethiopia's Nile River dam project. While those in the room made suggestions such as backing Ethiopian rebels to use as a bargaining chip, and politician Ayman Nour proposed, "We can leak information, for example intelligence information, that Egypt seeks to buy certain kinds of [military] planes... and that pressure, even if it wasn't actual, could have an impact in the diplomatic process" (Al Jazeera, 2013b), they were unaware that the cameras were still rolling. Egyptians could not believe that the politicians "didn't realize they were airing it live" and felt that the "minister of water sources was in a total coma about the Ethiopia dam." The general feeling about Morsi and those surrounding him was expressed by one man who said, "Really, every time he opened his mouth on TV, he or any of his people, or he traveled to anywhere in the world... that brought great anger and shame to me." While people listed many more instances of international missteps, the two cited above were the ones most frequently mentioned.

MIXING RELIGION AND POLITICS

Another problem for the Morsi presidency was that there were many in the country who just "didn't like the Muslim Brotherhood." As discussed in chapter 2, during the years prior to 2011, the Egyptian government's policy toward the Muslim Brotherhood vacillated between accommodation and repression, based on the government's perception of the strength of the organization, acts of violence committed by the group, and the political priorities of the Egyptian president in power. There were many in Egypt who were either members of the Muslim Brotherhood or sympathized with it. However, there were even more who opposed the group, particularly based on its history of violence and its aim to merge religion and politics.

While the Muslim Brotherhood made efforts to work peacefully within the system in the decade leading up to the Revolution, fielding independent candidates for parliament, one woman from Shubra explained her feelings toward the Morsi government as "I didn't like the Muslim Brotherhood's control of Egypt. I knew the history of the Muslim Brotherhood in terms of violence and their understanding of Islam." It was difficult for the Muslim Brotherhood to shake its reputation for bloodshed with some sectors of the population. Those who could not forget the violence of the 1980s and 1990s said, "We had a bad history with the Muslim Brotherhood since 1928. We don't need to try again." Many also used the term "liars" to describe the group, underlining that they were not trusted. "They're professional liars. They are murderers and liars and we know about them as liars and promising and not delivering on promises since Hassan al-Banna."

Other than the issue of associating the Muslim Brotherhood with violence, a large number of individuals, particularly from the upper class, did not favor the idea of mixing religion and politics. In Egypt, many people are satisfied with letting religion dictate family law, but they do not want their entire legal system governed by Islamic law. A 70-year-old, upper-middle-class lawyer related:

> I was against the Muslim Brotherhood. I belong to a generation that saw how nasty they were to the country. Some expectations were that Morsi was not the right man. Not acceptable to have a religious political party. It proved to be the case. . . . His mere existence as a president is contradictory to the past 200 years in Egypt. Mohammed Ali led to development in Egypt. The economy and society went in a very different direction from the Muslim Brotherhood. It didn't go in a religious direction, secularism. Secondly, when Morsi was elected he split the country into two or three parts. As an elected president he had supporters and opponents. After the election he should have brought people together. He divided people more.

Many Egyptians were dissatisfied with the vision that the Muslim Brotherhood put forth for the place of religion in politics. "There is a space for religion and a space for politics. The place for religion should not go into the place for politics and the place for politics should not go into the place for religion." Comments such as "[I did not like Morsi because] it was a religious state. I want a secular state" demonstrated discomfort with perceived attempts at theocratic rule.

Individuals also denounced the Morsi government and the Muslim Brotherhood for using religion to control the masses. A description of both Morsi and the Muslim Brotherhood as "hypocrites using religion to manipulate the people" expressed the view that Morsi was playing on religious sentiments in an effort to shore up his legitimacy. People saw Morsi as "trying to resurrect authoritarianism" through religious rhetoric rather than implementing the political freedoms that Egyptians had demanded during the 2011 Revolution. "There was no change. It was like having Mubarak with a beard; the only difference was that Morsi played the religion card."

People complained not only about Morsi's integration of religion into politics but also about his perceived attempts at ideological hegemony. Egyptians did not accept being told what to believe and what type of Islam they should practice. Many felt "[the Muslim Brotherhood] was trying to enforce its beliefs on us." During Morsi's time in office, there were many *imams* (prayer leaders) who used the Friday sermon to endorse the president, informing worshipers that it was their Islamic duty to support him. On May 17, 2013, a fight broke out at the Mostafa Mahmoud Mosque in the Mohandeseen district of Cairo between supporters and opponents of Morsi. Government opponents were angered when the *imam* offered a prayer for the Islamist president during the sermon (Ahram Online 2013a). Many Egyptians did not appreciate attending Friday prayers only to be told they were not "good Muslims" if they did not align themselves with the president. "The Muslim Brotherhood thinks that they're right and everyone else is wrong. They think they're Muslim and everyone else isn't."

POLITICAL APPOINTMENTS

In order to gain the backing that he needed from various other political parties to win the 2012 presidential election, on June 21, 2012, Morsi held a meeting at the Fairmont Hotel in Heliopolis where he promised influential members of civil society such as Wael Ghonim, administrator of the We are all Khaled Said Facebook page, and Ahmed Maher, founder of the April 6th Youth Movement, that he would adhere to their three main conditions in exchange for their support. These stipulations were the launching of a national unity project, the formation of a national salvation government that would include representatives from all political factions and would be headed by an independent political figure, and a presidential team that would reflect the diversity of the Egyptian political arena (Shukrallah 2013a). While it would seem that an Islamist party and liberal factions would make for strange bedfellows, the distaste for voting for Ahmed Shafiq, a member of the former Mubarak regime, led many liberal political movements and individuals to lend their support to Morsi.

The terms of the Fairmont talks were agreed upon, and Morsi gained the votes he needed.

Support for the Muslim Brotherhood had been estimated at 20–30% of the Egyptian population (Steinvorth 2011), which hardly gave Morsi the backing to push through decisions without coalition endorsement and consensus-building efforts. However, as his presidency progressed, the disregard for the agreements made with various political factions became strikingly obvious. A sizeable number of his non-Muslim Brotherhood political appointments were seen as "show" appointments, with the real power going to the Muslim Brotherhood Guidance Bureau. Many felt that "[Morsi] put all his people in positions of power and neglected the rest of the people."

The perception that Morsi was "making the country full of Muslim Brotherhood in every position from officers to ministers" was lent credibility by a number of his political appointments. On July 24, 2012, Morsi replaced outgoing Prime Minister Kamal el-Ganzouri with Islamist-supporting Hisham Qandil, who then appointed a cabinet with a large number of ministers from the Muslim Brotherhood and its supporters. Later in his presidency, on January 6, 2013, Morsi made a number of changes to the cabinet, increasing the number of appointees who were members of the Muslim Brotherhood's Freedom and Justice Party from five to eight. Morsi altered the cabinet again on May 7, 2013, when he appointed three more members of the Muslim Brotherhood to ministerial positions, bringing their number to eleven out of the thirty-five cabinet members. Finally, on June 17, 2013, in a move that shocked the country, Morsi appointed sixteen new governors, four of whom were members of the Muslim Brotherhood, and one, the governor of Luxor, who was from Muslim Brotherhood ally al-Gama'a al-Islamiyya. Egyptians were outraged at the Luxor appointment because al-Gama'a al-Islamiyya was the group that had committed the terror attack on foreign tourists in Luxor in 1997. The gubernatorial designations sparked protests and clashes between Muslim Brotherhood supporters and opponents in a number of governorates.

In addition to Morsi's political appointments and his marginalization of alternative voices, many criticized him for acting as a president of the Muslim Brotherhood and allowing its leaders to have undue influence on his decisions. Individuals pointed to Deputy Leader of the Muslim Brotherhood, Khairat al-Shater, and the Muslim Brotherhood Supreme Guide, Mohammed Badie, as the real decision-makers and claimed that the two spoke as if they represented the government when they held no official posts. "[Morsi] wasn't the actual ruler; the Supreme Guide was." During anti-regime protests in November and December 2012, demonstrators chanted, "Down with the Supreme Guide" rather than, "Down with Morsi," though they did declare, "The people want the downfall of the regime." People referred to Morsi as a "puppet," "sheep," and "robot taking orders from the Muslim Brotherhood."

Morsi's uncompromising approach to politics and his adherence to the demands of the Muslim Brotherhood, ignoring all others, lost him the goodwill of many of the non-Islamist citizens who had voted for him. "In the beginning I was hoping for the best, when he was in Tahrir saying he was a good man. After that I hated everything. He didn't act like a president. Everything was for the Muslim Brotherhood." Another student from Shubra who appreciated Morsi's religiosity and voted for him because he was a "man of the people" explained to me that in the first two or three months she was happy because Morsi was praying *fajr* (morning prayer) and walking around without guards. She recalled:

> He was eating like us. It was never like that with Mubarak. I thought Morsi was good and would change Egypt. He said his family was all the Egyptian people, but then I found that his family was only the Muslim Brotherhood. After three months I saw that the Muslim Brotherhood wanted to control the country alone and put Muslim Brotherhood members in the ministries.

As the Morsi presidency progressed, Egyptians sensed that the Muslim Brotherhood was overstepping its bounds and that Morsi was caving into its demands. These beliefs were a major factor in the perception of Morsi as a weak president incapable of independent thinking and consistent leadership and in a feeling of desperation as people saw their hopes being dashed by another regime veering toward authoritarianism.

CONCLUSION

This chapter examined a number of grievances against the Morsi government that contributed to individual decisions to protest on June 30, 2013. Egyptians held high expectations following the Revolution, expectations that Morsi was unable to meet. The president also made a number of political appointments and choices that angered his constituents. However, the decision that particularly incensed so much of the population was the November 22, 2012, constitutional declaration, which led to mass protests and violent clashes between Muslim Brotherhood supporters and opponents. The violence and torture committed by Muslim Brotherhood militias against the opposition during those clashes was one of the primary grievances cited. In the next chapter, I demonstrate how Morsi's constitutional declaration and the subsequent violence during the Ittihadiya protests generated mobilization against his presidency, eventually leading to the June 30th coup and his ouster.

7

The June 30th Coup

Amani, Yusra, and I were squeezed into the back seat of the taxi. It was not one of the modern taxis with air conditioning that had begun to appear on the Cairo streets in the past few years; it was an old black and white taxi with a back door roped shut and no meter. It was a sweltering June evening and we were trapped in an all too familiar traffic jam, inhaling smog and dripping with sweat. Amani was about to stick her head out of the window to see what was blocking the road when a young man approached the taxi and shoved a paper through the window. "Have you signed the petition yet?" Yusra grabbed the black and white photocopy and we immediately recognized it as the Tamarod petition demanding that President Mohamed Morsi step down from office. The taxi driver pulled to the side of the road, and Amani and Yusra filled out their personal information, signed the petition, and returned the paper to the young man. Then the taxi driver requested his own copy to fill out. When I turned to look at the other side of the road, I spotted a couple with their young children also stopping cars and encouraging passengers to sign the petition. This same scene was replayed throughout Cairo in the months leading up to June 30, 2013.

In the previous chapter, I outlined the Egyptian public's numerous grievances against the Morsi presidency. While grievances alone do not cause an uprising, grievances can be framed by a social movement organization in such a manner that individuals are mobilized to act on them. The Tamarod movement that emerged in April 2013 placed the people's grievances in a petition that called for nationwide protests on June 30th.

In this chapter, I argue that the events of June 30, 2013, exemplified a *popular participatory veto coup* facilitated by opposition co-optation. This new term, founded on Samuel Huntington's concept of a veto coup, describes not only the type of coup that took place but also the process by which it occurred. A thorough explanation of the processes surrounding the June 30th coup is important in order to understand that how it transpired differs slightly from Huntington's outlined characteristics of a veto coup. The chapter describes how the 2013 coup in Egypt was a veto coup triggered by the military's opposition to the Muslim Brotherhood as a militant organization and Morsi's infringement on the military's independence and political power. The coup took place through opposition co-optation when the military influenced and provided support to the Tamarod movement. The process involved popular participation of the public, the post-coup government's encouragement of demonstrations to support the military against the Muslim Brotherhood, and the Egyptian people's election of Abdel Fattah el-Sisi as president. In this chapter, I also contend that there was a difference between the general public's perception of political opportunities and actual political opportunities, and I outline how the military engaged in a retain and restrict policy that intensified repression and prevented a return to civilian rule out of fears of what would happen should it lose its veto power. Finally, I demonstrate how the Rabaa al-Adawiya massacre, subsequent actions by the military, and Sisi's election contributed to consolidating the coup.

COUP THEORY

Many works on military coups d'état rely on the typology of coups outlined in Samuel Huntington's *Political Order in Changing Societies*. In his book, Huntington describes different types of coups, from breakthrough coups, when junior officers attempt to implement a new social order, to guardian coups, when the military aims to protect the status quo against intra-elite conflict (Huntington 1968). The theoretical approach that informs this chapter is Huntington's concept of veto coup. A veto coup benefits the middle and upper classes and attempts to exclude mass participation by the lower class. It occurs when (1) a party or movement that the military opposes and wishes to exclude from political power wins an election (Huntington 1968, 223) and/or (2) the government in power "begins to promote radical policies or to develop an appeal to groups whom the military wishes to exclude from power" (Huntington 1968, 224). In these circumstances, the coup prevents the broadening of political participation by radical groups and slows the process of socioeconomic reform (Huntington 1968, 224). The military is opposed to any group or organization that threatens its position, and thus accepts a leader "only until he begins to organize his own mass following with which he can challenge the army's role as arbiter of national values" (Huntington 1968, 227). In Egypt, the military was opposed to Morsi's rule based on his membership in the Muslim Brotherhood, a group that previous governments had targeted due to its militant actions, and because he endeavored to undermine the independence and authority of the military. In Huntington's version of the veto coup, the military vetoes mass participation by the lower class. I argue that in Egypt, while the coup did benefit the upper class, it was more a veto of Islamist ideology and the power of the Muslim Brotherhood than a rejection of lower-class participation. In fact, the military was able to influence lower-class perceptions in a manner that allowed it to benefit from lower-class participation.

The stated purpose of the coup is for the military to become involved in politics for limited and intermittent purposes in order to guard and/

or purify the existing order (Huntington 1968, 225). According to Huntington:

> Military intervention, consequently, is prompted by the corruption, stagnation, stalemate, anarchy, subversion of the established political system. Once these are eliminated, the military claim that they can then return the purified polity to the hands of the civilian leaders. Their job is simply to straighten out the mess and then to get out. (Huntington 1968, 226)

Thus, the military presents itself as apolitical, intervening in politics because of a danger to the country based on the prospect of disorder. On June 30th, the Egyptian military claimed that its aim was to intervene to prevent chaos and to support the will of the people.

The dilemma for the military, once it assumes power, is that simply removing a leader cannot ameliorate the problems in the political system. In addition, once the group or leader is removed, the military's institutional and personal self-interest make it fearful of retaliation if it ever withholds its veto (Huntington 1968, 232-233). Therefore, while the military's initial rationale for intervention is founded on guarding the political order and a claim that the situation is temporary, with the country quickly returning to civilian rule, the military has a strong incentive to further intervene in politics so that the ousted group never returns to power.

Once the military removes the leader, it has four options of how to proceed: (1) *Return and Restrict*, where the military allows a return to civilian rule after purging government officials. In this case, the army continues to restrict the rise of specific new groups to political power; (2) *Return and Expand*, where the military allows a return to civilian rule and permits the ousted group to vie for power under particular restrictions and with new leadership; (3) *Retain and Restrict*, where the military retains power and restricts the expansion of political participation; in this case, the military is driven toward more repressive measures; and (4) *Retain and Expand*, where the military retains power and permits expansion of political participation (Huntington 1968, 233-236). As we will observe in the case of the June 30th coup, the military adopted a retain and restrict policy where it remained in power and engaged in severe repression.

Huntington's outline of the characteristics of a coup d'état include: (1) that the event must be an attempt by a political coalition to illegally overthrow the existing government by violence or the threat of violence, (2) if violence is employed it is usually limited, (3) the number of people participating is small, and (4) participants in the coup already have institutional bases of power within the political system (Huntington 1968, 218). A coup succeeds (a) when the number of participants in the political system is small, or (b) if the number of participants in the political system is large, but a substantial proportion of them support the coup (Huntington 1968, 218). In this chapter, we observe a novel coup characteristic, which is that the number of people participating in the coup was large. By co-opting the Tamarod movement, the military was able to use approximately 30 million people to unseat the government. It should be noted that these 30 million people were unwitting participants in the coup. However, once the coup had taken place its ultimate success relied on a large number of participants, a vast majority of the Egyptian population, to support continued military intervention. Thus, I label the events of June 30, 2013, a *popular participatory veto coup* facilitated by opposition co-optation. In the following pages, I outline the popular movement to oust Morsi, the military's co-opting of that movement, and how the military garnered support for its sustained intervention in Egyptian politics.

CONSTITUTIONAL DECLARATION

Sustained public opposition to the Morsi government began in November 2012 in response to the president's constitutional declaration. In order to explain the impact of the constitutional declaration, it is important to outline the events leading up to the proclamation, beginning with the history of the Constituent Assembly. The first elected constituent assembly charged with writing a new constitution following the 2011 Revolution was elected by the Islamist-dominated parliament. Non-Islamists felt that the Assembly was not representative of the range of perspectives in Egyptian society, as fully 66 out of 100 members were Islamists (Partlett 2012) and only 6 women held seats (Caspani 2013). "The Shura Council was all Muslim Brotherhood. The parliament was all Muslim Brotherhood. Everything in the country was Muslim Brotherhood," was the complaint of one young man who reflected the views of a number of his fellow citizens.

In April 2012, the Egyptian courts found the Constituent Assembly unconstitutional, and the Supreme Administrative Court dissolved it on the grounds that it included members of parliament and that the Islamist majority composition was not representative of the diversity in Egyptian society (Fahmy 2012b). The Assembly comprised too few youth, women, and minorities. In addition, according to the el-Salmi Document that had been issued on November 1, 2011, only 20 members of the Assembly could be partisan parliamentarians; the other 80 seats had to be filled by members of various specified sectors of Egyptian society (Trager 2016). A later judicial ruling had decreed that members of parliament were permitted to elect the members of the Constituent Assembly but were not allowed to elect themselves. By the time of the Assembly's dissolution many groups, including SCAF, had already withdrawn their members (Ottaway 2012).

In the June 2012 new Constituent Assembly Law regulating the work of the Assembly, drafted by Parliament's legislative committee, Article 3 stated, "The Constituent Assembly should be representative of all segments of Egyptian society to the fullest extent possible" (El Gundy 2012). However, the composition of the resulting newly elected assembly led an Egyptian administrative court to refer to the Supreme Constitutional Court a case seeking its dissolution, again on the basis that it was not inclusive and representative of Egyptian society and members of parliament were participating. For months there had been fights over Islamist domination of the Assembly, and many secular groups eventually staged a walk-out. These groups included those in the Egypt Bloc and the Revolution Continues Alliance, some in the Wafd Party, the Hurriyah Party, the Socialist Popular Alliance Party, the Egyptian-Arabic Union Party, and the Egyptian Citizen Party (Ottaway 2012). Many independent candidates also protested. Rather than serving as rubber stamps for an Islamist-created constitution, many secular groups believed that by withdrawing from the Assembly they would prompt its dissolution as an unrepresentative institution, thus pressuring Islamists to include other voices. This plan failed when, later in November, Morsi changed the rules of the game through his constitutional declaration.

In what was seen as a last-minute power grab, SCAF made a supplementary constitutional declaration only one week before Morsi's election was announced that placed it above the Constituent Assembly by stating that it was permitted to veto any clause drafted by the Assembly if the clause conflicted with the goals of the Revolution or the principles of previous constitutions. In addition, if the Assembly attempted to overturn the veto, the clause would be referred to the Supreme Constitutional Court. Finally, if the Assembly did not complete the constitution within three months and were dissolved, SCAF would then be responsible for appointing a new assembly (Labib 2012).

On November 22, 2012, with the Egyptian courts set to rule on the legality of the Assembly, the now-President Morsi issued a constitutional declaration giving the presidency powers that led many to call him the "new Pharaoh." Most controversial of the seven articles in this declaration was Article 2, which stated, "All constitutional declarations, laws and decrees made since Morsi assumed power on 30 June 2012 cannot be appealed or canceled by an individual or political or governmental body until a new constitution has been ratified and a new parliament has been elected. All pending lawsuits against them are void" (Egypt Independent 2012). The declaration also stated that the Shura Council and Constituent Assembly were immune from dissolution. The opposition began to mobilize against Morsi, claiming that the constitutional declaration granted the president dictatorial powers until a new constitution was passed. Those who disagreed with the politics surrounding the Constituent Assembly and how the constitution was being drafted were forced to choose between voting for a constitution that they did not support or accepting a dictator as president until a more satisfactory constitution could be created. When asked if she had voted in the 2012 constitutional referendum, one woman said,

"No. It would have been in vain. The Muslim Brotherhood did whatever they wanted. Voting wouldn't make a difference."

ITTIHADIYA

Morsi's constitutional declaration led to mass anti-government street protests in Tahrir Square and at the Ittihadiya Presidential Palace in November and December 2012. As was put by a student from Zamalek, "Morsi didn't understand what his mandate was. He got too big for his britches. People voted not-Shafiq. Morsi didn't understand they didn't vote *for* him."

Protests commenced on November 23, 2012, and continued for weeks. On November 27, 2012, more than 100,000 protested in the streets of Cairo against the declaration. Protest organizers set meeting points around the city and the marchers then descended on Tahrir Square. Demonstrators chanted "Leave" and "The people want the fall of the regime," reminiscent of the 2011 Revolution and anti-SCAF protests of the same year. The secular opposition, which had been fragmented for a while, overcame their differences in order to challenge the Morsi government and the Muslim Brotherhood. In response to the demonstrations, the Muslim Brotherhood mocked the protesters on one of its associated television networks, calling them "remnants" of the Mubarak regime (Fahim and Kirkpatrick 2012).

Protests intensified on December 4, 2012, with tens of thousands of demonstrators gathering at the Ittihadiya Presidential Palace and Tahrir Square to express their displeasure with the Islamist-drafted constitution. Protesters chanted "Bread, freedom and bring down the Brotherhood," a revised version of chants used in 2011, and "Shave your beard, show your disgrace, you will find that you have Mubarak's face!" (Kirkpatrick 2012b). Demonstrations also took place in Alexandria, Suez, and other Egyptian cities. Eleven newspapers made the decision to halt publication to protest restrictions on freedom of expression in the new constitution, and three television networks claimed that they would go dark the next day (Kirkpatrick 2012b).

Reaching the Ittihadiya Palace around 6:00 p.m., protesters began to push against police barricades. The police responded by firing tear gas at the approximately 10,000 demonstrators, some of whom broke through police lines and succeeded in protesting near the perimeter wall of the palace (Saleh and Awad 2012). The police, in an attempt to avoid further confrontations with protesters, retreated behind the walls of the palace. Eventually Morsi evacuated the presidential residence as two rows of riot police guarded his motorcade, clearing the way for it to pass (Kirkpatrick 2012b).

The most intense fighting between opposition protesters and Morsi's Islamist supporters took place on December 5, 2012. At 6:00 a.m. the Muslim Brotherhood Twitter account posted the message "Muslim Brotherhood & Islamist parties call for Million-Man March today afternoon outside Itehadyya palace in supprt the elected president." The Muslim Brotherhood bused supporters into Cairo from other governorates, and members of the group posted *istinfar* (en garde) on Facebook. In response to the Facebook posts calling for Brotherhood members to be prepared, the son of Muslim Brotherhood leader Mohamed Beltagy posted on Facebook that members should not circulate orders publicly on Facebook, as *istinfar* was an internal order. Clashes began when thousands of Morsi supporters approached an ongoing 300-person sit-in outside the Ittihadiya Palace. Muslim Brotherhood members tore down opposition tents, rifled through the possessions of the sit-in participants, and chased and beat anti-Morsi protesters. After a relative period of calm, hundreds of opposition protesters arrived at the palace, and opponents and supporters of the president began throwing Molotov cocktails and rocks at each other.

That evening, Freedom and Justice Party Deputy Secretary Essam al-Erian gave a television interview where he declared, "Everyone must go now to Ettihadiya and surround the thugs and separate the real revolutionaries out for one or two nights and then we can arrest them all" (Human Rights Watch 2012). Not long afterward, approximately 10,000 Morsi supporters were out putting up barricades to keep traffic away from the palace (Associated Press 2012b).

Throughout the night, opposition and pro-Morsi protesters attacked each other with stones, Molotov cocktails, rubber pellet rifles, and handguns, while Central Security Forces stood back and watched. The Muslim Brotherhood feared that security forces would not act to defend the president, and what appeared to be organized groups of militants were sent out to guard the palace (Youssef 2012). The actions of these seemingly coordinated "protection" groups during the protests went beyond those of security guards, as they set up outdoor torture chambers where members of the opposition were detained and tormented. At least 49 opposition protesters were unlawfully detained by Muslim Brotherhood supporters outside the palace gate, an area under the control of the Muslim Brotherhood and overseen by the police (Human Rights Watch 2012). According to Human Rights Watch, a police report from the New Cairo police station recorded that "youth from the Freedom and Justice Party handed the detainees over to the station" (Human Rights Watch 2012). The following day, the 49 detainees were turned over to state prosecutors. In total, 133 detainees were eventually released without charge because of lack of evidence (Human Rights Watch 2012).

By the end of the clashes, the Ministry of Health recorded 10 dead and 748 injured (Human Rights Watch 2012). This violence against citizens demanding their rights further inflamed the anti-Morsi movement. When asked whether he thought Morsi had been a legitimate president, one student replied, "He was because he won the election, but he wasn't when he sent guys out to beat up his own citizens."

Protests resumed on December 6, 2012, in Cairo, prompted by Vice-President Mahmoud Mekki's statement to the press that Morsi would not back down. In addition to four deaths and over 300 injuries in Cairo, protesters in the city of Ismailia burned down the headquarters of Morsi's Freedom and Justice Party (Hussein 2012). That same day, three members of Morsi's advisory team, Seif Abdel Fattah, Ayman al-Sayyad, and Amr al-Leithy, resigned. Morsi called for dialogue with opposition forces, but the National Salvation Front (NSF), a loosely formed group of the main opposition parties created after Morsi's declaration, declined the invitation. Opposition advocate Mohamed El Baradei made a statement, claiming,

"We hold President Morsi and his government completely responsible for the violence that is happening in Egypt today." He then continued by saying, "A regime that is not able to protect its people and is siding with his own sect, [and] thugs is a regime that lost its legitimacy and is leading Egypt into violence and bloodshed" (Hussein 2012).

As protests continued, over two dozen Muslim Brotherhood headquarters around the country were ransacked (Kirkpatrick 2012c). On December 9, 2012, Morsi issued a new constitutional declaration rescinding the old one that had sparked the recent protests (Hauslohner and Hassieb 2012). While the new declaration removed the president's immunity from judicial oversight, it still safeguarded the Constituent Assembly and Shura Council from dissolution. The declaration also maintained that the November 22nd declaration and all other constitutional declarations made by Morsi could not be challenged by the courts. The new declaration did not offer the concessions that protesters were demanding, namely canceling the constitutional referendum, which they saw as illegitimate. Thus, protesters remained active, and, in response, the president gave arrest powers to the military up until the day of the referendum (Kirkpatrick 2012c), a move that did nothing to stop demonstrations. Violent clashes between Morsi opponents and supporters, as well as confrontations between anti-Morsi protesters and police, continued through February 2013 in spite of a state of emergency, particularly on the days surrounding the anniversary of the 2011 Revolution, including January 26th when 21 people convicted of participation in the 2012 Port Said riot were sentenced to death. Many instances of violence were also reported in the following months.

TAMAROD

The Tamarod (Rebel) movement was founded on April 28, 2013, by five activists from the Kefaya movement (Kingsley 2013b). The face of the Tamarod movement was Mahmoud Badr, a 28-year-old journalist and activist (Giglio 2013). The other founders were Moheb Doss, Walid el-Masry, Mohammed Abdel Aziz, and Hassan Shahin. Not only did Tamarod call for Morsi's resignation but it also organized the June 30th protests to remove him. According to Abdel Aziz, "The president lost his legitimacy when he didn't follow the law or the constitution and when he put the interests of his group before those of the Egyptians" (Abdullah 2013).

Tamarod distributed a petition demanding President Morsi's resignation and the holding of early presidential elections. The petition was circulated online and in the streets by activists and everyday citizens alike, and Tamarod claimed to have gained 22 million signatures (BBC News 2013). A number of interviewees admitted having signed the petition multiple times, and I personally observed a woman from Yemen sign the petition without producing a national identification card. However, from the number of people who took to the streets on June 30th, one can reasonably assume that the number of valid signatories was large.

While the statements from Tamarod, particularly to the official press, centered on the anti-democratic character of Morsi's rule and the need to steer the Revolution back on track through a proposed road map, the petition itself appealed to the people's dissatisfaction with Morsi's performance as a whole and also with the ailing economy, which was leaving many of the population's basic needs unfulfilled. The petition included the statements "Because there is still no security in the streets . . . we don't want you," "Because the economy is collapsed and based on begging . . . we don't want you," and "Because there are still not rights for the martyrs . . . we don't want you" (Tamarod 2013).

The movement, which had organizers in every Egyptian governorate, grew with the participation of the April 6th Youth Movement, the National Salvation Front, the Constitution Party, the Egyptian Conference Party, and other movements opposed to the Muslim Brotherhood that also provided logistical support and office space. Activists covered the Egyptian streets, often blocking traffic and stopping cars to hand out petitions. They also circulated the petition on the Tamarod website, Facebook, and Twitter. Everyday citizens, too, took part in mobilization, paying to make their own copies of the petition, collecting signatures, and returning the signed petitions to Tamarod offices. Signatories were required to provide their name, proof of residence, and national ID number. The movement appeared to be a national grassroots effort.

By late June, BBC reported Tamarod's claim that it had collected 15 million signatures that had been checked against a recent interior ministry electoral register (BBC News 2013). At a June 29th press conference, Tamarod proposed a six-month transitional road map where an independent prime minister would lead a technocratic government, with the head of the constitutional court as president until presidential elections could be held. They also announced that they had collected over 22 million signatures (Abdullah 2013).

MILITARY CO-OPTATION OF TAMAROD

Mobilization for the June 30th protests was very different from mobilization for January 25, 2011. While 73% of protesters and 51% of non-protesters who were interviewed knew about plans for the January 25th protests before they occurred, 100% of interviewees knew about the June 30th protests before that date, and all but 9 knew about the Tamarod movement. The majority had seen the petition being circulated in the streets and in their offices, and many also knew about it from Facebook, television, and newspapers.

Before January 25, 2011, most mobilization had to take place online because of the threat of arrest for publicly distributing flyers or a petition challenging the regime. Prior to 2011, El Baradei's National Association for Change had circulated an online petition contesting the Mubarak regime. The petition, which required name, address, and national ID number, gained 10,000 signatories (Ghonim 2012, 47). However, the Tamarod petition represented the first time that a petition had been widely circulated on the streets, and the numbers willing to sign the El Baradei petition were insignificant in comparison to those who signed the Tamarod petition.

Mass public participation in the Tamarod effort and the ability to mobilize without interference implies that a drastic change in political opportunities had occurred. The change in political opportunities that everyday citizens who mobilized against Morsi perceived was that the people had become stronger than any regime. The success of prior protests had taught them that if the people demanded the downfall of the regime there was a high probability that the regime would fall. When interviewees were asked the questions "In the few days prior to the January 25th Revolution, did you believe that change was possible through protest?" and "In the few days prior to June 30, 2013, did you believe that change was possible through protest?" 54% of those who protested in 2011 and 57% who did not protest changed their answer from "no" for 2011 to "yes" for 2013. An additional 7% of protesters and 5% of non-protesters changed their answers from "not sure" or "I didn't think about it" to a definitive "yes." The common rationale for not believing in the success of protests in 2011 was that "[Mubarak] was autocratic. He was so tough. The government was so powerful. We are normal citizens. We didn't know we could do this." However, in regard to the 2013 protests, the most common answers were: "If we could change Mubarak who was there for 30 years, we could change Morsi after one," and "The people can do anything after January 25th. We broke the fear barrier." It should be noted that my data apparently suffered from what Timur Kuran calls an "I knew it would happen" fallacy where people exaggerate foreknowledge (Kuran 1991, 10-11). The reasons why many interviewees claimed to have "known" that the January 25th protests would result in the overthrow of Mubarak caused me to believe that at the time they did not actually believe that the protests would be successful. Thus, there were probably more changes from "no" to "yes" than my data indicates.

A striking statistic is that while only 40% of interviewees who protested in the 2011 Revolution began their participation before or on the first official day of protests, January 25th, 91% of interviewees who protested in 2013 claimed they had participated before or on the first official day of protests, June 30th. While those protesting in 2011 were influenced by the number of people already protesting or saying they would protest, in 2013 the majority of interviewees who protested claimed that neither the number of people saying they were going to protest on June 30th nor the number of people who signed the Tamarod petition had an effect on their decision. They wanted to "get Morsi out" and they were going to protest regardless of the number of people protesting in the streets. There had also been enough protests in the past two and a half years for individuals to feel assured that if there were a call to protest, a significant number of people would show up. Protest had become a common tool in the repertoire for contesting the government, and, as demonstrated in chapter 5, many individuals did not fear protesting even if there was a threat of violence.

For those opposed to Morsi's rule, the decision to protest on June 30th did not engender the complex emotional processes that emerged in January 2011. First, individuals were continuing to experience the *post-revolutionary emboldening effect*, whereby the enormous success of protests in 2011, and even 2012, led people to believe that the power of the people was greater than the people in power and that if Egyptians protested, they were almost certain to see results. When a student from Mohandessine was asked if prior to June 30th he had believed that change was possible through protest, he replied, "Yes. It had happened once before. The will on the street wouldn't be denied. It had gathered so much momentum." Second, while prior to 2011 anti-regime protests were rare, following the Revolution protesting as a means of addressing grievances and contesting the government was normalized. Mayer Zald (1996) argues that movements draw on the cultural stock of how to organize and protest. Between January 2011 and June 2013, Egyptians took to the streets thousands of times to push their political agendas forward. Thus, similar to the tradition of striking in France, in Egypt protesting became routine; it was the thing to do.

While very few individuals opposed to Morsi reported fear of violence as their reason for not protesting on June 30th, many claimed they did not protest because they had to work or knew that there would be a large number of people protesting so their participation was not needed. As one young woman who had protested in January 2011 explained, "On January 25th, I thought people needed me; the second time [June 30th] there were millions. I didn't think I'd count. There was no killing, shooting, or people dying. People didn't need my help." At the same time that large numbers embolden potential protesters to demonstrate, they may also deter others who believe that they can free ride, reaping the benefits of protest without participating.

One unique aspect of the June 30th events was the discrepancy between perceived political opportunities and actual ones. Many ordinary citizens, as well as social movement organizations that had previously contested the Mubarak regime, believed that their newfound strength relative to the Morsi government derived from a change in political opportunities initiated by the ouster of Mubarak. In reality, the political opportunities that opened the door to protests against Morsi were created by the military. Following is an examination of the actual change in political opportunities that occurred.

What the participating movements, everyday citizens, and even many members of Tamarod did not know prior to June 30th was that, not long after the establishment of the Tamarod movement, the campaign had been co-opted by the military and the Ministry of Interior. Officials in the Ministry of Interior helped collect signatures and even participated in the protests (Frenkel and Atef 2014). The Interior Ministry was also providing Tamarod with tactical and logistical support for the protests, which explains why, when protesters took to the streets on June 30th, hundreds of thousands of water bottles and mini Egyptian flags suddenly appeared for distribution throughout the crowds. Not all five founding members of Tamarod were involved in the collaboration. Doss, who separated himself from the movement after June 30th, described how in the lead-up to the massive demonstration, Badr, Aziz, and Shahin began attending meetings with Sisi and certain functionaries at the Ministry of Interior and returning with changed talking points (Frenkel and Atef 2014). One Tamarod activist resigned before June 30th, declaring that she was unhappy that the secret police and former Mubarak supporters were "infiltrating the movement" (Saleh and Taylor 2013).

Doss also claimed that the statement that was read on television on the evening of July 3, 2013, bore no resemblance to the one he had participated in drafting hours earlier (Frenkel and Atef 2014). Instead of calling for a peaceful transition to democracy, the presenter quoted Tamarod's request for the army to step in to protect the people from terrorists and chaos. Doss realized later that he was at the end of a process "in which the army and security officials slowly but steadily began exerting an influence over Tamarod, seizing upon the group's reputation as a grassroots revolutionary movement to carry out their own schemes for Egypt" (Frenkel and Atef 2014). The support given to Tamarod by the military and Ministry of Interior before June 30th demonstrates that the state's security institutions became key decision-makers and mobilizers in a campaign that the public thought was solely a grassroots popular movement against the Morsi government.

It was also reported that elite businessmen from the Mubarak era were providing financial support to the Tamarod movement. Some reports claimed that Naguib Sawiris, owner of Orascom, the largest private sector company in Egypt, transferred over $28 million to fund the Tamarod movement (Kirkpatrick and Hubbard 2013; SBWire 2013). While January 2011 was a protest organized against the Mubarak regime, some of the major funders of the June 30th protests were *falool* (supporters and sympathizers of the Mubarak regime) hoping to regain power through the overthrow of the Islamist government. It should be noted that *falool* funding of Tamarod and military participation in the campaign only became public after the June 30th uprising with the help of #SisiLeaks, a series of recordings that exposed Sisi and his staff's involvement in the Tamarod movement and implicated them in additional scandals (Kingsley 2015).

Prior to June 30th, Tamarod used frames directed toward Morsi such as "Because the economy is collapsed and based on begging . . . we don't want you" (Tamarod 2013) to mobilize the public by exploiting popular grievances. Framing its petition as a list of demands by "the people," Tamarod painted a picture of a return to January 25th when the people stood up to an oppressive regime to ask for their rights. However, in reality, June 30th was in large part funded and organized by supporters of that oppressive previous regime. Thus, Tamarod became a top-down organization disguised and promoted to those it mobilized as a bottom-up movement. The change in political opportunities that allowed for mass public mobilization was not an opening up of the system but instead an opportunity provided by one part of the state system challenging another part.

MILITARY OPPOSITION TO MORSI

As outlined in the beginning of the chapter, a veto coup usually occurs when a party or movement that the military opposes and wishes to exclude from political power wins an election and/or when the government in power "begins to promote radical policies or to develop an appeal to groups whom the military wishes to exclude from power" (Huntington 1968, 224). The Egyptian military opposed Morsi because it viewed the Muslim Brotherhood, a group that the military had been charged with targeting under previous regimes, as a terrorist organization. Displays such as the attendance of Tareq al-Zomor, convicted of assassinating President Anwar Sadat, at the 2012 official ceremony commemorating the 6 October War were unsettling, particularly given that al-Zomor was invited by Morsi. Additionally, chapter 5 outlined the military's manipulation of the legal system in an attempt to ensure its strength and independence under any future regime. While Morsi was president, he attempted to undercut the military's position by undermining its independence and authority, which contributed to the military's decision that he needed to go.

The major challenge to the military's authority occurred on August 12, 2012, when Morsi retired Defense Minister Mohammed Hussein Tantawi, Army Chief of Staff Sami Anan, and other senior generals, replacing Tantawi with the head of military intelligence, Abdel-Fattah el-Sisi. In addition, Morsi nullified the amendments to the Constitutional Declaration that SCAF issued in June 2012 with the intent to limit the power of the future president (Fahim 2012a). Thus, Morsi regained the executive and legislative power that had been delegated to the military. The move came after an embarrassing incident for the military earlier in the month when 16 Egyptian soldiers were killed in Sinai after their base was breached by armed militants (Fahim 2012a). Trying to ease the blow of what some called a "soft coup" against the military, on August 14, 2012,

Morsi awarded Tantawi and Anan the Order of the Nile medal, the most prestigious honor in the country (Shull and Hassieb 2012). Both Tantawi and Anan were also named presidential advisors. Morsi had thought that changing defense ministers would alter SCAF's attitude toward the Muslim Brotherhood, believing that Sisi would be more sympathetic to the group (Youssef 2013). Unfortunately for Morsi, he was wrong in his assessment. The military would not accept the reduction in its power resulting from the reversal of its June 2012 amendments, and Morsi's subsequent November 2012 Constitutional Declaration displeased them even further.

Morsi also challenged the judiciary, which had been a friend to SCAF. On October 11, 2012, Morsi sacked General Prosecutor Abdel-Meguid Mahmoud and appointed him envoy to the Vatican by presidential decree (Daily News Egypt 2012). However, a few days later Morsi reversed his decision after judges claimed that the move was illegal. On April 19, 2013, Islamists protested at the High Court demanding a purge of the judiciary, which had challenged Islamist domination of the parliament and Constituent Assembly on numerous occasions (AlSharif 2013). The judiciary was not pleased with the harassment it received from Islamists. Morsi's antagonism toward the military and the judiciary that supported it appeared to influence the military's decision to overthrow Morsi by co-opting the Tamarod movement. In the next section, I outline the countermovement to Tamarod.

TAGAROD

In response to the Tamarod campaign, on May 12, 2013, Assem Abdel Maged from al-Gama'a al-Islamiyya launched the Tagarod (Impartiality) counter-movement, which circulated a petition to maintain the "legitimately elected president in his post" (Mourad 2013). The petition stated, "We, the signatories, agreeing or disagreeing, with Dr. Mohamed Morsi, the elected president, insist that he should complete his term as long as we do not see from him outright blasphemy; we have in him a sign from

God, may God bless him and guide his footsteps" (Mourad 2013). Tagarod spokesman Ahmed Hosni later outlined the viewpoint of the Tagarod movement, stating, "Protests lead to violence and unrest. Real change comes through the ballot box, not through mass protests. Egyptians had elected Morsi as president and approved the constitution drafted." He then continued by saying, "The constitution stipulates that the elected president stays on for four years to see through his duty. That is what Tagarod is supporting" (El-Shenawi 2013).

By June 30, 2013, Hosni reported that the movement had gathered 26 million signatures (El-Shenawi 2013), but the number was suspect given that in the same statement he claimed, "June 30 is a successful day for Tagarod as it prevented millions of people from taking to the streets and protesting" (El-Shenawi 2013). Thus, it appeared that his sense of reality was a bit off.

Like Tamarod, Tagarod not only circulated a petition but also organized demonstrations. On June 21, 2013, Tagarod participated in a mass demonstration to support Morsi in front of the Rabaa al-Adawiya mosque in Nasr City. Tens of thousands of Morsi supporters waved Egyptian flags and carried pictures of the president (Al Akhbar 2013). Demonstrators claimed to be protesting in support of the president's legitimacy and/or Islamic law.

LEAD-UP TO JUNE 30TH

On June 25, 2013, the military called on all parties to reach a settlement that would "save the nation from serious political conflict," which implied that the military was sympathetic to the opposition's demands for change. This statement was supported by both Al-Azhar and the Coptic Orthodox Church and came after an ultimatum from the military referring to its "constitutional capacity as guarantor of national security" (Ahram Online 2013e). The next day, opposition leaders met with the Salafist Nour Party to express fears of political chaos if Morsi did not address the demands of the people. The Nour Party then communicated the points of this meeting to the Muslim Brotherhood leadership and offered to mediate between all parties (Ahram Online 2013e). This offer of mediation was supported by the military, which began to deploy into the streets without coordination with the president. Morsi then had a meeting with the defense minister in an attempt to reverse the deployment, and when that effort failed he sought support to remove the defense minister, a move that was also unsuccessful (Ahram Online 2013e).

On June 26, 2013, four days before the planned June 30th protests, Morsi made a speech, or "two and a half hours of headache," as protester Emile Azmy described it (Nagi 2013). Tensions in the country were running high, and many were hoping that Morsi would take a conciliatory stance, making concessions to the opposition and preventing political divisions from deepening. A young student from Muqattam described the speech as "declaring war on the people and [Morsi] in complete denial."

In his speech, Morsi mentioned "thugs" who were causing chaos in the streets. Many in the opposition were unhappy with this characterization, believing that the "thugs" of whom he spoke were the antigovernment protesters. Morsi criticized the opposition for failing to engage in constructive dialogue. He also blamed unspecified "enemies of Egypt" for sabotaging the democratic system and warned that Egypt would fall into chaos if the country continued to be politically polarized. Singling out political rivals as these "enemies," Morsi warned the judiciary to stay out of politics. One engineer from Garden City specifically mentioned being upset with this part of the speech "where he was naming judges."

During the two and a half hours, Morsi admitted to some failings and apologized to Egypt's youth for not involving them enough in the new political system. He also apologized for fuel shortages and long gas lines, saying, "The lines sadden me, and I wish I could join in and wait in line, too." However, such comments angered many Egyptians and led them to mock Morsi further, as he seemed out of touch with the grievances of his people. A newspaper report assessing the reaction of viewers described how "people laughed and cursed at the president while watching his lengthy remarks on a projector in the square" (Nagi 2013).

On June 27, 2013, the military deployed vehicles into the streets with stickers expressing its support for the opposition's demands. Then, on June 28, 2013, the Rabaa al-Adawiya sit-in commenced. While thousands of anti-Morsi demonstrators congregated at Tahrir Square and the Ittihadiya Presidential Palace, thousands of Morsi's supporters gathered at the Rabaa al-Adawiya Mosque in Nasr City to express their support for the president's legitimacy. The demonstration, called "Legitimacy is a Red Line," was said to be open-ended. In a press conference, 11 Islamist political parties launched the National Alliance to Support Legitimacy to "protect the Egyptian people's democratic gains" (Ahram Online 2013c). The alliance included the Freedom and Justice Party of the Muslim Brotherhood, the centrist al-Wasat Party, the Salafist Watan Party, the Building and Development Party of al-Gama'a al-Islamiyya, and the Professional Syndicates Union, composed of 24 syndicates and tribal coalitions from Sinai, Upper Egypt, and Marsa Matrouh. It was reported that on June 27th the military, police, and intelligence leadership made a decision to support the will of the people and that opposition activists were meeting with the military to discuss the political transition following Morsi's ouster (Ahram Online 2013e).

JUNE 30TH

On June 30, 2013, residents in the Dokki area of Giza decorated their apartment buildings with the Egyptian flag. One building had a long Egyptian flag running down the entire side of it. Around 2:30 p.m., a few protesters began to make their way down Tahrir Street toward Tahrir Square, and sometime after 3:00 p.m. a few more groups of protesters followed. Then, at 4:45 p.m., the crowds started. Tens of thousands of protesters marched down Tahrir Street chanting "Freedom," "The people want the downfall of the regime," "Get out," and "Get out, supreme guide." There were men and women of all ages filling both sides of the two-way street and the sidewalks. There were also microbuses, cars, and taxis flying the Egyptian flag, as well as pickup trucks with protesters on the back encouraging the chants. Beating drums, launching fireworks, and carrying Egyptian flags and signs, the crowd continued to grow. While exact numbers are not available, estimates place the number of protesters on June 30th at 30 million (Gomaa 2013). As protesters marched down Tahrir Street, police outside of the Dokki police station held up flags in support of them. Some officers held out signs saying "Leave!" By 11:00 p.m., helicopters were circling Tahrir Square and protesters were cheering because they saw them as a sign of support from the military. Egyptians on Facebook were labeling the event a revolution and saying the protests were bigger than anything they had ever seen.

By July 1, 2013, one day after the start of the June 30th protests, a large number of ministers and cabinet members had submitted their resignations. Later on that day, the military gave Morsi an ultimatum of 48 hours to resolve the political crisis. During the military's televised address, General Abdel Fattah el-Sisi said:

> If the demands of the people are not met within the given period of time, [the military] will be compelled by its national and historic responsibilities, and in respect for the demands of Egypt's great people, to announce a road map for the future, and procedures that it will supervise involving the participation of all the factions and groups. (Hauslohner 2013b)

Later in the day, the military put out another statement on Facebook, stating, "The ideology and culture of the Egyptian armed forces does not allow for the policy of a military coup," attempting to negate any claims that the military was staging a coup.

The military statement was supported by the Ministry of Interior, which issued its own statement:

> [The police force] is renewing its commitment to protect the people and the vital institutions of the country, and to ensure the security of the protesters, confirming that it will be under the service of the people, and that it will stand at an equal distance from all the

different groups and entities without taking sides. (Bradley and Abdellatif 2013b)

That evening, Tahrir Square took on a carnival-like atmosphere, with colorful fireworks bursting in the night sky. Families with children and women and men both young and old were crammed shoulder to shoulder enjoying what they already felt was a victory, based on the military's statement. Few people were chanting political slogans, as was usual at a Tahrir protest rally. Instead, people were waving Egyptian flags, smiling, and celebrating.

In response to the military's July 1st statement, Morsi sent out a tweet at 4:39 p.m. on July 2nd stating, "President Mohamed Morsi asserts his grasp on constitutional legitimacy and rejects any attempt to deviate from it, and calls on the armed forces to withdraw their warning and refuses to be dictated to internally or externally." However, by that time the military had already taken over the state newspaper, Al Ahram, using the front page of the newspaper to enforce the ultimatum that it would remove Morsi if he did not meet the protesters' demands (Kirkpatrick and Hubbard 2013). The military and security forces had also placed a number of Muslim Brotherhood allies under house arrest and stated that anyone resisting arrest would be put on trial in special courts (Kirkpatrick and Hubbard 2013). In Tahrir Square, the Interior Ministry removed the concrete blocks that had been erected as a barrier to assaults on the police during protests, saying that they were no longer needed because "the police had joined 'the people' in the new uprising against Mr. Morsi" (Kirkpatrick and Hubbard 2013).

On the evening of July 2nd, Morsi gave a speech that outraged many viewers watching from their homes. Rather than addressing protester demands, he took a defiant stance, using the term "legitimacy" to define his rule 57 times during the speech and implying that there would be bloodshed if his power were threatened. According to Morsi, this legitimacy came from the fact that he was elected in "free and clean elections, witnessed by everyone in Egypt and abroad," despite the fact that "there remained tails and claws, and there remained the deep state, and the vandals and many challenges remained." During the speech Morsi was mocked on Facebook by Egyptians for his excessive use of the word "legitimacy." One Egyptian posted, "If you missed it here's #Morsi's speech: Legitimacy is Me. Then he looks at his arms, and wonders if he's moving them convincingly. #Egypt," while another from an expat mocked, "Every time #Morsy says shar3aya (legitimacy) we drink . . . is gonna be a long night . . ."

While many jokes circulated about the president, Egyptians were truly aghast at the content of his speech and its allusion to retaliatory violence against anti-Morsi protesters. Some of the statements most disturbing to listeners included: "And the biggest responsibility now, is that we ensure [Egypt's] security and that of its people and keep their blood from being shed through holding onto the legitimacy that we have brought forth together . . ." "If the price of protecting legitimacy is my blood, I'm willing to pay it . . . it would be a cheap price for the sake of protecting this country," and "Legitimacy is the only thing that guarantees for all of us that there will not be any fighting and conflict, that there will not be bloodshed." Labeling the anti-Morsi protesters counter-revolutionaries, Morsi continued, "I see now, oh Egyptians, that this revolution is being stolen from us, and that it is desired for us to be submerged in a sea of never ending conflicts," and "What I see now, is that there are desperate attempts for this revolution to be stolen, so that we can return to square one, so we can start anew, which I absolutely refuse, I do not accept it and I do not agree to it."

After Morsi's speech, his cabinet resigned, stating on Twitter, "The cabinet declares its rejection of Dr. Morsi's speech and his pushing the country toward a civil war," and "The cabinet announces taking the side of the people." The military's response to the speech was to state that it is "more honorable for us to die than for the Egyptian people to feel threatened or terrorized," and that the military would "sacrifice our blood for Egypt and its people against every terrorist, extremist or ignorant person." The military's statement was one of the first during that time period to label the Muslim Brotherhood a terrorist organization. On July 2nd, there were reports of violence around the country, including fighting in Giza and Midan Kit Kat, as well as clashes near Cairo University that left 3 dead and 90 injured. There were gunfights in Dokki Square that continued until 7:00 a.m. the next day, and the sound of gunfire could be heard by nearby residents.

On the morning of July 3rd, the military held negotiations with El Baradei and various political factions. The Muslim Brotherhood's Freedom and Justice Party refused to participate (Haddon et al. 2013). At 4:30 p.m., the military deadline had passed and Egyptians were waiting to see what would happen next. State news agencies reported that the military had extended its deadline in an attempt to reach a consensus that would prevent further violence, offering a guarantee of the president's safety in exchange for the Muslim Brotherhood's agreement to contain bloodshed (Haddon et al. 2013). By 5:35 p.m., there were Twitter reports that Morsi was under house arrest and that other Muslim Brotherhood officials were barred from leaving the country via the airport. At 5:45 p.m., military helicopters began to fly over Cairo, and by 6:00 p.m., the military was deploying tanks throughout the city. Pictures on Twitter showed military tanks crossing Al Gamaa Bridge toward Cairo University and soldiers praying on another bridge. Armored personnel carriers (APCs) were rolling down Tahrir Street. At 7:00 p.m., the military informed Morsi that he was no longer president of the country (Haddon et al. 2013).

At 9:00 p.m., General Abdel-Fattah el-Sisi gave a live televised address. Attendees at the address included a number of top military and police officials who sat in two rows on either side of the podium, the Coptic Orthodox patriarch Pope Tawadros II, Grand Sheikh of Al-Azhar Ahmed El-Tayyeb, El Baradei, a representative of the Nour Party, Tamarod's Mohamed Abdel-Aziz, and a senior judicial figure. People in the streets roared with jubilation and set off fireworks during Sisi's speech, and by the time it finished car horns were honking, people were cheering wildly, and an enormous fireworks display erupted in Tahrir Square.

Sisi announced the ouster of Morsi to make way for new presidential elections and outlined the transitional road map. The road map included the temporary suspension of the constitution, the assignment of the head of Egypt's High Constitutional Court to run the country until a new presidential election could take place, the formation of a technocratic government, the intention to pass revised parliamentary election laws so that new parliamentary elections could take place, the formation of a committee to amend controversial articles in the temporarily suspended constitution, the creation of a media code of ethics to guarantee media professionalism, the formation of a committee to encourage national reconciliation, and the inclusion of youth in decision-making circles.

During the speech, Sisi explained that the military had made many attempts to resolve the issues between the president and opposition, beginning with the November 2012 constitutional declaration, but that Morsi would not compromise. The military intervention had occurred after a strategic assessment of the important challenges and dangers facing the country on the political, economic, and social levels. Sisi claimed that the military had no intention of interfering in politics, but it would "never turn a blind eye to the aspirations of the Egyptian people." After Sisi thanked the army, police, and judiciary for their sacrifices for Egypt, the Grand Sheikh of Al-Azhar Ahmed el-Tayeb, Coptic Orthodox Pope Tawadros II, and opposition figure Mohmed El Baradei gave speeches, demonstrating that the country's major institutions and political figures supported the military's actions. The next day, the Egyptian Air Force put on an airshow over Cairo, drawing hearts, Egyptian flags, and waterfalls in the sky.

UNDERSTANDING THE COUP

The military coup on July 3, 2013, displayed some elements of the veto coup as defined by Huntington. During the four days of the uprising and the speech on the final day, the military continued to highlight that the country risked being destabilized by chaos and that the current government posed political, economic, and social threats to the country. Thus, the military was forced to rectify the situation, with the support of the public, by temporarily intervening to set the country back on the right course. By outlining a road map for new parliamentary and presidential elections, Sisi emphasized that the military's intention was to remain out of politics in the long run and permit civilian rule.

In theory, the new transitional government, led by the head of Egypt's High Constitutional Court, Adly Mansour, was a civilian government. However, Huntington points out that while the military's role as guardian may have justifications and rationales, it has a corrupting and debilitating impact on the political system, since responsibility and power are divorced. "Civilian leaders may have responsibility, but they know they do not have power and are not allowed to create power because their actions are subject to military veto" (Huntington 1968, 228). In turn, the military has power, but they are not responsible for the consequences of their actions because authority is technically in the hands of the civilian government.

Another issue that arises after a veto coup is that the military must make the decision to proceed in one of the four ways outlined in the beginning of this chapter. They can engage in return and restrict, return and expand, retain and restrict, or retain and expand. While the military junta that comes to power following a veto coup promises a rapid return to civilian rule, hardliners in the military will argue that they must remain in power in order to permanently bar the ousted group from returning and to implement structural and political reforms in the system. These hardliners resist political expansion through public participation (Huntington 1968, 231–232). As discussed in the beginning of the chapter, while the military claims at the start of the coup that it intends to take power only temporarily, its desire to have control over political system reforms and its fear of retaliation if it relinquishes its veto power may lead to increased political intervention. "Hence the incentives to intervene escalate, and the army becomes irreversibly committed to insuring that the once-proscribed group never acquires office" (Huntington 1968, 232–233). In the case of Egypt post-June 30th, the fear of retaliation was intensified by the fact that the Rabaa al-Adawiya sit-in to support Morsi's legitimacy continued. Thus, the president and his organization may have been overthrown, but thousands were participating in a sit-in to demonstrate that they were not willing to leave quietly and were calling into question the legitimacy of the military's actions by claiming that Morsi had been legitimately and democratically elected and that the military had therefore overthrown a democracy. In response to this challenge, the military chose the option of *retain and restrict*, where the military retains power and restricts political expansion while being driven toward more repressive measures. In order to understand how the military implemented this policy, we must examine the Rabaa al-Adawiya sit-in and how the military crackdown on the demonstration led to events that helped facilitate the retain and restrict policy. Rather than implement retain and restrict by force, the military capitalized on the volatile environment in a manner that led the population to support the policy.

RABAA AL-ADAWIYA

The Rabaa al-Adawiya sit-in took place in Nasr City, Cairo, from June 28th to August 14th, 2013. The demonstration was organized by a number of Islamist groups that called themselves the National Alliance to Support Legitimacy. The stated purpose of the sit-in was to support the legitimacy of Morsi as president based on his democratic election and to refute the military coup. In addition to members of Islamist groups, among those in attendance were those who supported the Islamist agenda but were not members of any group or party, those who wanted an Islamic state, those who wanted "Islamic democracy," those who believed that Morsi was not given enough time in office to prove himself, those who believed that Morsi should have completed his four years as president, those who believed that they had been robbed of their vote after the Islamist parliament was dissolved and the Islamist president was deposed, and those who had protested for an Islamist government in the 2011 Revolution and thus believed that they were continuing the Revolution.

The protest site held a sea of tents lined up in the form of a makeshift city. Each tent was treated as a mosque, and those entering followed the custom of removing their shoes. The protest site reached right up to the sides of residential buildings, which had been evacuated by residents unhappy with being surrounded by the Islamist sit-in. Radio Shack, a bank, and other businesses were closed, but there was no evidence of damage to the stores. There was ample room to navigate the streets dividing the tents, and the level of organization was striking. There were security checkpoints at the entrances to the site, and security personnel with orange vests, hard hats, and large flashlights patrolled the sit-in to ensure that no sexual harassment or fights took place in the camp. There were also a few men lined up near the entrances with hard hats and large sticks, but there were no weapons in sight.

Many of the tents had posters hanging on them in Arabic, English, French, and occasionally German, or even Russian. There were posters depicting Morsi that read "No to the coup" in Arabic, and one in English showing a woman saying "Killing won't silence my voice." There were other posters with the words "We want the president and parliament," "Anti-coup," "Where is my ballot?" and "The revolution continues," referring to January 25, 2011. There was even a sign with a clenched fist. There were also a number of posters of martyrs with the picture of the victim before his martyrdom and then another of him on a respirator, or dead and mutilated. One poster portrayed a number of corpses lined up and said, "Paid for by U.S. tax dollars." Young men were also walking around with posters on sticks, some with faces of martyrs on them. There were Egyptian flags throughout the site.

A sex-segregated crowd assembled at a makeshift stage. Nearby was a hanging effigy of the Minister of Interior and a live donkey walking around with a boot hanging around its neck. Young children were lined up on the stage to sing, and small boys led the crowd in anti-American and anti-military chants. One of the chants was "Get out, get out, military rule." There were few, if any, televisions in the camp and most information was disseminated by a man on a loudspeaker on a 24-hour basis. Over and over again he drummed on the themes of legitimacy and democracy.

The entire area of the sit-in was remarkably clean, aided by sweepers who could be seen circulating through the streets. The atmosphere was almost festive, with swings and playground equipment for children, tents decorated with Sponge Bob and Mickey Mouse balloons, and street vendors selling clothes, accessories, and tea. Young men sprayed passersby with water to relieve the discomfort from the intense summer heat.

The people walking around Rabaa looked like a cross-section of those in the streets of Cairo. There were men with beards and men without beards, women in *niqab* (face covering), women in *hijab* (headscarf) wearing *abaya* (long robe), and others in *hijab* dressed in skirts. Only a few women were not wearing a *hijab*. There were a number of couples strolling, as well as families, children, and groups of men or women. Many people were going to work during the day and then returning to Rabaa before *iftar* (breaking the Ramadan fast) to stay for the evening or overnight.

There were no weapons displayed out in the open at the sit-in. However, there were some unconfirmed reports that torture was taking place under the stage, there were men with weapons in specific areas, and dead bodies with evidence of torture were found near the site (Lofty 2013). There were also speeches made by Morsi supporters and on the Rabaa stage that implied violence. During the June 30th protests, Mohamed al-Beltagy of the Muslim Brotherhood made the statement about violence in Sinai, "Events in Sinai are in retaliation for the military coup, and will stop immediately once the coup is withdrawn and Morsi is back" (Allam 2013). Later, on July 5, 2013, the Supreme Guide of the Muslim Brotherhood gave a speech on the Rabaa stage promising that "we will sacrifice our lives for Morsi and bring him back" (Allam 2013). On that same evening, there were nationwide clashes that left 30 dead and 1,100 injured. In addition to the violent clashes between supporters and opponents of Morsi that engulfed the country in the months following the coup, there was also sectarian violence, including the murder of four Christians in Luxor by Islamist attackers and the murder of a Coptic priest in a drive-by shooting in Sinai (Allam 2013).

The Rabaa al-Adawiya sit-in posed a direct challenge to the rationale behind the military coup. Refuting the military's argument that the president needed to be ousted in order to put the country on track, the claims of demonstrators at Rabaa al-Adawiya were that the military had overthrown a democratically elected president who held legitimacy based on the ballot box. The military, with the help of the media that supported it, countered the claims of the sit-in by describing the Muslim Brotherhood and those who supported them as terrorists. The media reported that the sit-in was filled with armed Islamists who tortured suspected infiltrators (Fahim and Gladstone 2013), and on July 26, 2013, the military called for all Egyptians to take to the streets to support the military and fight terror.

Around 3:00 p.m., on July 26th, pro-Morsi demonstrators began marching down Tahrir Street in Dokki, carrying colorful long flags with Morsi's picture over their heads, blasting music and dancing. Later, at 5:15 p.m., a pro-Sisi march made its way down the same street as military helicopters flew overhead. It was also reported that the military was using helicopters to drop Egyptian flags over the Rabaa al-Adawiya sit-in. By nightfall, Tahrir Square was packed with pro-military demonstrators. Men and women of all ages, some with their children, were waving Egyptian flags and holding up posters of General Sisi. Street vendors were selling masks with Sisi's face on them and posters of Morsi's face with an X on it. In Maadi, many apartment buildings were draped with Egyptian flags, which were also planted in the divider area of two-way streets. People waved Egyptian flags from their cars, and there were posters of Sisi on the backs of tuk-tuks. The mood was jovial. Television networks played live video of mass demonstrations in Cairo, Alexandria, Suez, and Port Said.

The following day security forces killed at least 72 members of the Rabaa sit-in who were protesting at an overpass near Rabaa (Fahim and El Sheikh 2013), but a large portion of the Egyptian population that supported Sisi did not seem to care. They were convinced by the military's statements that the Rabaa protesters were terrorists and were happy to support the military against Muslim Brotherhood supporters, even if violent measures were involved. The killing of protesters on July 27th was not the first time that security forces had attacked Morsi supporters. On July 8, 2013, at least 51 pro-Morsi protesters had been killed in front of the Republican Guard compound in Cairo (Dziadosz and Nasralla 2013).

THE RABAA AL-ADAWIYA MASSACRE

By August 2013, the Egyptian military had had enough of the Rabaa al-Adawiya sit-in, as well as its sister sit-in at Al-Nahda Square, and it decided to end them. Doing so would assist the military in completing its coup and eliminating vocal opposition. While the government had already shut down Islamist television networks, conducted nationwide arbitrary arrests of Islamists, and frozen the assets of Muslim Brotherhood and Islamist leaders (Allam 2013), it had yet to quell the protests and media statements challenging the coup. In theory, clearing the protests would also end the nationwide violence and clashes between supporters and opponents of Morsi.

On July 31, 2013, the military-backed government instructed security forces to disperse the sit-ins. In a televised address, the government stated that the sit-ins were disruptive and represented "a threat to the Egyptian national security and an unacceptable terrorizing of citizens" (Fahim and Gladstone 2013). However, the government did not set a date for the dispersal. The statement came in the middle of Ramadan, and many believed that the military would not end the sit-ins during the holy month or the following Eid holiday.

At 6:00 a.m., on August 14, 2013, central security forces, supported by the military, began their violent dispersal of the Al-Nahda Square sit-in. Smoke could be seen emanating from the protest site, and videos of participants who were burned alive in their tents because they did not hear the warning announcements were later circulated on YouTube. At 7:00 a.m., police officers encircled the Rabaa al-Adawiya sit-in, firing tear gas at the protest camps and destroying tents with bulldozers. According to a *New York Times* report, while the Interior Ministry had stated that it would leave safety exits and move in gradually, "Soon after the attack began several thousand people appeared trapped inside the main camp, near the Rabaa al-Adawiya mosque, as snipers fired down on those trying to flee and riot police officers with tear gas and birdshot closed in from all sides" (Kirkpatrick 2013c). Human Rights Watch found that security forces fired on protesters using live ammunition, killing hundreds with bullets to the head, neck, and chest. Lethal force was used indiscriminately, "with snipers and gunmen inside and alongside APCs firing their weaponry on large crowds of protesters" (Human Rights Watch 2014, 6). There were also reports of snipers firing from helicopters over Rabaa Square. The Human Rights Watch report additionally stated that there had not been any notification of a specific day on which the dispersal would take place and that many protesters did not hear the warnings that were announced on the loudspeakers at two entrances early in the morning. Only minutes later, security forces opened fire, thus providing virtually no time for people to escape. They attacked protesters from all five main entrances to the Square, leaving no safe exit until the end of the day (Human Rights Watch 2014, 6). While debate continues over whether security forces gave adequate warning to sit-in participants, whether exits for escape were provided to demonstrators, and whether demonstrators were armed and fired on security forces, what cannot be disputed is that in one day over 1,000 people were killed in what Human Rights Watch called the largest killing of protesters in a single day in recent history (Human Rights Watch 2014).

Following the massacre, Prime Minister Hazem El Beblawi made a televised speech where he said that security forces "observed the highest degrees of self-restraint" in clearing the camp and that they "were forced to intervene" (The Guardian 2013). In his statement, the prime minister also claimed that the government had "exhausted all opportunities" before deciding to disperse the sit-in. Mohamed El Baradei refuted the government's claim when he resigned as vice-president on August 14th and wrote in his resignation letter, "As you know, I saw that there were peaceful ways to end this clash in society, there were proposed and acceptable solutions for beginnings that would take us to national consensus." He continued, "It has become difficult for me to continue bearing responsibility for decisions that I do not agree with and whose consequences I fear. I cannot bear the responsibility for one drop of blood" (Hill 2013).

The peaceful proposals to address the sit-in to which El Baradei referred were many. El Baradei had invited a number of international mediators to Cairo, including European Union (EU) Foreign Minister Catherine Ashton. European Union envoy Bernardino Leon, who co-led mediation efforts with U.S. Deputy Secretary of State William Burns, claimed that there had been a political plan on the table that was acceptable to the Muslim Brotherhood (Taylor 2013), an option that could have been embraced by the government. El Baradei also attempted to negotiate a deal whereby Rabaa protesters would scale back their encampment in exchange for the prison release of Saad El-Katatni, head of the Muslim Brotherhood's Freedom and Justice Party, and Al-Wasat leader Abul Ela Madi (Howeidy 2013). After approval of the deal by both sides, the government reneged and refused to release El-Katatni. There were additional confidence-building measures proposed by negotiators from Qatar, the United Arab Emirates, the United States, and the European Union that included prisoner releases and Morsi's honorable exit from politics, an amended constitution, and new elections (Taylor 2013). Despite the numerous deals put on the table by negotiators, some to which the Muslim Brotherhood agreed, the government chose the option of a violent dispersal of the sit-in.

Large segments of the Egyptian public reacted to the Rabaa al-Adawiya massacre with enthusiastic approval of the government's actions. When on August 16, 2013, an Egyptian journalist posted on Facebook that he had witnessed the police violently attacking pro-Morsi protesters in Ramses Square, the responses to his post included "Yabny stop looking one way because you hate the police the police have every right to kill those son of a bitch terrorists when they go around burning churches and killing innocent people fuck THE MB and i hope they all die a slow painful death" and "THE MB ARE NOT HUMAN not even animals even animals have more humanity then those beasts." These comments were not necessarily from marginal extremists because they echoed remarks heard all over the Cairo streets in reference to the Muslim Brotherhood. Significant portions of the Egyptian public had been whipped into a frenzy and were out for blood, emphatically supporting any actions that the military took against the Islamist group and its supporters, no matter how violent.

Any criticisms of the government's handling of the Rabaa sit-in were met with rationales for the government's actions. Many Egyptians believed that there was no other way to clear Rabaa, and that the military had looked at all other options before settling on the dispersal. They continued to maintain that the blocking of roads, residential buildings, and businesses by the anti-coup protests necessitated the drastic action. Additionally, many claimed that the demonstrators in Rabaa had been sufficiently warned that the protest would be cleared and were given opportunities to leave.

Thus, anyone who stayed, knowing there were gunmen among the protesters, was clearly a terrorist. Claims were also made that sit-in participants knew that they were supporting a terrorist group because of some of the speeches inciting violence made on the Rabaa stage.

CONSOLIDATING THE VETO COUP

At 4:00 p.m., on the day of the Rabaa massacre, the Egyptian government declared a state of emergency and announced that a military curfew would begin at 9:00 p.m. that same day. While there are no reports or interviews with military officials that would explain the intentions behind this decision, the fact that the state of emergency was declared prior to the end of clearing the Rabaa sit-in implies that the military knew that a violent attack on the sit-in would precipitate a violent response by Islamists in the following days. International negotiators had presented the government with peaceful options to address the sit-in that were rejected in favor of a violent response. However, the government argued to the Egyptian public that violence was the only alternative after all others had been exhausted. Thus, it appears that a violent response may have been what the government was seeking. Statements made by international negotiators implied that from the beginning the Egyptian government had no intention of implementing a peaceful approach to the sit-in; they were committed to violent tactics despite mediators' warnings that moves to disperse the sit-in "would likely cause hundreds of deaths and drive many conservative Salafi Muslim activists, initially supportive of Mursi's overthrow, to join forces with the Brotherhood in fierce opposition to the authorities" (Taylor 2013).

Whether or not it was the intention of the military to provoke the violence committed by Islamists in response to the government's dispersal of Rabaa, the reaction provided the military with a pretext for implementing repressive measures and consolidating its hold on the country. Egypt had been experiencing violent clashes across the nation prior to the Rabaa dispersal, but without a highly visible incident of mass violence, it would have been difficult for the military to impose the extremely repressive measures that would follow. In its rationale for the state of emergency, the government did not refer to the slaughtering of Rabaa protesters by security forces but instead painted a picture of armed terrorists from within the sit-in attacking government forces.

The Rabaa massacre and the associated state of emergency was a watershed moment for the military's retain and restrict policy. In one day, the military was able to virtually wipe out the possibility of a political return by the Muslim Brotherhood, engage in mass arrests and suppression of both Islamists and anti-military secular opponents with little challenge, and intensify its retaking of the country. Similar to support for the repressive Patriot Act in United States following the 9/11 attacks because of the population's fear of terrorism, a large percentage of the Egyptian public wildly supported the military's repressive measures. Day after day the words "Egypt fighting terror" were displayed on the upper right-hand side of the television screen on state channels, and programming included patriotic films and documentaries on the Egyptian military. Egyptians were worked up by the idea of a terrorist threat, promoted by the government and state media, into supporting a "war" effort against the Islamist terrorists attacking their country. At the beginning of this chapter, I labeled what occurred in Egypt a *popular participatory veto coup*. The popular participatory aspect of the coup was confirmed on July 26, 2013, when Egyptians took to the streets to support the military in its fight on terror and was further consolidated after the Rabaa massacre. Egyptians' support for, and justification of, the military's repressive measures and their participation in rallies that the military promoted to manifest popular support for its actions demonstrated the popular participatory characteristic of the coup.

Not only was there a demonstration of passionate, patriotic support for the military by the Egyptian people but a personality cult surrounding General Sisi also began to develop. Earlier in the chapter, I described the posters and masks of Sisi at the July 26th rally. That day was only the beginning. Sisi paraphernalia popped up around the country. Shops sold Sisi sandwiches, Sisi chocolates, Sisi jewelry, Sisi T-shirts, and Sisi perfume. Street vendors sold fake "Sisi" ID cards where under "profession" the card read "Savior of Egypt" and, under address, "The Presidential Office" (Nour and Robinson 2014). It should be noted that this was a time before Sisi officially ran for president. A woman who sold a Sisi jewelry line said that she believed Sisi had "liberated Egypt and freed it from fascism" and that her line was called "The Second Victory" because the army's ousting of Morsi was its biggest success since the 1973 Arab-Israeli War (Nour and Robinson 2014). In the streets and on the doors of residential apartment buildings hung posters of Sisi next to a lion, couples threw military-themed wedding parties, and pro-military songs such as "Teslem al Ayadi" (May those hands be safe) became popular mobile phone ringtones.

One young woman described Sisi's appeal in great detail:

> For once in years and years, we have a president who actually listens, that sits there and talks to people from his heart without being scripted. I don't think he's pulling an act. He's a sensitive guy, I think, and people can actually sense that. Finally, we have someone who can listen to us and we can respond to. Also he's charismatic to a lot of the females. He's soft spoken and elegant in the way he talks and the way he handles things. He doesn't get angry and he doesn't get all crazy when he talks. He's like a romantic singer, let's put it that way. Also, people see him as a safe haven after everything we endured from the Muslim Brotherhood, from the Morsi time. Finally we have some relief, finally someone who is normal. He's not extremely liberal and he's not extremely religious. He's someone just in the middle.

The media also fawned over Sisi. Columnist Ghada Sherif described Sisi as Nasser's "reincarnation" and wrote, "He doesn't need to order or command us, all he needs to do is give us a wink with one eye, or even just flutter his eyelashes," continuing, "This is a man adored by Egyptians. And if he wants to take four wives, we're at his service" (AFP 2013). Egypt's airwaves were flooded with songs praising the defense minister's victory against terrorism, and an editorial in the state newspaper described Sisi's "bronzed, gold skin" and "herculean strength" (CBS News 2013).

There were too many political incidents in the months following the Rabaa massacre to chronicle in this chapter, but to provide a brief summary: The nation saw violent attacks by Islamist militants on police and military institutions and personnel, including bombings, drive-by shootings, and attempted assassinations of government officials, such as the Minister of Interior. Ansar Bayt al-Maqdis, a terrorist group that later aligned with the Islamic State, began to strengthen its organization and attack soldiers in the Sinai Peninsula. There were also attacks on soldiers by Islamist militants in other areas of the country, Islamist attacks on Christians and their houses of worship, and a bombing of a tourist bus in Taba. Both peaceful and violent protests by Morsi supporters continued across the country and were met with a violent response by security forces. The assets of those associated with Islamist groups were frozen, Islamists were imprisoned en masse, and mass death sentences were handed out to Islamist protesters.

The military's repressive tactics were not limited to Islamists. The Third Square, a movement opposed to both the Muslim Brotherhood and military rule, had its protests shut down; international journalists such as Mohamed Fadel Fahmy, Peter Greste, and Baher Mohamed of Al Jazeera who did not toe the party line were imprisoned; and secular activists who had initiated the 2011 Revolution, such as Mohamed Adel and Ahmed Maher of the April 6th Youth Movement, along with blogger Ahmed Douma, were fined E£50,000 each and sentenced to three years of hard labor for violating the new protest law.

The protest law, or anti-protest law, was signed on November 24, 2013. The law forced protesters to obtain seven separate permissions before organizing a demonstration and banned overnight sit-ins. If an application were rejected, activists would have to appeal to the courts. The law banned unsanctioned gatherings in private or public of more than ten people, and the police would have the final say on whether or not a protest could take place (Kingsley 2013e). Heavy fines and prison sentences were imposed on those who broke the law, which was especially utilized to mete out long prison sentences to prominent secular political activists who challenged the legislation by protesting without obtaining prior permission. Activists began to cease protesting because they either were imprisoned, had fled the country, or realized they were no longer able to garner popular support for their public challenges to the regime. Explaining why people no longer protested, one young man proclaimed, "If anyone protests now, they would call him a terrorist, Muslim Brotherhood or Daesh. People would go to jail for nothing or get killed for nothing. So, I don't think [protesting] is really important right now. I don't think it's useful."

As the months went on, the military-backed government became more repressive and the people grew more in love with Sisi. As early as September 2013, there were calls to elect Sisi president, months before presidential elections were even announced. A popular campaign called "Finish the Job" was collecting signatures urging Sisi to run for president, and most of the candidates from the previous presidential election had already endorsed him. Participants in the campaign said that it was their way of expressing their appreciation for the general. The name "Finish the Job" is ironic because that is exactly what Sisi did through a military-backed constitution that freed the military from oversight and was passed in a January 2014 referendum, and through his run for president in May 2014. He was finishing the job of consolidating the veto coup through a retain and restrict policy. With Sisi as a candidate for president, both he and the military would ensure that there would be no challenges to, or retaliation for, their veto.

On March 26, 2014, Sisi announced his formal resignation from the Armed Forces and his intention to run for president, claiming that it was his duty and desire to serve the nation (Ezzat 2014). In Egypt, the president must be a civilian; therefore, Sisi had to resign from office before announcing his candidacy. However, one Egyptian man posted on Facebook that Sisi's taking off his uniform and calling himself a civilian was the same as his putting on a bra and calling himself the first female president of Egypt.

On June 3, 2014, when Sisi was proclaimed the winner of the presidential election, the popular participatory aspect of the coup was complete.

Sisi had won more than 96% of the vote, while his challenger, Hamdeen Sabahi, had received only 3.9% of the vote (CNN 2014). Responding to the violence committed by Islamist militants, one voter said that the army was the "only body stronger than the Muslim Brotherhood, and it would have been impossible to free the country from the Brotherhood without the army. For this reason, we need the chief of the army to be president. The conflict with the Brotherhood is not over yet" (Ezzat 2014). The people gave their support to a military president and his retain and restrict approach to politics because they were convinced that the military's repressive tactics were the only way to combat Islamist extremism. "I don't think he's the best person ever, but I do believe he is the best for this era," explained one young woman. "In this situation, in this time and place now, he's the best option we have. After what happened with the Muslim Brotherhood, Mohamed Morsi, and all the horrible events that went down, after we saw all the other politicians unable to unite and make one legitimate party or anything that could actually run for the presidency and we wasted three full years out of Egypt's history just running in vicious circles, it was exhausting." Three years of political turmoil, weekly and sometimes daily protests, and increasing incidents of violence had left Egyptians with revolutionary fatigue. "People in Egypt don't protest [anymore] because they're searching for stability," one young man explained. They just wanted to return to their normal lives and abandon the constant uncertainty that the Revolution had brought about.

Sisi was not perceived as a civilian candidate; he was regarded as a representative of the military establishment. Egyptians voted for Sisi because the military was seen as the only institution that could return order to the country. It was "not just security, people just lost their minds, and in situations like that, we are not following the law, we do not respect the police force, we do not have any institutions going on in the country, we don't have any economy going on. The only institution we can put some trust in, and I'm not saying it's the greatest but it's the best for this specific time, is the military. Seriously, we don't have anything else. There's absolutely nothing there to hold on to. Someone with a military background is the only person who is able to fight."

The fight about which this young health administrator spoke was real. "We have fights on the border with Libya, we have fights on the border of Palestine, we have fights in Sinai and in the South near Sudan. We seriously have fights everywhere. We cannot pick a civilian who doesn't understand anything about military work to do these fights." The perception was that a president with military experience was necessary because the army would not respect or listen to a civilian president. "Do you think that if we have a civilian as president the military will listen to him if he says let's go to Sinai to fight ISIS? Let's go to Libya to fight whoever? Do you think the military will even blink? They wouldn't listen to him because they wouldn't respect him. That's the mind of the military people," explained an affluent doctor. "[The military] would never listen to him or they would try to make it worse for him. The military would try to stall him. They would want to embarrass him because the military does not want a civilian. So the only solution at this point to stop the blood on the streets and grab ahold of the country and start building again is to have someone with a military background that the military will listen to and respect, someone who can control all the violence that's going on, the terrorism that's going on, and that will fight on the borders."

Even many Egyptians who were not Sisi supporters looked around their regional neighborhood to the chaos and destruction in Syria and Libya and decided that any qualms they had about their government were not worth the disorder that protests could potentially cause. The violent Islamist threat had become the main focus and primary fear for most Egyptians. When asked why there were no longer protests in the streets, one former protester replied, "Because people are sick of it. We tried that. It was only a constant bleeding of our economy and it made things worse, not better. You've seen the results in Libya, Lebanon, and Syria, and we're not willing to be like those countries, so we're not going to do this now. People are much, much wiser now. Even though our parliament is still a joke, politics is like that everywhere. Now we are more politically educated. Especially now we know we're in a state of war with terror, so we're not going to deal with interior issues when we're fighting ISIS and jihadi people over the borders. Now people are wiser than to do that."

CONCLUSION

Explaining the events surrounding June 30th is challenging because doing so requires differentiating the perspectives of multiple parties from the reality of what occurred. Analysis of the coup is also made difficult by the fact that the military's decision-making process during a coup is not usually made public. However, from the information available, I was able to determine that June 30th was a *popular participatory veto coup* facilitated by opposition co-optation. The military and the Interior Ministry were successful in their attempts to influence leaders of the Tamarod movement and co-opted both the social movement organization and the popular uprising. When people rose up against the Morsi government, the military staged a veto coup that ousted the president from power. In the following months, the military labeled the Muslim Brotherhood a terrorist organization and mobilized the public against the group through calls for mass demonstrations in support of the military in their fight on terror. Later, the military used the violent dispersal of the Rabaa al-Adawiya sit-in as a justification for imposing a state of emergency and for intensifying repression. By creating an atmosphere of fear, the government and media were able to influence the public to support the imposition of repressive measures. Additionally, the glorification of Sisi by the media, portraying him as the savior of the country, contributed to a cult of personality that developed around the general, which in turn led the people to petition for his presidential run. Sisi's win in the presidential elections consolidated the coup and conserved the military's veto power as a key element of Egyptian politics. It also demonstrated that the military was successful in galvanizing popular support for its coup.

While the overwhelming majority of the electorate voted for Sisi, it should be noted that there were still many who opposed military rule in the country. In addition to Islamists, there were many secular activists and members of the general public who continued to advocate for civilian rule and oppose the military regime. What we can observe from this chapter is that after the 2011 Revolution remnants of the old regime remained. These remnants capitalized on an opportune moment to regain power, returning stronger than they had ever been under Mubarak's rule.

8

Conclusion

The primary aim of my study was to uncover why and how individuals who are not members of political groups or organizers of political movements choose to engage or not engage in anti-government protest under a repressive regime. I employed elements of the Synthetic Political Opportunity Theory (SPOT) and the Collective Action Research Program (CARP) approaches to investigate protest mobilization leading up to and during the 18 days of the 2011 Egyptian Revolution, the 2011-2012 SCAF transitional government, and the June 30, 2013, uprising in Cairo, Egypt. Through the lens of these two approaches, this work explored how the interplay of political opportunity structures, mobilizing structures, and framing processes affected decisions to protest or not protest. It also examined the role of emotions in ordering preferences in the decision-making process. In this final chapter, I summarize my findings from each chapter and the main arguments of the book, after which I briefly explore the generalizability of my work and its implications for future research. The last segment discusses increased state repression in the years following the 2013 coup.

This book traced the experiences and decision-making processes of individuals in Cairo in the years preceding the 2011 Revolution through the 2013 June 30th protests. Chapter 2 demonstrated that leading up to the 2011 Revolution individuals of all classes shared similar grievances against the Mubarak regime regarding dissatisfaction with the economy and the high rate of unemployment, police brutality, and corruption. Many Egyptians felt that the regime had robbed them of their dignity, through the brutality and humiliation they experienced at the hands of the police and through their inability to provide for their families because of unemployment and underemployment. Many also experienced hopelessness because high levels of corruption had made it difficult to obtain employment or maneuver successfully in society without connections. Grievances alone do not lead to revolution; however, activists may use grievances as a starting point for mass mobilization against a regime if they are able successfully to frame them in a way whereby individuals are led to attribute these problems to failures of the regime and can be convinced that the way to address them is through protest. Chapter 3 documented how social movement organizers reinforced these grievances by disseminating information on police brutality, corruption, and labor issues online, intensifying exasperation and anger against the state and then channeling the resulting discontent into a call for collective action to contest the Mubarak regime.

In chapter 3, social media was found to be the most influential tool for disseminating information and mobilizing individuals to protest in the weeks leading up to the 2011 Revolution and on January 25th. While social media is not a necessary element of the revolutionary process, nor does it always accelerate the rate of mobilization, in the Egyptian case Facebook facilitated the building of a politically conscious civil society over the course of a number of years prior to the Revolution. In addition, it contributed to reinforcing grievances and mobilizing opposition to the regime in three important ways: (1) exposing corruption and human rights abuses, (2) allowing people to realize that they were not alone in their opposition to the regime, and (3) lowering the threshold for engaging in political participation and dissent by providing a relatively safe, easily accessible space for political expression in a country that outlawed gatherings of five or more people that could threaten public order or security. Many Egyptians were hesitant to protest in the streets in the years leading up to the Revolution because of the harsh crackdowns on demonstrations by state security. Thus, Facebook was seen as a more secure place to express grievances and share ideas. Additionally, the large number of people politically active online lowered the threshold for political participation based on the normalization of online political discussion, even for individuals who were not initially intending to use Facebook for political purposes.

The advent of new technologies leads to novel spaces for mobilization and protest. In chapter 3, I also reconceptualized Timur Kuran's (1991) idea of private and public preference by adding an intermediate step, online preference. While Kuran's explanation for first protesters out centers on their being selfless individuals who possibly have a higher moral standard than the rest of the population, I demonstrated that individuals are able to break the barrier of fear quite early by estimating how many people will attend a protest based on the number of people who accept the Facebook invitation to a protest event and by the number of groups that publicly proclaim that they will participate. Thus, revolutionary bandwagoning takes place online before anyone even begins protesting in the streets. I found that Facebook not only mobilized individuals online but also served as a stepping stone to on-the-ground protests. Regarding the non-protester population, these individuals were less likely to have a Facebook account than protesters, and those who were on Facebook were less likely to have been exposed to political information on the site.

Chapter 4 explained how government violence against protesters influenced individual decisions to join the demonstrations. The key emotional mechanism that contributed to ordering individual preferences and producing the decision to protest was moral shock. People at home experienced moral shock when they viewed the brutal treatment of protesters and experienced a sense of injustice that their compatriots were being killed for demanding their rights. One component of the emotion was empathy with protesters. In the chapter, I outlined how the empathy felt by those deciding to protest was based on feelings of collective identity, a newly developing form of nationalism that could be defined as "bottom-up." This national collective identity was founded on perceptions of collective victimization stemming from the regime's persecution of its people and failure to meet their needs. When individuals sitting at home observed expressions of this national identity in the chants of protesters in the streets and this particular form of collective identity resonated with them, it produced empathy, which moved them to become protesters themselves. However, individuals were less likely to protest when they did not empathize with those protesting in the streets or did not perceive that the injustices taking place were solely against protesters.

Chapter 5 investigated protest dynamics under the transitional rule of the Supreme Council of the Armed Forces (SCAF) and how protesters were able to successfully pressure SCAF to facilitate parliamentary and presidential elections. Protesters had opened political opportunities through their actions during the 18 days of the Revolution and their ousting of Mubarak, and they attempted to sustain and further open those opportunities through continuing to protest against SCAF rule. Protesters believed that the goals of the Revolution could only be achieved through a swift transition to civilian rule, which was the primary demand of the anti-SCAF protests. At the same time, SCAF aimed to remain in power long enough to manipulate laws and institutions in its favor; therefore, it tried to close political opportunities through violent crackdowns on its opponents. As explained in chapter 4, violent repression increased protesters' anger, furthering mobilization against SCAF. In chapter 5, I also introduced the term *post-revolutionary emboldening effect* to describe an emotional mechanism which occurs when protesters feel empowered because they attribute victory in a revolution to their own act of having protested and are therefore motivated to protest further.

When protesters overthrew Mubarak, they redefined the terms of regime legitimacy in Egypt so that a ruler required approval from the people. Because the military prided itself on being a military of the people, it was susceptible to challenges based on this definition. Each time protesters publicly challenged SCAF's rule and the military government used violence to quell demonstrations, SCAF further eroded its legitimacy. After failing to suppress protests with either superficial concessions or violence, SCAF eventually conceded to protester demands for democratic elections because it could not maintain its legitimacy while continuing to use violence against protesters in an attempt to close political opportunities. The chapter is important not only theoretically but also because, at the time of writing, it is one of the few scholarly pieces to summarize political and protest events under SCAF. Therefore, I hope that it can be useful as a source of information and a foundation for further research on political events in Egypt during that particular time period.

Chapter 6 outlined the individual grievances arising from political, economic, social, and religious conditions under the government of Mohamed Morsi that became the foundations of opposition to his presidency. Chapter 7 identified the discrepancy between real and perceived political opportunities and the effect this gap had on political mobilization for the 2013 coup. I outlined how the Tamarod movement inserted popular grievances in its petition to mobilize the mass protest against Morsi on June 30, 2013. Chapter 7 also assessed the intricate details and step-by-step process of the military coup. I introduced new terminology by labeling the coup a *popular participatory veto coup* that was facilitated by opposition co optation. Opposition co-optation occurred when the military and the Interior Ministry successfully influenced leaders of the Tamarod movement. During the four days of the June 30th uprising, the military intervened with a veto coup that ousted the president from power. In the months that followed, the military designated the Muslim Brotherhood a terrorist organization and mobilized the public against the group by organizing mass demonstrations in support of the military in its fight on terror. The public's participation in such events exemplified the popular participatory aspect of the coup.

The military used the violent reaction of some Morsi supporters to the dispersal of the Rabaa al-Adawiya sit-in as a pretext for imposing a state of emergency and intensifying repression. By fostering an atmosphere of fear, the government and state-aligned media influenced the Egyptian public to support the repressive measures. Additionally, the cult of personality that developed around General Sisi was so magnetic that it even led some people to petition for his presidential run. Sisi's victory in the presidential elections consolidated the coup and again reflected the popular participatory dimension of the coup.

The central argument in this study is that individuals are rational actors and their decisions to protest or not protest are affected by the interplay of three sets of factors conveniently grouped under the following headings: political opportunity structures, mobilizing structures, and framing processes. Ordering of individual preferences in the decision-making process takes place through emotional mechanisms that are activated by specific combinations of these factors. In Part I, I integrated the SPOT and CARP approaches using CARP to explore the emotional mechanisms involved in the decision-making process to protest and SPOT to identify the causes of such decisions. In Part II, I moved toward a SPOT-centered approach after finding in my data that changes in political opportunity structures and the discrepancy between perceived and actual opportunities were some of the most important explanatory factors for understanding protest dynamics during the period of time under study.

Each stage of the political process was associated with different emotions. Chapter 2 delineated how the political opportunity structures created by the Mubarak regime produced emotions of anger and exasperation, which social movement organizations were able to manipulate for mobilization against the government. Chapter 3 examined social media and online networks as tools for protest mobilization. I found that online participation was produced through the mechanisms of resentment formation, threshold-based safety calculations with Facebook-wide referents, and status considerations linked to Facebook community. Later, I uncovered that triggering mechanisms that caused individuals to move offline and into the streets were belief in the possibility of success based on the victory in Tunisia, status considerations linked to Facebook community, and threshold-based safety calculations with Facebook-wide referents, which were enhanced by community encouragement linked to work, family, and friend communities. Chapter 4 returned to political opportunities and how government violence against demonstrators caused individuals to protest. Regime violence produced moral shock and moral outrage, which were reinforced through empathy based on collective national identity.

Chapters 5 through 7 focused more heavily on structural factors rather than individual calculations and emotions. While emotions and individual decisions to protest were relevant aspects of mobilization during the SCAF transitional period and Morsi government, I found, particularly in chapters 6 and 7, that structural elements of the mobilization process were more important for understanding these events. Chapter 5 was similar to chapter 4 in its exploration of regime violence against protesters and the resulting activation of the moral shock emotion. However, the protests in chapter 5 took place under SCAF rather than Mubarak. In this chapter, I found that individuals were also invigorated to protest because of the post-revolutionary emboldening effect, which developed as a response to their success in removing Mubarak. Chapter 6 outlined the structural problems and actions taken by the Morsi regime that Tamarod was able to play upon in its mobilization for June 30th. Finally, in chapter 7, I explained the various political opportunities, mobilizing structures, and framing processes that contributed to the June 30th coup.

This study did not aim to produce a grand theory of revolution or collective action. However, I do believe that many of the elements and processes found in the Egyptian case may be useful for understanding protest events under other repressive regimes. I hope that my contributions to the literature on revolutionary bandwagoning and thresholds, such as online preference, encourage scholars to rethink these concepts, particularly given the advent of new media and communication technologies. Additionally, further research into emotional mechanisms, such as moral shock, may help to identify how and when individuals protest in the face of violent repression.

My research highlights the importance of understanding both the micro-foundations of protest and broader structural mechanisms. The two can be uncovered by interviewing individuals about their experiences.

It would be interesting to pose the same questions I used in Egypt to individuals who participated in another uprising, such as the Tunisian Revolution or the 8888 Uprising in Burma, to uncover whether individuals had similar experiences or went through similar emotional processes in their decisions of whether or not to protest. While interviewing allowed me to identify causal mechanisms and the intricacies of decision-making processes, the number of interviews in my study was not large enough to determine solid statistical significance for some of my findings. A mass survey that asked similar questions would further confirm my claims.

Finally, this study aimed to operationalize the relationship between structure and emotional mechanisms in individual decisions to protest or not protest. In order to do so, I relied on qualitative research methods including interviews and participant observation. In the political science field, where there is an increasing emphasis on quantitative methods, the value of qualitative research methods cannot be overstated. The emphasis on quantitative methods has, in a few cases, led to studies suffering from an ecological fallacy where aggregate data is used to explain individual decision-making. Let us not allow methods to guide our research. Instead, we should seek out the methods that best help us answer the questions posed. Despite the difficult research conditions presented by the current political climate in Egypt, further investigation of the events covered in this study, as well as those that occurred after the time period of my project, may prove very fruitful.

On January 25, 2016, Sanaa Seif stood in Tahrir Square sporting a shirt that read: "It is still the January revolution." The 21-year-old woman, whose older brother Alaa Abdel-Fattah was serving a five-year prison sentence for illegal protesting, was staging a one-woman demonstration on the fifth anniversary of the 2011 Revolution. Sanaa hailed from a prominent activist family and had herself been handed a three-year sentence in 2014 for violating the protest law, though she was later released following a presidential pardon. An Egyptian news outlet reported Sanaa's saying, "I am alone but I am sure that next year thousands will return to walk again from Mostafa Mahmoud to Tahrir Square" (Ahram Online 2016). Was Sanaa correct in her assessment of

Egyptians' intolerance for repression and their potential to protest again, or was the Revolution over?

In the lead-up to the fifth anniversary of the January 25th Revolution, Egyptian police searched over 5,000 apartments in central Cairo, questioning residents and arresting youth who fit the profile of activists. These sweeping raids, combined with the targeting of Facebook page administrators advocating protest, publishing houses, and cultural centers such as Townhouse Gallery, aimed to prevent any type of street protest. According to the Associated Press, the search campaign focused on pro-democracy activists, including foreigners, both inside and outside of Egypt, and was assisted by intelligence gathered through months of surveillance by security personnel. The government's use of arrest and intimidation tactics proved effective. Activist groups warned their followers to remain at home, and while on January 25th there were a few small anti-government protests in Cairo, Alexandria, and Kafr El-Sheikh, they were quickly dispersed. The tight security across the country, including the presence of anti-riot vehicles and army tanks in the streets, prevented any major protest incidents.

Since the 2013 coup, the Egyptian government has been leading an active campaign to silence any and all voices of dissent. Officials have played on popular fears of an Islamist insurgency similar to the situation in Iraq and Syria and declared a "war on terror." Initially, the crackdown targeted Islamists, both violent and peaceful, as well as followers of the banned Muslim Brotherhood. However, soon the government cast a wider net to include liberal and pro-democracy activists, who were either placed in the terrorist category or labeled traitors seeking to undermine Egypt's stability. Some activists have been handed long prison sentences on a range of trumped up charges or for illegal protest, while others have gone into exile. "Two years after the ousting of President Mohamed Morsi, mass protests have been replaced by mass arrests. By relentlessly targeting Egypt's youth activists, the authorities are crushing an entire generation's hopes for a brighter future," observed Hassiba Hadj Sahraoui, Deputy Director of the Middle East and North Africa Program at Amnesty International, in June 2015 (Amnesty International 2015).

Increased repression by the Sisi government has not been limited to officially documented detentions. Citizens, mostly Islamists and suspected civil society activists, have also been subjected to arbitrary arrest and forced disappearances, where individuals are secretly abducted and imprisoned by the state and authorities refuse to acknowledge the person's whereabouts or even confirm that she is being held. Under Sisi, hundreds of Egyptians have been forcibly disappeared into a network of security forces–run detention centers, without charges or access to a lawyer, and usually subjected to torture. Some have been held for weeks or months, or in rare cases years, before their release; others have turned up in the morgue. During their detention, individuals have often been forced to provide passwords to their social media accounts, offer information on friends and acquaintances, or testify to wrongdoing. One of the most prominent cases of forced disappearance was Esraa el-Taweel, a 23-year-old disabled photojournalist who had incurred a spinal injury from a bullet discharged by security forces during their aggressive dispersal of protesters on the third anniversary of the Revolution. Along with her friends Omar Mohamed and Sohaib Saad, Esraa was plucked from the street and held incommunicado for two weeks before being sighted at Qanater Women's Prison. After six months of detention, Esraa was released on health grounds but her charges were not dismissed. In January 2016, the National Council for Human Rights (NCHR) released the names and whereabouts of over 100 Egyptians who had been forcibly disappeared. After months of denials, the Ministry of Interior finally released information under pressure from rights groups and families searching for loved ones.

In addition to spreading fear and intimidation, the Sisi government's modus operandi has been the elimination of any person or group that seeks to expose the human rights abuses, extrajudicial killings, and violations of international law perpetrated by the regime and, more particularly, the security forces that act with impunity. On January 10, 2016, the Egyptian Commission for Rights and Freedoms reported that plainclothes security agents had attempted to abduct Ahmed Abdullah, one of its board members (Ismail and Walsh 2016). In February 2016, Egyptian authorities closed the Nadeem Center for Rehabilitation for Victims of

Violence and Torture, a prominent local nongovernmental organization (NGO) that documented human rights abuses and provided support to torture victims. The Nadeem Center was not the first NGO to be shuttered. In 2014, members of the Human Rights Watch staff were barred from entering Egypt following the organization's damning report on the Egyptian government's handling of the Rabaa al-Adawiya sit-in dispersal, forcing the group to move its operations outside the country.

The government has also taken unprecedented steps to restrict research and writing that might place Egypt in a negative light. In May 2015, Emad Shahin, a world-renowned political science professor at the American University in Cairo, was sentenced to death in absentia on fabricated charges of espionage. In the ruling by a Cairo court, death sentences were also handed down to former President Mohamed Morsi and one hundred others. Dr. Shahin's writings had focused on the brutality of the military coup, sexual assaults on students, and the judiciary's practice of mass death sentences, such as in March 2014 when more than five hundred people were sentenced to death for allegedly killing one police officer. Foreign researchers, such as French graduate student Fanny Ohier, have been arrested in Egypt and deported, while others, such as Tunisian professor Amel Grami, have been detained at the airport and denied entry into the country.

One of the most shocking cases that garnered international attention was the murder of Cambridge University graduate student Giulio Regeni in 2016. Mr. Regeni was conducting research on labor movements and was writing articles anonymously that were critical of the Sisi regime in the Italian daily *Il Manifesto*. Although the Egyptian government vehemently denied involvement in Mr. Regeni's death, the horrific marks of torture on the student's body, which had been discarded on the side of the road, held the signature signs of torture methods used by Egyptian police. Additionally, the *New York Times* reported that witnesses observed Mr. Regeni being led away by two men believed to be security agents, and three security officials admitted that Mr. Regeni had been taken into custody. The international community was outraged by Mr. Regeni's killing because it was almost unheard of for foreigners, excepting those with dual

Egyptian citizenship, to be physically assaulted by the regime. However, there are an unknown number of Egyptians who have been tortured and killed in a similar manner without a single line written about them in the press.

In the years following the Revolution, Egyptians gradually found that social media, initially used for mobilization against the regime, could also be used by the government as an apparatus of repression. In 2014, See Egypt, the sister company of American cybersecurity firm Blue Coat, won a government contract to monitor Egyptians' online communications. For the first time, the Egyptian government would be able to widely use deep packet inspection technology for tracking, geolocation, and heavy monitoring of Internet traffic. This newly acquired technology would be combined with training for security forces in methods for combing through data from email and social media accounts, as well as in how to access WhatsApp, Viber, and Skype accounts. In addition to monitoring Islamists, liberal activists, and the LGBTQ community, the authorities' main targets, the Interior Ministry announced that they would be searching for the following types of online communications:

> Blasphemy and skepticism in religions; regional, religious, racial, and class divisions; spreading of rumors and intentional twisting of facts; throwing accusations; libel; sarcasm; using inappropriate words; calling for the departure of societal pillars; encouraging extremism, violence and dissent; inviting demonstrations, sit-ins and illegal strikes; pornography, looseness, and lack of morality; educating methods of making explosives and assault, chaos and riot tactics; calling for normalizing relations with enemies and circumventing the state's strategy in this regard; fishing for honest mistakes, hunting flesh; taking statements out of context; and spreading hoaxes and claims of miracles. (Egypt Independent 2014)

Vasileios Karagiannopoulos stated it best when he observed: "The democratizing and revolutionizing potential of the Internet for these struggles can also be doubted due to the regime's capacity to infiltrate and manipulate information production and exchange, therefore transforming the Internet from a tool of dissent to a tool of oppression" (Karagiannopoulos 2012, 165). In January 2011, the Mubarak government imposed an Internet blackout because, at the time, authorities were not technologically sophisticated enough to address the mass mobilization for street protests taking place online in any other way. Security forces quickly realized that in order to prevent successive protests they would have to nip online mobilization in the bud. The concerted efforts to increase their monitoring capacity allowed the regime to block a Facebook page with 50,000 likes calling for new protests leading up to the fifth anniversary of the Revolution (TheWashington Post 2016).

Protesters in the January 25th Revolution demanded bread, freedom, and social justice. Their dissatisfaction centered on police brutality, corruption, and the poor economy. Five years later the situation in Egypt was worse than the conditions that drove Egyptians into the streets in 2011. Corruption persisted, annual tourism revenue had plunged 18%, and unemployment stood at 12% with even higher numbers recorded for youth. As a consequence of the government's floating the currency and slashing fuel subsidies in November 2016, by January 2017, the Egyptian pound was trading at 19 EGP to the dollar, and the inflation rate had risen to 24.3% (Agence France-Presse 2017). In order to compete with Islamists' claims to represent the Islamic faith in politics, the Sisi government under took the role of morality police, imprisoning homosexuals, as well as novelists such as Ahmed Naji who dared to "infringe on public decency" in their writing. Available spaces for dissent had virtually disappeared, record numbers of journalists and political activists had been incarcerated, and government repression and police brutality had risen to terrifying levels. Egyptians' enthusiasm for political engagement had waned, and participation in the 2015 parliamentary elections was reported as less than 26%.

Sanaa Seif was incorrect in her prediction that the sixth anniversary of the 2011 Revolution would see a return of thousands to Tahrir Square. In May 2016, Seif was sentenced to six months in prison for insulting the judiciary, and on January 25, 2017, Cairo remained relatively quiet. Despite the momentary lull in protest activity, the future for Egypt remains unknown. Brave journalists and liberal activists persist in exposing human rights violations in the country, politically subversive artists continue to create, and in April 2016 over a thousand people gathered in Cairo to protest Sisi's transfer of two Red Sea islands to Saudi Arabia. However, the question remains: Will the Egyptian people take to the streets again en masse to remove the regime?

NOTES

CHAPTER 1
1. I have used pseudonyms throughout to protect the identities of my informants.

CHAPTER 2
1. It should be noted that there were also a few women who were dissatisfied with the lack of employment opportunities.

CHAPTER 5
1. While protesters never reflect the opinion of the entire population and may not even represent the perspective of the majority, their place as vocal and public actors often allows them to dominate narratives of the "people's" views on the regime. There is also no reliable survey evidence to identify how much legitimacy was granted to the regime by the people.
2. This idea developed out of a conversation with Derek Ludovici, an anthropology PhD candidate at the CUNY Graduate Center.

BIBLIOGRAPHY

678. 2010. Dir. Mohamed Diab. New Century Productions. Film.
Abdel Kouddous, Sharif. 2011. "University Professors in Egypt Stage Open Sit-In, Call for Reform." Truthout, July 11. http://www.truth-out.org/news/item/2100-university-professors-in-egypt-stage-open-sitin-call-for-reform.
Abdel Kouddous, Sharif, and Nicole Slazar. 2011. *Tahrir Square: The July Sit-In*. Cairo: Pulitzer Center.
Abdelrahman, Maha M. 2004. *Civil Society Exposed: The Politics of NGOs in Egypt*. New York: Tauris Academic Studies.
Abdoun, Safaa, and Dalia Rabie. 2011. "SCAF Accepts Cabinet Resignation, MOI to Pull Police from Tahrir." *Daily News Egypt*, November 22.
Abdullah, Salma. 2013. "Tamarod Surpasses 22 Million Signatures." *Daily News Egypt*, June 29.
Aboulenien, Ahmed. 2012. "Decree Expands SCAF Authority and Curbs President's Remit over Defence." *Daily News Egypt*, June 19.
Aboulenein, Ahmed. 2013. "Labour Strikes and Protests Double under Morsi." *Daily News Egypt*, April 28.
Abul-Magd, Zeinab. 2011. "The Army and the Economy in Egypt." *Jadaliyya*, December 23. http://www.jadaliyya.com/pages/index/3732/the-army-and-the-economy-in-egypt
Afify, Heba. 2011. "Activists Hope 25 January Protest Will Be Start of 'Something Big.'" *Egypt Independent*, January 24.
Afify, Heba, and Nadim Audi. 2011. "Egyptian Forces Roust Tahrir Square Sit-In." *New York Times*, August 1.
AFP. 2008. "Egypt Demanding Data from Cyber Cafe Users: NGO." AFP, August 9.
AFP. 2009. "Protesters Arrested on Egypt 'Day of Anger.'" AFP, April 6.
AFP. 2013. "Cult Growing around Egypt's General Sisi." *Al Arabiya English*, August 1.
Agence France-Presse. 2017. "Egyptian Inflation Quickens to Highest Level in Years." Agence France-Presse, January 20.
Ahmed, Amir. 2011. "Egypt's New Cabinet: 14 New Ministers; 13 Stay in Place." CNN, July 18.

Ahmed, Amira, Safaa Abdoun, and Tamim Elyan. 2011. "Prison Inmates Escape amid Security Vacuum." *Daily News Egypt*, January 30.

Ahram Online. 2012a. "Official: The 100 Members of Egypt's Revamped Constituent Assembly." Ahram Online, June 12. http://english.ahram.org.eg/News/44696.aspx.

Ahram Online. 2012b. "Morsi's First 100 Days: A Report Card." Ahram Online, October 9. http://english.ahram.org.eg/NewsContent/1/140/55089/Egypt/The-Balance-Sheet/Morsis-first--days-A-report-card.aspx.

Ahram Online. 2013a. "Imam at Morsi's Friday Prayers Warns against 'Haters of Islam'." Ahram Online, May 17. http://english.ahram.org.eg/NewsContent/1/64/71682/Index.aspx.

Ahram Online. 2013b. "Shura Council Verdict Likely to Change Little: Political Figures." Ahram Online, June 2. http://english.ahram.org.eg/NewsContent/1/64/72936/Egypt/Politics-/SendToFriend.aspx?Title=Shura%20Council%20verdict%20likely%20to%20change%20little:%20Political%20figures&ID=72936.

Ahram Online. 2013c. "11 Islamist Parties Launch 'Legitimacy Support' Alliance." Ahram Online, June 28. http://english.ahram.org.eg/NewsContent/1/64/75145/Egypt/Politics-/-Islamist-parties-launch-Legitimacy-Support-allian.aspx.

Ahram Online. 2013d. "Egypt Military Unveils Transitional Roadmap." Ahram Online, July 3. http://english.ahram.org.eg/News/75631.aspx.

Ahram Online. 2013e. "Egypt's President Morsi in Power: A Timeline." *Jadaliyya*, July 22. http://www.jadaliyya.com/pages/index/13101/egypts-president-morsi-in-power_a-timeline-.

Ahram Online. 2016. "Activist stages single-person demonstration in Tahrir Square." *Ahram Online*, January 25.

Al Akhbar. 2012. "Egyptian Protests Continue; Egypt–Israel Pipeline Hit." *Al Akhbar*, February 5. http://english.al-akhbar.com/node/3913.

Al Akhbar. 2013. "Thousands of Mursi Supporters Rally in Egypt." *Al Akhbar*, June 21. http://english.al-akhbar.com/node/16197.

Al Arabiya. 2012a. "Want to Save Power? Wear Cotton and Stay in One Room: Egyptian PM." *Al Arabiya*, August 12. https://english.alarabiya.net/articles/2012/08/12/231786.html.

Al Arabiya. 2012b. "Egypt's Constitutional Assembly Case Referred to Supreme Court." *Al Arabiya*, October 23. https://english.alarabiya.net/articles/2012/10/23/245476.html.

Al Jazeera. 2011a. "Hosni Mubarak Resigns as President." Al Jazeera, February 11. http://www.aljazeera.com/news/middleeast/2011/02/201121125158705862.html.

Al Jazeera. 2011b. "Timeline: Egypt's Revolution." Al Jazeera, February 14. http://www.aljazeera.com/news/middleeast/2011/01/201112515334871490.html.

Al Jazeera. 2013a. "Death Sentences over Egypt Football Massacre." Al Jazeera, January 26. http://www.aljazeera.com/news/middleeast/2013/01/20131268947448319.html.

Al Jazeera. 2013b. "Egypt's Worst Hot-Mic Gaffe?" Al Jazeera, June 4. http://stream.aljazeera.com/story/201306042350-0022805.

Al Jazeera. 2013c. "Egypt Declares State of Emergency." Al Jazeera, August 14. http://www.aljazeera.com/news/middleeast/2013/08/201381413509551214.html.

Allagui, Ilhem, and Johanne Kuebler. 2011. "The Arab Spring and the Role of ICTs." *International Journal of Communication* 5: 1435–1442.

Allam, Rana. 2013. "If You Are Not with Us, You Are against Us." *Daily News Egypt*, July 29.
AlSharif, Asma. 2013. "Egyptian Islamists Rally at High Court, Demand Judiciary Purge." Reuters, April 19. http://uk.reuters.com/article/uk-egypt-protest-idUKBRE93I0XQ20130419.
Alterman, Jon B. 2011. "The Revolution Will Not Be Tweeted." *Washington Quarterly* 34(4): 103–116.
Amenta, Edwin, and Neal Caren. 2004. "The Legislative, Organizational, and Beneficiary Consequences of State-Oriented Challengers." In *The Blackwell Companion to Social Movements*, edited by David A. Snow, Sarah A. Soule, and Hanspeter Kriesi, 461–488. Malden, MA: Blackwell Publishing.
Amin, Shahira. 2011. "Egyptian General Admits 'Virginity Checks' Conducted on Protesters." CNN, March 31. http://www.cnn.com/2011/WORLD/meast/05/30/egypt.virginity.tests/.
Amnesty International. 2007a. *Egypt: Continuing Crackdown on Muslim Brotherhood*. London: Amnesty International.
Amnesty International. 2007b. *Egypt—Systematic Abuses in the Name of Security*. London: Amnesty International.
Amnesty International. 2009. *Egypt—Amnesty International Report 2009: Human Rights in the Arab Republic of Egypt*. London: Amnesty International.
Amnesty International. 2010. *Egypt—Amnesty International Report 2010: Human Rights in Arab Republic of Egypt*. London: Amnesty International.
Amnesty International. 2015. "Egypt: Generation of young activists imprisoned in ruthless bid to crush dissent." *Amnesty International*, June 30.
April 6 Youth Movement. 2009a. "6 April Movement." Facebook, April 4.
April 6 Youth Movement. 2009b. "6 April Movement." Facebook, April 6.
April 6 Youth Movement. 2011. "6 April Movement." Facebook, January 11.
Arabic Network for Human Rights Information 2005. "Egypt: Increasing Curb over Internet Usage Harassments against Net Cafes Should Immediately End." www.anhri.net, February 23.
Armbrust, Walter. 1996. *Mass Culture and Modernism in Egypt*. Cambridge: Cambridge University Press.
Aronoff, Myron J., and Jan Kubik. 2013. *Anthropology & Political Science: A Convergent Approach*. New York: Berghahn Books.
Associated Press. 2005. "Violence Mars Egypt's Election Law Referendum." Associated Press, May 25. http://usatoday30.usatoday.com/news/world/2005-05-25-egypt-referendum_x.htm.
Associated Press. 2011. "Egyptian Protesters Break into Israeli Embassy in Cairo." *The Guardian*, September 9. https://www.theguardian.com/world/2011/sep/10/egyptian-protesters-israeli-embassy-cairo.
Associated Press. 2012a. "Egypt Military Issues Interim 'Constitutional Declaration.'" *The World Post*, June 17. http://www.huffingtonpost.com/2012/06/17/egypt-constitutional-declaration-military_n_1604154.html.
Associated Press. 2012b. "Morsi Supporters Clash with Protesters outside Presidential Palace in Cairo." *The Guardian*, December 5. https://www.theguardian.com/world/2012/dec/05/morsi-supporters-protest-presidential-palace-cairo.

Associated Press in Cairo. 2011. "Egypt's Prime Minister, Ahmed Shafiq, Resigns on Eve of Rally." *The Guardian*, March 3.

Assran, Mahitab. 2013. "Further Competition between Tamarod and Tagarod." *Daily News Egypt*, June 22.

Atteya, Ahmed. 2013. "'Rebel' Egyptian Movement Defies Morsi through Petitions." *Al-Monitor*, May 17.

Audi, Nadim, and Michael Slackman. 2009. "Bomb Blast Kills Tourist in Cairo." *New York Times*, February 22.

Awadi, Hesham al-. 2005. "Mubarak and the Islamists: Why Did the 'Honeymoon' End?" *Middle East Journal* 59(1): 62–80.

Azzam, Maha. 2012. *Egypt's Military Council and the Transition to Democracy*. London: Chatham House.

Badawi, Nada. 2013. "US Dollar Soars to 8.25 Egyptian Pounds on Black Market." *Daily News Egypt*, April 3.

Baiasu, Kira D. 2009. "Sustaining Authoritarian Rule: The Rise of the Business Class and Descent of the Ulama in Saudi Arabia." *Northwestern Journal of International Affairs* 10(1): 92–109.

Barany, Zoltan. 2011. "The Role of the Military." *Journal of Democracy* 22(4): 24–35.

Baston, Daniel C., and Laura L. Shaw. 1991. "Evidence for Altruism: Toward a Pluralism of Prosocial Motives." *Psychological Inquiry* 2: 107–122.

BBC News. 1997. "World Tourists Massacred at Temple." BBC News, November 17. http://news.bbc.co.uk/2/hi/32179.stm.

BBC News. 2011a. "Egypt Unrest: Elbaradei Returns as Protests Build." BBC News, January 27. http://www.bbc.com/news/world-africa-12300164.

BBC News. 2011b. "Egypt Protests Escalate in Cairo, Suez and Other Cities." BBC News, January 28. http://www.bbc.com/news/world-middle-east-12303564.

BBC News. 2011c. "Cairo Clashes Leave 24 Dead after Coptic Church Protest." BBC News, October 9. http://www.bbc.com/news/world-middle-east-15235212.

BBC News. 2012a. "Egyptian Steel Magnate Ahmed Ezz Convicted." BBC News, October 4. http://www.bbc.com/news/world-middle-east-19830922.

BBC News. 2012b. "Egypt: The Legacy of Mohammed Mahmoud Street." BBC News, November 19. http://www.bbc.com/news/world-middle-east-20395260.

BBC News. 2013. "Profile: Egypt's Tamarod Protest Movement." BBC News, July 1. http://www.bbc.com/news/world-middle-east-23131953.

Behairy, Nouran el-. 2013. "Morsi Appoints 17 New Governors." *Daily News Egypt*, June 17.

Beinin, Joel, and Frederic Vairel. 2011. *Social Movements, Mobilization, and Contestation in the Middle East and North Africa*. Stanford, CA: Stanford University Press.

Bellin, Eva. 2004. "The Robustness of Authoritarianism in the Middle East: Exceptionalism in Comparative Perspective." *Comparative Politics* 36(2): 139–157.

Bellin, Eva. 2012. "Reconsidering the Robustness of Authoritarianism in the Middle East: Lessons from the Arab Spring." *Comparative Politics* 44(2): 127–149.

Benford, Robert D. 1997. "An Insider's Critique of the Social Movement Framing Perspective." *Sociological Inquiry* 67: 409–430.

Benford, Robert D., and David A. Snow. 2000. "Framing Processes and Social Movements: An Overview and Assessment." *Annual Review of Sociology* 26: 611–639.

Bennett, W. Lance, and Alexandra Sergerberg. 2012. "The Logic of Connective Action." *Information, Communication & Society* 15(5): 739–768.

Berbrier, Mitch. 1998. "Half the Battle: Cultural Resonance, Framing Processes and Ethnic Affectations in Contemporary White Separatist Rhetoric." *Social Problems* 45(4): 431–450.

Bermeo, Nancy, and Philip Nord. 2000. *Civil Society before Democracy: Lessons from Nineteenth-Century Europe*. New York: Rowman & Littlefield Publishers.

Bhatty, Ayesha, and Michael Hirst. 2011. "As It Happened: Egypt Unrest Day Five." BBC, January 29.

Bikhchandani, Sushil, David Hirshleifer, and Ivo Welch. 1998. "Learning from the Behavior of Others: Conformity, Fads, and Informational Cascades." *Journal of Economic Perspectives* 12(3): 151–170.

Blair, Edmund. 2012. "Train Plows into School Bus in Egypt, 50 Killed." Reuters, November 17. http://www.reuters.com/article/us-egypt-crash-idUSBRE8AG03V20121117.

Bourdieu, Pierre. 1991. "On Symbolic Power." In *Language and Symbolic Power*, edited by John B. Thompson, translated by Gino Raymond and Matthew Adamson, 163–170. Cambridge, MA: Harvard University Press.

Bradley, Matt, and Reem Abdellatif. 2013a. "Egypt's Subsidies Stall Its IMF Aid." *Wall Street Journal*, April 2.

Bradley, Matt, and Reem Abdellatif. 2013b. "Egypt Army Issues Ultimatum." *Wall Street Journal*, July 2.

Bryman, Alan. 2012. *Social Research Methods*. 4th ed. Oxford: Oxford University Press.

Bueno de Mesquita, Bruce. n.d. "Foreign Policy Analysis and Rational Choice Models." International Studies Compendium Project, 1–29.

Bush, Ray, ed. 2002. *Counter-Revolution in Egypt's Countryside: Land and Farmers in the Era of Economic Reform*. London: Zed Books.

Calhoun, Craig. 1997. *Nationalism*. Minneapolis: University of Minnesota Press.

Carey, Sabine C. 2006. "The Dynamic Relationship between Protest and Repression." *Research Quarterly* 58(1): 1–11.

Carter Center, The. 2012. *Presidential Elections in Egypt: Final Report*. Atlanta, GA: Carter Center.

Caspani, Maria. 2013. "Infographic: Egypt's Constituent Assembly." Thomas Reuters Foundation, September 3.

CBS News. 2013. "Egyptian General Abdul Fattah al-Sisi's Growing Cult-like Following." CBS News, December 26. http://www.cbsnews.com/news/egyptian-general-abdul-fattah-al-sisis-growing-cult-like-following/.

Central Intelligence Agency. n.d. *The World Factbook*.

Chick, Kristen. 2011a. "Egyptian Army Empties Tahrir Square." *Christian Science Monitor*, August 1. http://www.csmonitor.com/World/Middle-East/2011/0801/Egyptian-Army-empties-Tahrir-Square.

Chick, Kristen. 2011b. "Egypt's Tahrir Square Protests: A Second Revolution Unfolding Now?" *Christian Science Monitor*, November 20. http://www.csmonitor.

com/World/Middle-East/2011/1120/Egypt-s-Tahrir-Square-protests-A-second-revolution-unfolding-now.

Chong, Dennis. 1991. *Collective Action and the Civil Rights Movement.* Chicago: University of Chicago Press.

Clark, Janine A. 2000. "The Economic and Political Impact of Economic Restructuring on NGO-State Relations in Egypt." In *Economic Liberalization, Democratization and Civil Society in the Developing World*, edited by Remonda Bensabat Kleinberg and Janine A. Clark, 157–179. New York: St. Martin's Press.

Clark, Terry Nichols, and Seymour Martin Lipset. 1991. "Are Social Classes Dying?" *International Sociology* 6(4): 397–410.

CNBC. 2011. "Egypt's Mubarak Steps Down, Hands Power to Military." CNBC, February 11. http://www.cnbc.com/id/41531755.

CNN. 2011a. "Egyptian Police Crack Down on Second Day of Protests." CNN, January 27. http://www.cnn.com/2011/WORLD/africa/01/26/egypt.protests/.

CNN. 2011b. "Egyptians Brace for Friday Protests as Internet, Messaging Disrupted." CNN, January 27. http://www.cnn.com/2011/WORLD/africa/01/27/egypt.protests/.

CNN. 2011c. "Egypt Cracks Down on Mass Protests as Mubarak Dissolves Government." CNN, January 29. http://www.cnn.com/2011/WORLD/africa/01/28/egypt.protests/.

CNN. 2014. "Egypt Declares El-Sisi Winner of Presidential Election." CNN, June 4. http://www.cnn.com/2014/06/03/world/africa/egypt-presidential-election/.

Cogburn, Derrick L., and Fatima K. Espinoza-Vasquez. 2011. "From Networked Nominee to Networked Nation: Examining the Impact of Web 2.0 and Social Media on Political Participation and Civic Engagement in the 2008 Obama Campaign." *Journal of Political Marketing* 10(1–2): 189–213.

Collier, David, and Steven Levitsky. 1997. "Democracy with Adjectives: Conceptual Innovation in Comparative Research." *World Politics* 49(3): 430–451.

Cooper, Mark N. 1983. "State Capitalism, Class Structure, and Social Transformation in the Third World: The Case of Egypt." *International Journal of Middle East Studies* 15(5): 451–469.

Cousin, Eduard. 2013. "Egyptian Army in Privileged Position with One-Third Share of GDP." Hoqook News Network, July 8.

Cowell, Alan, and Douglas Jehl. 1997. "Luxor Survivors Say Killers Fired Methodically." *New York Times*, November 24.

Cowen, Tyler. 1998. "Do Economists Use Social Mechanisms to Explain?" In *Social Mechanisms: An Analytical Approach to Social Theory*, edited by Peter Hedstrom and Richard Swedberg, 125–146. New York: Cambridge University Press.

Dabh, Basil el-. 2013. "99.3% of Egyptian Women Experienced Sexual Harassment: Report." *Daily News Egypt*, April 28. http://www.dailynewsegypt.com/2013/04/28/99-3-of-egyptian-women-experienced-sexual-harassment-report/.

Dahan, Maha, and Tamim Elyan. 2011. "Egyptian Soldiers Battle Protesters, Three Dead." Reuters, December 26. http://www.reuters.com/article/us-egypt-protest-idUSTRE7BF0IQ20111216.

Daily News Egypt. 2012. "Morsy Sacks Prosecutor General." *Daily News Egypt*, October 11. https://www.dailynewsegypt.com/2012/10/11/morsy-sacks-prosecutor-general/.

Dajani, Nabil. 2012. "Technology Cannot a Revolution Make: Nas-Book Not Facebook." *Arab Media & Society* 15. http://www.arabmediasociety.com/?article=782.
Damasio, Antonio. 2003. *Looking for Spinoza: Joy, Sorrow, and the Feeling Brain*. London: William Heinemann.
Davis, Nancy J., and Robert V. Robinson. 2009. "Overcoming Movement Obstacles by the Religiously Orthodox: The Muslim Brotherhood in Egypt, Shas in Israel, Comunione e Liberazione in Italy, and the Salvation Army in the United States." *American Journal of Sociology* 114(5): 1302–1349.
Dawisha, Adeed. 2003. *Arab Nationalism in the Twentieth Century: From Triumph to Despair*. Princeton, NJ: Princeton University Press.
Deeb, Sarah el-. 2011. "Egypt Police Fire at Rally outside Israel Embassy." *The San Diego Union Tribune*, May 16. http://www.sandiegouniontribune.com/sdut-egypt-police-fire-at-rally-outside-israel-embassy-2011may16-story.html.
Deeb, Sarah el-. 2013. "Egypt Appoints 9 Ministers in Limited Reshuffle." *Washington Examiner*, May 7. http://www.washingtonexaminer.com/egypt-appoints-9-ministers-in-limited-reshuffle/article/2529142.
De Koning, Anouk. 2009. *Global Dreams: Class, Gender, and Public Space in Cosmopolitan Cairo*. Cairo: American University in Cairo Press.
Della Porta, Donatella, and Mario Diani. 1999. *The Symbolic Dimension of Collective Action*. Oxford: Blackwell Publishers.
Demertzis, Nicolas, ed. 2013. *Emotions in Politics: The Affect Dimension in Political Tension*. New York: Palgrave Macmillan.
DPA. 2012. "Egypt Unveils New Cabinet, Tantawi Keeps Defense Post." *Haaretz*, August 2. http://www.haaretz.com/middle-east-news/egypt-unveils-new-cabinet-tantawi-keeps-defense-post-1.455638.
Drake, Harold A. 2002. *Constantine and the Bishops: The Politics of Intolerance*. Baltimore: Johns Hopkins University Press.
Dreyfuss, Bob. 2011. "Obama and Egypt's Revolution." *The Nation*, February 14. https://www.thenation.com/article/obama-and-egypts-revolution/.
Dubai Press Club. 2012. *Arab Media Outlook: 2011–2015*. Dubai: Dubai Press Club.
Duncan, Riley. 2009. "More Assistance from Anonymous for Iran." *The Inquisitr*, June 18. http://www.inquisitr.com/26534/more-assistance-from-anonymous-for-iran-iranelection-mrh/.
Dziadosz, Alexander, and Shadia Nasralla. 2013. "At Least 51 Killed in Egypt as Islamists Urge Defiance." Reuters, July 8. http://www.reuters.com/article/us-egypt-protests-idUSBRE95Q0NO20130708.
Early, Evelyn A. 1993. *Baladi Women of Cairo: Playing with an Egg and a Stone*. London: Lynne Rienner.
Egyptian Streets. 2014. "Steel Tycoon and Mubarak-Era Politician Ahmed Ezz Released from Prison." *Egyptian Streets*, October 8. https://egyptianstreets.com/2014/08/08/steel-tycoon-and-mubarak-era-politician-ahmed-ezz-released-from-prison/.
Egypt Independent. 2011. "New Egyptian Law Criminalizes Protests." *Egypt Independent*, March 23.
Egypt Independent. 2012. "Morsy Issues New Constitutional Declaration." *Egypt Independent*, November 22.

Egypt Independent. 2014. "Interior Ministry denies monitoring Internet activity." *Egypt Independent*, September 18.

Egypt Independent. 2013a. "CAPMAS Says Tourist Numbers Improved almost 20% in 2012." *Egypt Independent*, March 13.

Egypt Independent. 2013b. "Google 'No Ability' to Count Protesters in Egypt." *Egypt Independent*, July 21.

"Egypt: Seeds of Change." 2011. People & Power, Al Jazeera. February 9. Television.

Einhorn, Bruce, and Ben Elgin. 2006. "The Great Firewall of China." *Bloomberg Businessweek*, January 3.

Eisenberg, Nancy, and Natalie D. Eggum. 2008. "Empathy-Related and Prosocial Responding: Conceptions and Correlates during Development." In *Cooperation: The Political Psychology of Effective Human Interaction*, edited by Brandon A. Sullivan, Mark Snyder, and John L. Sullivan, 53–74. Malden, MA: Blackwell Publishing.

Ekiert, Grzegorz, and Jan Kubik. 2014. "Myths and Realities of Civil Society." *Journal of Democracy* 25(1): 46–58.

Elaasar, Aladdin. 2010. "Is Egypt's Economy in Crisis?" *World Post*, May 22.

Elster, Jon. 1989. *The Cement of Society*. Cambridge: Cambridge University Press.

Elster, Jon. 1996. "Rationality and the Emotions." *Economic Journal* 106(438): 1386–1397.

Elyachar, Julia. 2011. "The Political Economy of Movement and Gesture in Cairo." *Journal of the Royal Anthropological Institute* 17: 82–99.

Esterman, Isabel. 2013. "Natural Gas Dilemma Forces Egypt to Import." *Business Monthly Magazine*, February. http://www.amcham.org.eg/publications/business-monthly/issues/206/February-2013/2961/natural-gas-dilemma-forces-egypt-to-import.

Esterman, Isabel. 2014. "Egypt's Natural Gas Quagmire." *Mada Masr*, May 8.

Eyerman, Ron. 2005. "How Social Movements Move: Emotions and Social Movements." *Emotions and Social Movements*, edited Helena Flam and Debra King, 41–56. New York: Routledge.

Ezzat, Dina. 2014. "Al-Sisi Announces His Candidacy." *Al Ahram Weekly*, March 27. http://weekly.ahram.org.eg/News/5817/17/Al-Sisi-announces-his-candidacy.aspx.

Fahim, Kareem. 2012a. "In Upheaval for Egypt, Morsi Forces Out Military Chiefs." *New York Times*, August 12.

Fahim, Kareem. 2012b. "Egypt Requests $4.8 Billion from I.M.F." *New York Times*, August 22.

Fahim, Kareem, and Mona El-Naggar. 2011. "Violent Clashes Mark Protests against Mubarak's Rule." *New York Times*, January 25.

Fahim, Kareem, and Mayy El Sheikh. 2013. "Crackdown in Egypt Kills Islamists as They Protest." *New York Times*, July 27.

Fahim, Kareem, and Rick Gladstone. 2013. "Egypt Vows to End Sit-Ins by Supporters of Deposed President." *New York Times*, July 31.

Fahim, Kareem, and David D. Kirkpatrick. 2012. "Egypt Protesters Gather to Denounce Morsi in Scenes Recalling Uprising." *New York Times*, November 27.

Fahim, Kareem, Michael Slackman, and David Rohde. 2011. "Egypt's Ire Turns to Confidant of Mubarak's Son." *New York Times*, February 6.

Fahmy, Dalia Fikry. 2011. "Muslim Democrats: Moderating Islam, Modifying the State." PhD diss., Rutgers.

Fahmy, Mohamed Fadel. 2012a. "Eyewitnesses: Police Stood Idle in Egypt Football Massacre." CNN, February 2. http://www.cnn.com/2012/02/02/world/africa/egypt-soccer-deaths-color/.

Fahmy, Mohamed Fadel. 2012b. "Court Disbands Egypt's Constitutional Group." CNN, April 11. http://www.cnn.com/2012/04/11/world/africa/egypt-constitution/.

Faris, David M. 2013. *Dissent and Revolution in a Digital Age: Social Media, Blogging, and Activism in Egypt*. New York: I. B. Tauris.

Farouk, Dalia. 2012. "Egypt Tourism Shows Little Recovery in 2012." AhramOnline, December 27. http://english.ahram.org.eg/NewsContent/3/12/61366/Business/Economy/Egypt-tourism-shows-little-recovery-in-.aspx.

Fathi, Yasmine. 2012. "Egypt's 'Battle of the Camel': The Day the Tide Turned." AhramOnline, February 2. http://english.ahram.org.eg/News/33470.aspx.

Federal Communications Commission. 2017. *Communications Assistance for Law Enforcement Act*. February 9. Accessed May 26, 2017. https://www.fcc.gov/public-safety-and-homeland-security/policy-and-licensing-division/general/communications-assistance.

Ferrara, Federico. 2003. "Why Regimes Create Disorder: Hobbes's Dilemma during a Rangoon Summer." *Journal of Conflict Resolution* 47(3): 302–325.

Ferree, Myra Marx. 1992. "The Political Context of Rationality: Rational Choice Theory and Resource Mobilization." In *Frontiers in Social Movement Theory*, edited by Aldon D. Morris and Carol McLurg Mueller, 29–52. New Haven, CT: Yale University Press.

Fireman, Bruce, and William Gamson. 1979. "Utilitarian Logic in the Resource Mobilization Perspective." In *The Dynamics of Social Movements*, edited by Mayer N. Zald and John D. McCarthy, 8–44. Cambridge, MA: Winthrop.

Fisher, Max. 2013. "Is What Happened in Egypt a Revolution or a Coup? It's Both." *Washington Post*, July 3. https://www.washingtonpost.com/news/worldviews/wp/2013/07/03/is-what-happened-in-egypt-a-coup-or-a-revolution-its-both/.

Fitzpatrick, Alex. 2013. "Egypt's President Morsi Defies Army with One Tweet." *Mashable*, July 2.

Fouad, Viviane, Nadia Ref'at, and Samir Murcos. 2005. "From Inertia to Movement: A Study of the Conflict over the NGO Law in Egypt." In *NGOs and Governance in the Arab World*, edited by Sarah Ben Nefissa, Nabil Abd al-Fattah, Sari Hanafi, and Carlos Milani, 101–122. New York: American University in Cairo Press.

FoxNews. 2012. "Egypt's Muslim Brotherhood Accused of Paying Gangs to Rape Women." FoxNews, December 5. http://www.foxnews.com/world/2012/12/05/egypt-muslim-brotherhood-accused-paying-gangs-to-rape-women.html.

Francisco, Ronald A. 1995. "The Relationship between Coercion and Protest: An Empirical Evaluation in Three Coercive States." *Journal of Conflict Resolution* 39(2): 263–282.

Francisco, Ronald A. 2010. *Collective Action Theory and Empirical Evidence*. New York: Springer.

Freedom House. 2012. "Freedom on the Net 2011." 2011. Freedomhouse.org. January 5. https://freedomhouse.org/report/freedom-net/freedom-net-2011.

Frenkel, Sheera, and Maged Atef. 2014. "How Egypt's Rebel Movement Helped Pave the Way for a Sisi Presidency." BuzzFeed News, April 15.

Freud, Sigmund. 1959. *Group Psychology and Analysis of the Ego*. New York: Norton.

Gamson, William A. 1975. *The Strategy of Social Protest*. Homewood, IL: Dorsey.

Gamson, William A. 1992. *Talking Politics*. Cambridge: Cambridge University Press.

Gamson, William A., and David S. Meyer. 1996. "Framing Political Opportunity." In *Comparative Perspectives on Social Movements: Political Opportunities, Mobilizing Structures, and Cultural Framing*, edited by Doug McAdam, John D. McCarthy, and Mayer N. Zald, 275–290. New York: Cambridge University Press.

Gause, Gregory F. 2011. "Why Middle East Studies Missed the Arab Spring: The Myth of Authoritarian Stability." *Foreign Affairs* 90(4): 81–90.

Gaventa, John. 1980. *Power and Powerlessness: Quiescence and Rebellion in an Appalachian Valley*. Urbana: University of Illinois Press.

Gavious, Arieh, and Shlomo Mizrahi. 2001. "A Continuous Time Model of Bandwagon Effect in Collective Action." *Social Choice and Welfare* 18(1): 91–105.

Gellner, Ernest. 1994. *Conditions of Liberty: Civil Society and Its Rivals*. New York: Allen Lane/Penguin Press.

Gellner, Ernest. 2008. *Nations and Nationalism*. Ithaca, NY: Cornell University Press.

George, Alexander L., and Andrew Bennett. 2005. *Case Studies and Theory Development in the Social Sciences*. Cambridge, MA: MIT Press.

Gerges, Fawaz A. 2000. "The End of the Islamist Insurgency in Egypt?: Costs and Prospects." *Middle East Journal* 54(4): 592–612.

Gerson, Kathleen, and Ruth Horowitz. 2002. "Observation and Interviewing: Options and Choices in Qualitative Research." In *Qualitative Research in Action*, edited by Tim May, 199–224. London: Sage.

Ghanem, Amina. 2010. *Egyptian Economic Monitor*. Cairo: Arab Republic of Egypt Ministry of Finance.

Ghannam, Farha. 2013. *Live and Die Like a Man: Gender Dynamics in Urban Egypt*. Stanford, CA: Stanford University Press.

Ghonim, Wael. 2012. *Revolution 2.0: The Power of the People Is Greater than the People in Power*. New York: Mariner Books.

Giglio, Mike. 2011. "The Facebook Freedom Fighter." *Newsweek*, February 21. https://www.highbeam.com/doc/1G1-249163445.html.

Giglio, Mike. 2013. "Mahmoud Badr Is the Young Face of the Anti-Morsi Movement." *Daily Beast*, July 2.

Ginkel, John, and Alastair Smith. 1999. "So You Say You Want a Revolution: A Game Theoretic Explanation of Revolution in Repressive Regimes." *Journal of Conflict Resolution* 43(3): 291–316.

Gladwell, Malcolm. 2010. "Small Change: Why the Revolution Will Not Be Tweeted." *The New Yorker*, October 4. http://www.newyorker.com/magazine/2010/10/04/small-change-malcolm-gladwell.

Gladwell, Malcolm, and Clay Shirky. "From Innovation to Revolution: Do Social Media Make Protests Possible?" *Foreign Affairs*, March/April 2011.

Glaser, Barney G., and Anselm L. Strauss. 1967. *The Discovery of Grounded Theory: Strategies for Qualitative Research*. Chicago: Aldine.

Goldberg, Ellis. 1992. "Peasants in Revolt—Egypt 1919." *International Journal of Middle East Studies* 24(2): 261–280.

Goldstone, Jack. 2003. "Comparative Historical Analysis and Knowledge Accumulation in the Study of Revolutions." *Comparative Historical Analysis in the Social Sciences*, edited by James Mahoney and Dietrich Reuschemeyer, 41–90. Cambridge: Cambridge University Press.

Gomaa, Mahmoud. 2013. "Egypt's June 30 Protest: Day 19 of a Revolution Reignited." CNN, July 1. http://ireport.cnn.com/docs/DOC-998347.

Goodwin, Jeff, and James M. Jasper. 1999. "Caught in a Winding, Snarling Vine: The Structural Bias of Political Process Theory." *Sociological Forum* 14(1): 27–54.

Goodwin, Jeff, James M. Jasper, and Francesca Polletta. 2000a. "Emotional Dimensions of Social Movements." In *The Blackwell Companion to Social Movements*, edited by David A. Snow, Sarah A. Soule, and Hanspeter Kriesi, 413–432. Malden, MA: Blackwell Publishing.

Goodwin, Jeff, James M. Jasper, and Francesca Polletta. 2000b. "The Return of the Repressed: The Fall and Rise of Emotions in Social Movement Theory." *Mobilization: An International Journal* 5(1): 65–83.

Gordon, Cynthia, and James M. Jasper. 1996. "Overcoming the 'NIMBY' Label: Rhetorical and Organizational Links for Local Protesters." *Research in Social Movements, Conflicts and Change* 19: 153–175.

Gramsci, Antonio. 1957. *The Modern Prince & Other Writings*. New York: International Publishers.

Green, Donald P., and Ian Shapiro. 1994. *Pathologies of Rational Choice Theory: A Critique of Applications in Political Science*. New Haven, CT: Yale University Press.

Gribbon, Laura, and Sarah Hawas. 2012. "Signs and Signifiers: Visual Translations of Revolt." *Translating Egypt's Revolution: The Language of Tahrir*, edited by Samia Mehrez. Cairo: American University in Cairo Press.

Guardian, The. 2011. "Egypt's Prime Minister, Ahmed Shafiq, Resigns on Eve of Rally." *The Guardian*, March 3. https://www.theguardian.com/world/2011/mar/03/egypt-prime-minister-shafiq-resigns.

Guardian, The. 2012a. "Egypt: Port Said Football Disaster-2." *The Guardian*, February 2. https://www.theguardian.com/world/middle-east-live/2012/feb/02/egypt-port-said-football-dsaster-live-updates.

Guardian, The. 2012b. "Egypt Protest Continue after Football Deaths." *The Guardian*, February 3. https://www.theguardian.com/world/middle-east-live/2012/feb/03/egypt.

Guardian, The. 2012c. "Egyptian Police Incited Massacre at Stadium, Say Angry Footballers." *The Guardian*, February 4. https://www.theguardian.com/world/2012/feb/05/egypt-football-massacre-police-arab-spring.

Guardian. 2012d. "Egyptian Opposition Masses in Tahrir Square—Tuesday 27 November." *The Guardian*, November 27. https://www.theguardian.com/world/middle-east-live/2012/nov/27/egypt-morsi-compromise-protests-live.

Guardian, The. 2013. "Egyptian Military Government Declares Month-Long Emergency." *The Guardian*, August 14. https://www.theguardian.com/world/2013/aug/14/egypt-clear-cairo-sitins-live.

Gundy, Zeinab el-. 2012. "Egypt Parliament Issues Law Regulating Constitution-Drafting Body." Ahram Online, June 11. http://english.ahram.org.eg/NewsContent/

1/64/44573/Egypt/Politics-/Egypt-Parliament-issues-law-regulating-constitutio. aspx.

Gupta, Dipak, Harinder Singh, and Tom Sprague. 1993. "Government Coercion of Dissidents: Deterrence or Provocation?" *Journal of Conflict Resolution* 37: 301–339.

Gurr, Ted Robert. 1970. *Why Men Rebel*. Princeton, NJ: Princeton University Press.

Haddon, Hazel, Salma Shukrallah, Mina Adel, Ayat Al-Tawy, Nada Rashwan, and Randa Ali. 2013. "Live Updates: Morsi Ousted; Head of Constitutional Court to Take over Egypt Presidency." Ahram Online, July 3. http://english.ahram.org.eg/News/75594.aspx.

Hakim, Karim el-. 2012. "The Director of ½ Revolution Recounts His Experience on the Front Lines of the Egyptian Revolution." Sundance Institute, January 25. https://www.sundance.org/blogs/the-director-of-revolution-recounts-his-experience-on-the-front-lines-of-th.

Halime, Farah. 2013. "Egypt's Long-Term Economic Recovery Plan Stalls." *New York Times*, May 2.

Hall, Peter A. 2006. "Systematic Process Analysis: When and How to Use It." *European Management Review* 3: 24–31.

Halliday, Fred. 1997. "The Formation of Yemeni Nationalism: Initial Reflections." In *Rethinking Nationalism in the Arab Middle East*, edited by James Jankowski and Israel Gershoni, 26–41. New York: Columbia University Press.

Halliday, Fred. 2005. *The Middle East in International Relations: Power, Politics and Ideology*. Cambridge: Cambridge University Press.

Handoussa, Heba. 2010. *Egypt Human Development Report 2010*. Tampa, FL: United Nations Development Programme.

Hatina, Meir. 2004. "History, Politics, and Collective Memory: The Nasserist Legacy in Mubarak's Egypt." In *Rethinking Nasserism: Revolution and Historical Memory in Modern Egypt*, edited by Elie Podeh and Onn Winckler, 100–124. Gainesville: University Press of Florida.

Hauslohner, Abigail. 2011. "Egypt's Protesters Return in Force but Don't Speak with One Voice." *Time*, July 8. http://content.time.com/time/world/article/0,8599,2082172,00.html.

Hauslohner, Abigail. 2013a. "Egypt's Morsi Remakes Cabinet." *Washington Post*, January 6.

Hauslohner, Abigail. 2013b. "Egypt's Military Threatens to Step In to Resolve Political Crisis." *Washington Post*, July 2.

Hauslohner, Abigail, and Ingy Hassieb. 2012. "Confusion Pervades Egypt's Opposition after Morsi Rescinds Decree." *Washington Post*, December 9.

Hawke, Jack. 2009. "Internet Underground Takes on Iran." *MSN News*, June 19.

Hawthorne, Amy. 2005. "Is Civil Society the Answer?" In *Uncharted Journey: Promoting Democracy in the Middle East*, edited by Thomas Carothers and Marina Ottaway, 81–113. Washington, DC: Carnegie Endowment for International Peace.

He, Baogang, and Mark Warren. 2011. "Authoritarian Deliberation: The Deliberative Turn in Chinese Political Development." *Perspectives on Politics* 9(2): 269–289.

Hearst, David, and Rahman Hussein. 2012. "Egypt's Supreme Court Dissolves Parliament and Outrages Islamists." *The Guardian*, June 14. https://www.theguardian.com/world/2012/jun/14/egypt-parliament-dissolved-supreme-court.

Hedstrom, Peter, and Richard Swedberg. 1998. "Social Mechanisms: An Introductory Essay." In *Social Mechanisms: An Analytical Approach to Social Theory*, edited by Peter Hedstrom and Richard Swedberg, 1–31. New York: Cambridge University Press.

Hendawi, Hamza. 2013. "Mohammed Morsi, Egypt's President, Acknowledges Making Mistakes in Televised Speech." *Huffington Post*, June 26.

Hendawi, Hamza, Sarah El Deeb, and Maggie Michael. 2013. "Egypt's Military Gives Morsi 48-Hour Ultimatum." *The Jakarta Post*, July 1. http://www.thejakartapost.com/news/2013/07/02/egypts-military-gives-morsi-48-hour-ultimatum.html.

Hermida, Alfred. 2002. "Behind China's Internet Red Firewall." BBC News Online, September 3. http://news.bbc.co.uk/2/hi/technology/2234154.stm.

Herrera, Linda. 2014. *Revolution in the Age of Social Media: The Egyptian Popular Insurrection and the Internet*. New York: Verso.

Hill, Evan. 2010. "A Bittersweet Release." Al Jazeera, November 25.

Hill, Evan C. 2013. "What Values Could El-Baradei Mean?" *Tahrir Squared*, August 9. http://evanchill.com/blog/2013/8/24/what-values-could-elbaradei-mean.

Hochschild, Arlie Russell. 1983. *The Managed Heart*. Berkeley: University of California Press.

Hoodfar, Hooma. 1997. *Between Marriage and the Market: Intimate Politics and Survival in Cairo*. Berkeley: University of California Press.

Howard, Philip N. 2011. *The Digital Origins of Dictatorship and Democracy: Information Technology and Political Islam*. New York: Oxford University Press.

Howeidy, Amira. 2013. "The Road Not Taken." Middle East Institute, September 2.

Human Rights Watch. 2011a. *Egypt: End Torture, Military Trials of Civilians*. New York: Human Rights Watch.

Human Rights Watch. 2011b. *Work Him Until He Confesses: Impunity for Torture in Egypt*. New York: Human Rights Watch.

Human Rights Watch. 2012. *Egypt: Investigate Brotherhood's Abuse of Protesters*. New York: Human Rights Watch.

Human Rights Watch. 2014. *All According to Plan: The Rab'a Massacre and Mass Killings of Protesters in Egypt*. New York: Human Rights Watch.

Human Rights Watch. 2013. "Egypt: Lynching of Shia Follows Months of Hate Speech; Police Fail to Protect Muslim Minority." Human Rights Watch.

Huntington, Samuel P. 1968. *Political Order in Changing Societies*. New Haven, CT: Yale University Press.

Hussein, Abdel-Rahman. 2012. "Egypt Erupts as Muslim Brotherhood Supporters Clash with Protesters." *The Guardian*, December 6. https://www.theguardian.com/world/2012/dec/05/egypt-clashes-protesters-muslim-supporters.

Ibish, Hussein. 2013. "The Mexican Standoff in Egypt." *Daily Beast*, July 3. http://www.thedailybeast.com/articles/2013/07/03/the-mexican-standoff-in-egypt.

Ibrahim, Ekram. 2012a. "9 April, 2011: When the SCAF, People Went Their Separate Ways." Ahram Online, April 9. http://english.ahram.org.eg/NewsContent/1/64/38881/Egypt/Politics-/-April,--When-the-SCAF,-people-went-their-separate.aspx.

Ibrahim, Ekram. 2012b. "Justice Denied: Egypt's Maspero Massacre One Year On." Ahram Online, October 9. http://english.ahram.org.eg/NewsContent/1/64/54821/Egypt/Politics-/Justice-denied-Egypts-Maspero-massacre-one-year-on.aspx.

Ibrahim, Ekram. 2012c. "Mohamed Mahmoud Clashes, 1 Year On: 'A Battle for Dignity.'" Ahram Online, November 19. http://english.ahram.org.eg/NewsContent/1/64/58444/Egypt/Politics-/Mohamed-Mahmoud-clashes,--year-on-A-battle-for-dig.aspx.

IkhwanWeb. 2012. "President Mohamed Morsi's Speech in Tahrir Square, Friday June 29, 2012." IkhwanWeb, June 30.

Indexmuni. 2011. "Historical Data Graphs per Year." January 1.

International Monetary Fund. 2010. *Arab Republic of Egypt—2010 Article IV Consultation Mission, Concluding Statement.* Cairo: International Monetary Fund.

Ismael, Tareq Y. 2001. *Middle East Politics Today: Government and Civil Society.* Gainesville: University Press of Florida.

Ismail, Amina, and Declan Walsh. 2016. "Hundreds Vanishing in Egypt as Crackdown Widens, Activists Say." *New York Times*, January 26.

Ismail, Salwa. 2006. *Political Life in Cairo's New Quarters: Encountering the Everyday State.* Minneapolis: University of Minnesota Press.

Jackman, Robert W. 1993. *Power without Force: The Political Capacity of Nation States.* Ann Arbor: University of Michigan Press.

Jankowski, James. 1991. "Egypt and Early Arab Nationalism, 1908-1922." In *The Origins of Arab Nationalism*, edited by Rashid Khalidi, Lisa Anderson, Muhammad Muslih, and Reeva S. Simon, 243-270. New York: Columbia University Press.

Jankowski, James. 2002. *Nasser's Egypt, Arab Nationalism, and the United Arab Republic.* London: Lynne Rienner.

Jasper, James M. 1997. *The Art of Moral Protest: Culture, Biography, and Creativity in Social Movements.* Chicago: University of Chicago Press.

Jasper, James M. 1998. "The Emotions of Protest: Affective and Reactive Emotions in and around Social Movements." *Sociological Forum* 13(3): 397-424.

Jasper, James M., and Jane D. Poulsen. 1995. "Recruiting Strangers and Friends: Moral Shocks and Social Networks in Animal Rights and Anti-Nuclear Protests." *Social Problems* 42(4): 493-512.

Jenkins, Craig J., and Charles Perrow. 1977. "Insurgency of the Powerless: Farm Worker Movements (1946-1972)." *American Sociological Review* 42: 249-268.

Johnston, Hank. 2014. "The Mechanisms of Emotion in Violent Protest." In *Dynamics of Political Violence: A Process-Oriented Perspective on Radicalization and the Escalation of Political Conflict*, edited by Lorenzo Bosi, Chares Demetriou, and Stefan Malthaner, 27-50. Burlington, VT: Ashgate Publishing.

Joudeh, Safa. 2014. *Egypt's Military: Protecting Its Sprawling Economic Empire.* Washington, DC: Atlantic Council.

Jumet, Kira. 2012. "Social Media: A Force for Political Change in Egypt." San Diego, CA: International Studies Association. http://www.atlanticcouncil.org/blogs/mena-source/egypt-s-military-protecting-its-sprawling-economic-empire.

Karagiannopoulos, Vasileios. 2012. "The Role of the Internet in Political Struggles: Some Conclusions from Iran and Egypt." *New Political Science* 34(2): 151-171.

Karawan, Ibrahim A. 2011. "Politics and the Army in Egypt." *Survival: Global Politics and Strategy* 53(2): 43-50.

Kassem, Maye. 2004. *Egyptian Politics: The Dynamics of Authoritarian Rule.* London: Lynne Rienner.

Kepel, Gilles. 1995. "Islamists versus the State in Egypt and Algeria." *The Quest for World Order* 124(3): 109–127.

Kershaw, Sarah. 2003. "Cairo, Once 'the Scene,' Cracks Down on Gays." *New York Times*, April 3. http://www.nytimes.com/2003/04/03/world/cairo-once-the-scene-cracks-down-on-gays.html?mcubz=2.

Khamis, Sahar. 2011. "The Transformative Egyptian Media Landscape: Changes, Challenges and Comparative Perspectives." *International Journal of Communications* 5: 1159–1177.

Khamis, Sahar, and K. Vaughn. 2012. "We Are All Khaled Said: The Potentials and Limitations of Cyberactivism in Triggering Public Mobilization and Promoting Political Change." *Journal of Arab & Muslim Media Research* 4: 145–163.

Khawaja, Marwan. 1993. "Repression and Popular Collective Action: Evidence from the West Ban." *Sociological Forum* 8: 47–71.

Khawly, Mohammad. 2012. "Egypt's Military Junta: The Road from Hero to Villain." *Al Akhbar English*, February 12. http://english.al-akhbar.com/node/4119.

Kholy, Heba Aziz el-. 2002. *Defiance and Compliance: Negotiating Gender in Low-Income Cairo.* New York: Berghahn Books.

Kingsley, Patrick. 2013a. "Egypt's Mohamed Morsi: I Have Made Mistakes." *The Guardian*, June 26. https://www.theguardian.com/world/2013/jun/26/egypt-mohamed-morsi-mistakes.

Kingsley, Patrick. 2013b. "Tamarod Campaign Gathers Momentum among Egypt's Opposition." *The Guardian*, June 27. https://www.theguardian.com/world/2013/jun/27/tamarod-egypt-morsi-campaign-oppsition-resignation.

Kingsley, Patrick. 2013c. "80 Sexual Assaults in One Day—The Other Story of Tahrir Square." *The Guardian*, July 5. https://www.theguardian.com/world/2013/jul/05/egypt-women-rape-sexual-assault-tahrir-square.

Kingsley, Patrick. 2013d. "Egypt: Dozens of Protesters Killed as Rival Factions Tear Cairo Apart." *The Guardian*, October 6. https://www.theguardian.com/world/2013/oct/06/egypt-cairo-morsi-yom-kippur.

Kingsley, Patrick. 2013e. "Egypt's Interim President Adly Mansour Signs 'Anti-Protest Law.'" *The Guardian*, November 24. https://www.theguardian.com/world/2013/nov/24/egypt-interim-president-anti-protest-law.

Kingsley, Patrick. 2014. "Egypt's Human Rights Groups 'Targeted' by Crackdown on Foreign Funding." *The Guardian*, September 24. https://www.theguardian.com/world/2014/sep/24/egypt-human-rights-crackdown-foreign-funding.

Kingsley, Patrick. 2015. "Will #SisiLeaks be Egypt's Watergate for Abdel Fatah al-Sisi?" *The Guardian*, March 5. https://www.theguardian.com/world/2015/mar/05/sisileaks-egypt-watergate-abdel-fatah-al-sisi.

Kirkpatrick, David D. 2011a. "Egypt Revamps Cabinet as Protesters Seem to Lose Steam." *New York Times*, July 18.

Kirkpatrick, David D. 2011b. "Egypt News Media Clash over Cause of Violence." *New York Times*, December 18.

Kirkpatrick, David D. 2012a. "Hoarding Is Seen as a Cause of Fuel Shortage in Egypt." *New York Times*, January 15.

Kirkpatrick, David D. 2012b. "Thousands of Egyptians Protest Plan for Charter." *New York Times*, December 4.

Kirkpatrick, David D. 2012c. "Backing Off Added Powers, Egypt's Leader Presses Vote." *New York Times*, December 8.

Kirkpatrick, David D. 2013a. "Short of Money, Egypt Sees Crisis on Fuel and Food." *New York Times*, March 30.

Kirkpatrick, David D. 2013b. "Morsi Defies Egypt Army's Ultimatum to Bend to Protest." *New York Times*, July 2.

Kirkpatrick, David D. 2013c. "Hundreds Die as Egyptian Forces Attack Islamist Protesters." *New York Times*, August 14.

Kirkpatrick, David D., and Ben Hubbard. 2013. "Sudden Improvements in Egypt Suggest a Campaign to Undermine Morsi." *New York Times*, July 10.

Kiser, Edgar, and Michael Hechter. 1991. "The Role of General Theory in Comparative-Historical Sociology." *American Journal of Sociology* 97: 1–30.

Kitschelt, Herbert. 1986. "Political Opportunity Structures and Political Protest." *British Journal of Political Science* 16(1): 57–85.

Kortam, Hend. 2013. "The Battle of the Camel: The Final Straw for Mubarak's Regime." *Daily News Egypt*, February 3. http://www.dailynewsegypt.com/2013/02/03/the-battle-of-the-camel-the-final-straw-for-mubaraks-regime/.

Koslowski, Barbara. 1996. *Theory and Evidence: The Development of Scientific Reasoning*. Cambridge, MA: MIT Press.

Kriesi, Hanspeter. 1996. "The Organizational Structure of New Social Movements in a Political Context." In *Comparative Perspectives on Social Movements: Political Opportunities, Mobilizing Structures, and Cultural Framings*, edited by Doug McAdam, John D. McCarthy, and Mayer N. Zald, 152–184. Cambridge: Cambridge University Press.

Kriesi, Hanspeter. 2004. "Political Context and Opportunity." In *The Blackwell Companion to Social Movements*, edited by David A. Snow, Sarah A. Soule, and Hanspeter Kriesi, 67–90. Malden, MA: Blackwell Publishing.

Kuran, Timur. 1991. "Now Out of Never: The Element of Surprise in the East European Revolution of 1989." *World Politics* 33(1): 7–48.

Labib, Sara. 2012. "The New Constitutional Declaration of 17 June 2012." *Tabula Sara*, June 17. http://tabulasara.blogspot.be/2012/06/new-constitutional-declaration-of-17.html.

Laws of Rule. 2011. "Illegitimate Privatization in Egypt." The Laws of Rule, October 15.

Le Bon, Gustave. 2002. *The Crowd: A Study of the Popular Mind*. Mineola, NY: Dover Publications.

Lesch, Ann M. 2011. "Egypt's Spring: Causes of the Revolution." *Middle East Policy Council* 18(3).

Levy, Jack. 2003. "Political Psychology and Foreign Policy." In *Oxford Handbook of Political Psychology*, edited by David O. Sears, Leonie Huddy, and Robert Jervis, 253–284. New York: Oxford University Press.

Lichbach, Mark I. 1987. "Deterrence of Escalation? The Puzzle of Aggregate Studies of Repression and Dissent." *Journal of Conflict Resolution* 31(2): 266–297.

Lichbach, Mark I. 1995. *The Rebel's Dilemma*. Ann Arbor: University of Michigan Press.

Lichbach, Mark I. 1996. *The Cooperator's Dilemma*. Ann Arbor: University of Michigan Press.

Lichbach, Mark I. 1998. "Contending Theories of Contentious Politics and the Structure-Action Problem of Social Order." *Annual Review of Political Science* 1: 401–424.

Lindsey, Ursula. 2013. "The Cult of Sisi." *New York Times*, September 12. https://latitude.blogs.nytimes.com/2013/09/12/the-cult-of-sisi/?mcubz=2.

Lofty, Mohamed. 2013. "Special Tour of the Pro-Morsi Sit-In after Torture Allegations." *Live Wire*, August 9.

Lotan, Gilad, Erhardt Graeff, Mike Ananny, Devin Gaffney, Ian Pearce, and danah boyd. 2011. "The Revolutions Were Tweeted: Information Flows during the 2011 Tunisian and Egyptian Revolutions." *International Journal of Communication* 5: 1375–1405.

Loveluck, Louisa. 2013. "Morsi's Speech: Too Little, Too Late for Opposition." *Christian Science Monitor*, June 27. http://www.csmonitor.com/World/Middle-East/2013/0627/Morsi-s-speech-too-little-too-late-for-opposition-video.

Luce, Duncan R., and Howard Raiffa. 1957. *Games and Decisions*. New York: John Wiley & Sons.

Lukes, Steven. 1974. *Power: A Radical View*. London: Macmillan.

Lupia, Arthur, and Gisela Sin. 2003. "Which Public Goods Are Endangered?: How Evolving Communication Technologies Affect the Logic of Collective Action." *Public Choice* 117: 315–331.

Lynch, Marc. 2013. *The Arab Uprising: The Unfinished Revolution of the New Middle East*. New York: Public Affairs.

Lynch, Sarah. 2011. "The Aftermath of Another Clash at Egypt's Tahrir Square." *Christian Science Monitor*, June 29. http://www.csmonitor.com/World/Middle-East/2011/0629/The-aftermath-of-another-clash-at-Egypt-s-Tahrir-Square.

Lynch, Sarah. 2013. "Egypt Pyramid Vendors Grow Violent, Embassy Says." *USA Today*, June 3. https://www.usatoday.com/story/news/world/2013/06/03/egypt-pyramids-tourism-violent/2384601/.

Maass, Alan, and Aaron Petkov. 2012. "What Caused the Soccer Massacre in Egypt?" *Socialist Worker*, February 7.

Macey, Jennifer. 2011. "US Puts Pressure on Mubarak to Step Down Now." Australian Broadcasting Corporation, February 4.

Mackell, Austin G. 2013. "Morsi's Post-Coup Speech Translated." *The Moon under Water*, July 4.

Mackey, Robert. 2012. "Clashes in Cairo after Morsi Supporters Attack Palace Sit-In." *New York Times*, December 5.

Mada Masr. 2014. "Corrupt Gas Contracts Cost Egypt 10 Billion Dollars, Says Report." *Mada Masr*, March 20.

Mahdi, Rabab el-. 2011. *Empowered Participation or Political Manipulation? State, Civil Society and Social Funds in Egypt and Bolivia*. Boston: Brill.

Mahoney, James. 2001. "Beyond Correlational Analysis: Recent Innovations in Theory and Methods." *Sociological Forum* 26(3): 575–593.

Markič, Olga. 2009. "Rationality and Emotions in Decision Making." *Interdisciplinary Description of Complex Systems* 7: 54–64.

Marroushi, Nadine. 2012. "Egypt Tries Undoing Mubarak Deals." *Bloomberg Businessweek*, October 25. https://www.bloomberg.com/news/articles/2012-10-25/egypt-tries-undoing-mubarak-deals.

Marshall, Shana. 2012. "Egypt's Other Revolution: Modernizing the Military-Industrial Complex." *Jadaliyya*, February 10. http://www.jadaliyya.com/pages/index/4311/egypts-other-revolution_modernizing-the-military-i.

Marshall, Shana, and Joshua Stacher. 2012. "Egypt's Transnational Capital." *Middle East Report*: 12–18.

Marx, Karl, and Friedrich Engels. 2014. *The Communist Manifesto*. New York: International Publishers.

Masoud, Tarek E. 1999. "The Arabs and Islam: The Troubled Search for Legitimacy." *The Next Generation: Work in Progress* 128(2): 127–145.

McAdam, Doug. 1982. *Political Process and the Development of Black Insurgency, 1930–1970*. Chicago: University of Chicago Press.

McAdam, Doug. 1996. "Conceptual Origins, Current Problems, Future Directions." In *Comparative Perspectives on Social Movements: Political Opportunities, Mobilizing Structures, and Cultural Framings*, edited by Doug McAdam, John D. McCarthy, and Mayer N. Zald, 23–40. Cambridge: Cambridge University Press.

McAdam, Doug, John D. McCarthy, and Mayer N. Zald. 1996. *Comparative Perspectives on Social Movements*. New York: Cambridge University Press.

McAdam, Doug, and Dieter Rucht. 1993. "The Cross-National Diffusion of Movement Ideas." *Annals of the American Academy of Political and Social Science* 528: 56–74.

McAdam, Doug, Sidney Tarrow, and Charles Tilly. 2001. *Dynamics of Contention*. New York: Cambridge University Press.

McAdam, Doug, Sidney Tarrow, and Charles Tilly. 2009. "Comparative Perspectives on Contentious Politics." In *Comparative Politics: Rationality, Culture, and Structure*, edited by Mark Irving Lichbach and Alan S. Zuckerman, 260–290. Cambridge: Cambridge University Press.

McCarthy, John. 1996. "Constraints and Opportunities in Adopting, Adapting, and Inventing." In *Comparative Perspectives on Social Movements: Political Opportunities, Mobilizing Structures, and Cultural Framing*, edited by Doug McAdam, John McCarthy, and Mayer N. Zald, 141–151. Cambridge: Cambridge University Press.

McCarthy, John D., and Mayer N. Zald. 1977. "Resource Mobilization and Social Movements: A Partial Theory." *American Journal of Sociology* 82(6): 1212–1241.

McFarlane, Sarah. 2013. "Egypt's Wheat Problem: How Mursi Jeopardized the Bread Supply." Reuters, July 25. http://www.reuters.com/article/us-egypt-mistakes-wheat-idUSBRE96O07N20130725.

Michael, Maggie. 2011. "Egypt Protests: New Clashes between Military Police and Demonstrators." *The World Post*, December 16.

Middle East Voices. 2011. "After Civilian Cabinet Resigns, Egypt's SCAF Scrambles for Crisis Talks." *Middle East Voices*, November 21.

Mokhtari, Mona El. 2012. "Confessions of a Tunisian Hacktivist." *Tech Crunch*, January 6. https://techcrunch.com/2011/10/23/confessions-of-a-tunisian-hacktivist/.

Monroe, Kristen R. 1991. *A Critical Reassessment of the Theory of Rational Choice*. New York: Harper Collins Publishers.

Moriyama, Kenji. 2011. *Inflation Inertia in Egypt and Its Policy Implications*. Washington, DC: International Monetary Fund.

Morozov, Evgeny. 2011. *The Dark Side of Internet Freedom: The Net Delusion*. New York: PublicAffairs.

Mourad, Menna. 2013. "Tagarod Campaign to Counter Tamarod." *Daily News Egypt*, May 13. https://www.dailynewsegypt.com/2013/05/13/tagarod-campaign-to-counter-tamarod/.

Mowafi, Timmy. 2012. "Morsi's Got Balls." *Cairo Scene*, September 26. http://www.cairoscene.com/BusinessAndPolitics/Morsi's-Got-Balls.

Muller, Edward N., and Karl-Dieter Opp. 1986. "Rational Choice and Rebellious Collective Action." *American Political Science Review* 80: 471–487.

Musekamp, Catherine. 2010. "Negotiating Egyptian Nationalism: Militant Islamist Confrontations with the State and the Fragmentation of Political Authority." *Journal of the Centre for Studies in Religion and Society Graduate Students Association* 9(1): 21–44.

Nagi, Mohamad. 2013. "Tahrir Masses React to Morsi's Speech." *Daily News Egypt*, June 27. http://www.dailynewsegypt.com/2013/06/27/tahrir-masses-react-to-morsis-speech/.

Nawawy, Mohammed el-, and Sahar Khamis. 2013. *Egyptian Revolution 2.0: Political Blogging, Civic Engagement, and Citizen Journalism*. New York: Palgrave Macmillan.

Neidhardt, Friendhelm, and Dieter Rucht. 1991. "The Analysis of Social Movements: The State and the Art and Some Perspectives for Further Research." In *Research on Social Movements: The State of the Art in Western Europe and the USA*, edited by Dieter Rucht, 421–460. Boulder, CO: Westview Press.

Newsmax. 2011. "Egypt's Poverty, Unemployment, Push Youths to Breaking Point." *Newsmax*, January 31. http://www.newsmax.com/Newsfront/Egypt-poverty-unemployment-unrest/2011/01/31/id/384555/.

New Sources. 2011. "Egypt's Military Barrier to Democracy." *News Sources*, October 8.

Nicholas, Peter. 2011. "Obama's Strategy was to Pressure Mubarak without Intruding." *Los Angeles Times*, February 13. http://warincontext.org/2011/10/28/egypts-military-barrier-to-democracy/.

Norton, Augustus Richard. 2005. "Thwarted Politics: The Cast of Egypt's Hizb al-Wasat." In *Remaking Muslim Politics: Pluralism, Contestation, Democratization*, edited by Robert W. Hefner. Princeton, NJ: Princeton University Press.

Nour, Ahmed, and Adam Robinson. 2014. "Egypt's Abdul Fattah al-Sisi 'Cult' Sees Surge in Merchandise." BBC News, March 31. http://www.bbc.com/news/world-middle-east-26775516.

Oberschall, Anthony. 1973. *Social Conflict and Social Movements*. Englewood Cliffs, NJ: Prentice-Hall.

Oliner, Pearl M., and Samuel P. Oliner. 1992. "Promoting Extensive Altruistic Bonds: A Conceptual Elaboration and Some Pragmatic Implications." In *Embracing the Other: Philosophical, Psychological, and Historical Perspectives on Altruism*, edited by Pearl M. Oliner, Samuel P. Oliner, Lawrence Baron, and Lawrence Blum, 369–389. New York: New York University Press.

Oliver, Pamela E. 1993. "Formal Models of Collective Action." *Annual Review of Sociology* 19: 271–300.

Olson, Mancur. 1965. *The Logic of Collective Action: Public Goods and the Theory of Groups*. Cambridge, MA: Harvard University Press.

Ondetti, Gabriel. 2006. "Repression, Opportunity, and Protest: Explaining the Takeoff of Brazil's Landless Movement." *Latin American Politics and Society* 48(2): 61–94.

Onians, Charles. 2004. "Supply and Demand Democracy in Egypt." *World Policy Journal* 21(2): 78–84.

Onodera, Henri. 2009. "The Kifaya Generation: Politics of Change among Youth in Egypt." *Suomen Antropologi: Journal of the Finish Anthropological Society* 34(4): 44–64.

OpenNet Initiative. 2012. "Internet Filtering in Egypt." 2009. OpenNet Initiative, January 5. https://opennet.net/research/profiles/egypt.

Opp, Karl-Dieter, and Wolfgang Roehl. 1990. "Repression, Micromobilization and Political Protest." *Social Forces* 69: 521–547.

Ossowski, Stanislaw. 1963. *Class Structure in the Social Consciousness*. London: Routledge.

Ottaway, Marina. 2012. "Egypt: Death of the Constituent Assembly?" Carnegie Endowment for International Peace, June 13. http://carnegieendowment.org/2012/06/13/egypt-death-of-constituent-assembly-pub-48501.

Partlett, William. 2012. "Constitution-Making by 'We the Majority' in Egypt." Brookings, November 30.

Passy, Florence. 2001. "Political Altruism and the Solidarity Movement: An Introduction." In *Political Altruism? Solidarity Movements in International Perspective*, edited by Marco Giugni and Florence Passy, 3–25. Boulder, CO: Rowman & Littlefield Publishers.

Pearlman, Wendy. 2013. "Emotions and the Microfoundations of the Arab Uprisings." *Perspectives on Politics* 11(2): 387–408.

Peralta, Eyder. 2014. "That 'I'm a Voter' App at the Top of Your Newsfeed Actually Makes a Difference." NPR.org, November 4. http://www.npr.org/sections/thetwo-way/2014/11/04/361407161/that-im-a-voter-app-at-the-top-of-your-newsfeed-actually-makes-a-difference.

Petersen, Roger D. 2001. *Resistance and Rebellion: Lessons from Eastern Europe*. New York: Cambridge University Press.

Petersen, Roger D. 2002. *Understanding Ethnic Violence: Fear, Hatred, and Resentment in Twentieth-Century Eastern Europe*. Cambridge: Cambridge University Press.

Peterson, Mark Allen. 2011. *Connected in Cairo: Growing up Cosmopolitan in the Modern Middle East*. Bloomington: Indiana University Press.

Popovic, Srdja. 2011. Interview. Kira Jumet. April 27.

Pratt, Nicola. 2005. "Hegemony and Counter-Hegemony in Egypt: Advocacy NGOs, Civil Society, and the State." In *NGOs and Governance in the Arab World*, edited by Sarah Ben Nefissa, Nabil Abd al-Fattah, and Carlos Milani, 123–150. New York: American University in Cairo Press.

SBWire. 2013. "Naguib Sawiris Transfers $28 Million USD to Tamarod Organizers." *SBWire*, July 18. http://www.sbwire.com/press-releases/naguib-sawiris-transfers-28-million-usd-to-tamarod-organizers-285324.htm.

Putnam, Robert D. 2000. *Bowling Alone: The Collapse and Revival of American Community*. New York: Simon & Schuster.

Raphaeli, Nimrod. 2013. *Egyptian Army's Pervasive Role in National Economy*. Washington, DC: Middle East Media Research Institute.

Rasler, Karen. 1996. "Concessions, Repression, and Political Protest in the Iranian Revolution." *American Sociological Review* 61(1): 132–152.

Reed, Jean-Pierre. 2004. "Emotions in Context: Revolutionary Accelerators, Hope, Moral Outrage, and Other Emotions in the Making of Nicaragua's Revolution." *Theory and Society* 33(6): 653–703.

Rees, John. 2011. "Egypt's Second Revolution." *The Occupied Times*, December 2. http://theoccupiedtimes.org/?p=1368.

Reproductive Health Matters. 2009. "In a Time of Torture: From the Human Rights Watch Report." *Reproductive Health Matters* 34: 173–177.

Reuters. 2011. "Egypt Police Break Up Largest Protest since Mubarak's Ouster." *Haaretz*, April 9. http://www.haaretz.com/world-news/egypt-police-break-up-largest-protest-since-mubarak-s-ouster-1.354941.

Reuters. 2013a. "Egyptian Government Faces Blame in Mob Sectarian Killing." *The National*, June 25.

Reuters. 2013b. "Egypt Forex Reserves Dip to $17.8 bln in Nov." Reuters, December 8.

"Revolution in Cairo." 2011. *Frontline*, PBS, February 22. Television.

Reza, Sadiq. 2007. "Endless Emergency: The Case of Egypt." *New Criminal Law Review: An International and Interdisciplinary Journal* 10(4): 532–553.

RFI. 2011. "Army Deployed to Tahrir Square to Oust Demonstrators." RFI, August 1. http://en.rfi.fr/africa/20110801-army-deploys-soldiers-tahrir-square-oust-demonstrators.

Richtel, Matt. 2011. "Egypt Cuts Off Most Internet and Cell Service." *New York Times*, January 28.

Riker, William H. 1990. "Political Science and Rational Choice." In *Perspectives on Positive Political Economy*, edited by James E. Alt and Kenneth A. Shepsle. Cambridge: Cambridge University Press.

Roudi-Fahimi, Farzaneh, Shereen El Feki, and Tyjen Tsai. 2011. "Youth Revolt in Egypt, a Country at the Turning Point." Population Reference Bureau, February. http://www.prb.org/Publications/Articles/2011/youth-egypt-revolt.aspx.

Rozen, Laura. 2011. "Egyptian Military Delegation at Pentagon for Annual Meeting." *Politico*, January 27.

Rucht, Dieter. 1996. "The Impact of National Contexts on Social Movement Structures: A Cross-Movement and Cross-National Comparison." In *Comparative Perspectives on Social Movements: Political Opportunities, Mobilizing Structures, and Cultural Framings*, edited by Doug McAdam, John D. McCarthy, and Mayer N. Zald, 185–204. Cambridge: Cambridge University Press.

Rutherford, Bruce K. 2008. *Egypt after Mubarak: Liberalism, Islam, and Democracy in the Arab World*. Princeton, NJ: Princeton University Press.

Rutherford, Bruce, Steven A. Cook, and Geoffrey Wawro. 1976. "The Arab Conundrum." *The Wilson Quarterly* 34(2): 5–7.

Sabry, Bassem. 2012. "A Guide to Egypt's Challenges: Fuel & Electricity Shortages." AhramOnline, August 16. http://english.ahram.org.eg/News/49603.aspx.

Sabry, Sarah. 2014. "Pause for a Second and Visualize This-Poverty in Egypt." *MadaMasr*, January 20.

Sadat, Anwar el-. 1977. *In Search of Identity*. New York: Harper & Row.

Said, Edward W. 2003. *Orientalism*. London: Penguin Books.

Saleh, Yasmine, and Marwa Awad. 2012. "Egypt's Mursi Leaves Palace as Police Battle Protester." Reuters, December 4. http://www.reuters.com/article/us-egypt-politics-idUSBRE8B30GP20121204.

Saleh, Yasmine, and Paul Taylor. 2013. "Mahmoud Badr, Tamarod Protest Leader, 'Owns the Streets' in Egypt." Reuters, September 6.

Salvage, Charlie. 2010. "U.S. Tries to Make It Easier to Wiretap the Internet." *New York Times*, September 27.

Sattar, Noman. 1995. "'Al Ikhwan Al Muslimin' (Society of Muslim Brotherhood) Aims and Ideology, Role and Impact." *Pakistan Horizon* 48(2): 7–30.

"Saudi Wasta. 2010. Does More Wishes than a Genie." YouTube, uploaded by Ali Farahat, June 20. https://www.youtube.com/watch?v=eQH8wioFHUQ.

Sayyid, Mustapha Kamil al-. 1995. "A Civil Society in Egypt?" In *Civil Society in the Middle East*, edited by Augustus Richard Norton, 269–293. New York: E. J. Brill.

Schattschneider, Elmer Eric. 1960. *The Semi-Sovereign People: A Realist's View of Democracy in America*. New York: Holt, Rinehart and Winston.

Schechla, Joseph. 2015. "Land Grabs and the Arab Spring: A Chronicle of Corruption as Statecraft." Housing & Land Rights Network, January 2. http://www.hlrn.org/img/documents/Fasad_asas_al-umran2.pdf.

Schelling, Thomas C. 1998. "Social Mechanisms and Social Dynamics." In *Social Mechanisms: An Analytical Approach to Social Theory*, edited by Peter Hedstrom and Richard Swedberg, 32–44. New York: Cambridge University Press.

Shahine, Alaa, and Tarek El-Tablawy. 2012. "Egypt Pound Weakens to Record after Central Bank Sells Dollars." *Daily Herald*, December 31. http://www.dailyherald.com/article/20121231/business/712319942/.

Sheikh, Mayy el-, and David Kirkpatrick. 2013. "Rise in Sexual Assaults in Egypt Sets Off Clash over Blame." *New York Times*, March 25.

Shenawi, Eman el-. 2012. "Egypt Pulls TV Ads Warning Foreigners May Be Spies after 'Xenophobia' Fears." *Al Arabiya*, June 10.

Shenawi, Eman el-. 2013. "Tamarod vs. Tagarod: Egyptians in Virtual War." *Saudi Gazette*, July 2.

Shenker, Jack. 2011. "Egypt's Prime Minister Reshuffles Cabinet in Response to Protests." *The Guardian*, July 17.

Sherry, Virginia N. 1993. "Security Forces Practices in Egypt." *Criminal Justice Ethics* 12(2): 42–44.

Shirky, Clay. 2011. "The Political Power of Social Media: Technology, the Public Sphere, and Political Change." *Foreign Affairs*, January/February.

Shukrallah, Salma. 2013a. "Once Election Allies, Egypt's 'Fairmont' Opposition Turn against Morsi." AhramOnline, June 27.

Shukrallah, Salma. 2013b. "Egypt Protesters Tell Stories of Torture, Abuse at Ittihadiya Presidential Palace." AhramOnline, November 4.

Shull, Henry, and Ingy Hassieb. 2012. "Egypt's Morsi Decorates Generals He Dismissed." *Washington Post*, August 14.

Siegel, David A. 2009. "Social Networks and Collective Action." *American Journal of Political Science* 53(1): 122–138.
Simpson, Cam, and Mariam Fam. 2011. "Egypt's Army Marches, Fights, Sells Chickens." Bloomberg, February 7. https://www.bloomberg.com/news/articles/2011-02-17/egypts-army-marches-fights-sells-chickens.
Sin, Ray. 2009. "Emotionally Contentious Social Movements: A Tri-Variate Framework." *Conflict and Inequality* 30: 87–116.
Singerman, Diane. 1995. *Avenues of Participation: Family, Politics, and Networks in Urban Quarters of Cairo*. Princeton, NJ: Princeton University Press.
Skocpol, Theda. 1979. *States and Social Revolutions: A Comparative Analysis of France, Russia and China*. Cambridge: Cambridge University Press.
Slackman, Michael. 2005. "Assault on Women at Protest Stirs Anger, Not Fear, in Egypt." *New York Times*, June 10. http://www.nytimes.com/2005/06/10/world/africa/assault-on-women-at-protest-stirs-anger-not-fear-in-egypt.html?mcubz=2.
Slackman, Michael. 2008. "Egypt's Problem and Its Challenge: Bread Corrupts." *New York Times*, January 17.
Smith, Anthony D. 1991. *National Identity*. Reno: University of Nevada Press.
Snow, David A. 2004. "Framing Processes, Ideology, and Discursive Fields." In *The Blackwell Companion to Social Movements*, edited by David A. Snow, Sarah A. Soule, and Hanspeter Kriesi, 380–412. Malden, MA: Blackwell Publishing.
Snow, David A., E. Burke Rochford, Jr., Steven K. Worden, and Robert D. Benford. 1986. "Frame Alignment Processes, Micromobilization, and Movement Participation." *American Sociological Review* 51(4): 464–481.
Stack, Liam. 2013. "With Cameras Rolling, Egyptian Politicians Threaten Ethiopia over Dam." *New York Times, News Blog*, June 6. https://thelede.blogs.nytimes.com/2013/06/06/with-cameras-rolling-egyptian-politicians-threaten-ethiopia-over-dam/?mcubz=2.
Stack, Megan K. 2005. "Assailants Hit 2 Cairo Attractions." *Los Angeles Times*, May 1.
Stein, Ewan. 2012. "Revolution or Coup? Egypt's Fraught Transition." *Survival: Global Politics and Strategy* 54(4): 45–66.
Steinvorth, Daniel. 2011. "'We Are on Every Street': What the Future May Hold for Egypt's Muslim Brotherhood." *Der Spiegel*, February 1. http://www.spiegel.de/international/world/we-are-on-every-street-what-the-future-may-hold-for-egypt-s-muslim-brotherhood-a-742940.html.
Strauss, Anselm, and Juliet M. Corbin. 1998. *Basics of Qualitative Research: Techniques and Procedures for Developing Grounded Theory*. London: Sage Publications.
Sutter, John D. 2011. "The Faces of Egypt's 'Revolution 2.0.'" CNN, February 21. http://www.cnn.com/2011/TECH/innovation/02/21/egypt.internet.revolution/.
Swidler, Ann. 1995. "Cultural Power and Social Movements." In *Social Movements and Culture*, edited by Hank Johnston and Bert Klandermans, 25–40. Minneapolis: University of Minnesota Press.
Taha, Rana Muhammad. 2013. "Democracy Index: 9427 Protests during Morsi's First Year." *Daily News Egypt*, June 24. http://www.dailynewsegypt.com/2013/06/24/democracy-index-9427-protests-during-morsis-first-year/.

Taha, Rana Muhammad, and Hend Kortam. 2013. "The Remains of Mohamed Mahmoud." *Daily News Egypt*, November 19. http://www.dailynewsegypt.com/2013/11/19/the-remains-of-mohamed-mahmoud/.

Tamarod. 2013. Tamarod Petition. Cairo, April 28.

Tanner, Lindsey. 2011. "Docs Warn about Teens and 'Facebook Depression.'" Associated Press, March 29.

Tapscott, Don. 2011. "The Debate on Social Media and Revolutions: Reality Steps In." *Huffington Post*, February 14.

Tarrow, Sidney. 1988. "National Politics and Collective Action: Recent Theory and Research in Western Europe and the United States." *Annual Review of Sociology* 14: 421–440.

Tarrow, Sidney. 1989. *Democracy and Disorder: Protest and Politics in Italy, 1965–1975*. Oxford: Oxford University Press.

Tarrow, Sidney. 1994. *Power in Movement: Social Movements, Collective Action and Politics*. Cambridge: Cambridge University Press.

Tarrow, Sidney. 2013. *The Language of Contention: Revolutions in Words, 1688–2012*. Cambridge: Cambridge University Press.

Taylor, Alan. 2011. "Deadly New Clashes in Egypt's Tahrir Square." *The Atlantic*, November 21. https://www.theatlantic.com/photo/2011/11/deadly-new-clashes-in-egypts-tahrir-square/100192/.

Taylor, Charles. 1995. *Philosophical Arguments*. Cambridge, MA: Harvard University Press.

Taylor, Paul. 2013. "Exclusive—West Warned Egypt's Sisi to the End: Don't Do It." Reuters, August 14. http://www.reuters.com/article/us-egypt-protests-west-idUSBRE97D16920130814.

Taylor, Verta, and Nella Van Dyke. 2004. "'Get up, Stand up': Tactical Repertoires of Social Movements." In *The Blackwell Companion to Social Movements*, edited by David A. Snow, Sarah A. Soule, and Hanspeter Kriesi, 262–293. Malden, MA: Blackwell Publishing.

The President's Chef. 2008. Dir. Said Hamed. Elsobky Film. Film.

Telegraph, The. 2011. "Most US Aid to Egypt Goes to Military." *The Telegraph*, January 29.

Tibi, Bassam. 1997. *Arab Nationalism: Between Islam and the Nation-State*. New York: St. Martin's Press.

Tignor, Robert L. 1976. "The Egyptian Revolution of 1919: New Directions in the Egyptian Economy." *Middle Eastern Studies* 12(3): 41–67.

Tilly, Charles. 1978. *From Mobilization to Revolution*. Reading, MA: Addison-Wesley.

Tilly, Charles. 2006. *Regimes and Repertoires*. Chicago: University of Chicago Press.

Tilly, Charles, and Sidney Tarrow. 2007. *Contentious Politics*. Boulder, CO: Paradigm Publishers.

Trager, Eric. 2016. *Arab Fall: How the Muslim Brotherhood Won and Lost Egypt in 891 Days*. Washington, DC: Georgetown University Press.

Transparency International. 2007. "Corruption Perceptions Index 2007." Transparency International, September 25. https://www.transparency.org/research/cpi/cpi_2007/0/.

Transparency International. 2010. "Corruption Perception Index 2010." Transparency International, https://www.transparency.org/cpi2010/results.

Tufekci, Zeynep, and Christopher Wilson. 2012. "Social Media and the Decision to Participate in Political Protest: Observations from Tahrir Square." *Journal of Communication* 62(2): 363–379.
Turner, John C. 1999. "Some Current Themes in Research on Social Identity and Self-Categorization Theories." In *Social Identity: Context, Commitment, Content*, edited by Naomi Ellemers, Russell Spears, and Bertjan Doosje, 6–34. Oxford: Blackwell.
Twitchy. 2012. "Ballsy Move: Egyptian President Manhandles Himself on Live TV." Twitchy, September 26. http://twitchy.com/sd-3133/2012/09/26/ballsy-move-egyptian-president-manhandles-himself-on-live-tv/.
UNDP. 1999. "Human Development Report 1999." United Nations Development Program.
United Nations Economic Commission for Africa. 2013. "The Economic Situation in Egypt in the Context of Political Instability and a Risky Transition."
U.S. Department of State. 2013. "2013 Investment Climate Statement—Egypt." U.S. Department of State, February. https://www.state.gov/e/eb/rls/othr/ics/2013/204635.htm.
van Stekelenburg, Jacquelien, and Bert Klandermans. 2013. "The Social Psychology of Protest." *Current Sociology* 61(5-6): 1–13.
Verhulst, Joris, and Stefaan Walgrave. 2009. "The First Time is the Hardest? A Cross-National and Cross-Issue Comparison of First-Time Protest Participation." *Political Behavior* 31(3): 455–484.
Wahba, Abdel Latif, and Alaa Shahine. 2010. "Egypt's Economic Growth Accelerates to 5.6% in Third Quarter of 2010." Bloomberg, October 13.
Warkentin, Craig. 2001. *Reshaping World Politics: NGOs, the Internet, and Global Civil Society*. New York: Rowman & Littlefield Publishers.
Waterbury, John. 1983. *The Egypt of Nasser and Sadat: The Political Economy of Two Regimes*. Princeton, NJ: Princeton University Press.
Watson, Ivan, and Mohamed Fadel Fahmy. 2011. "Army Officers Join Cairo Protest." CNN, April 8. http://www.cnn.com/2011/WORLD/meast/04/08/egypt.protests/.
Watts, Jonathan. 2005. "China's Secret Internet Police Target Critics with Web Propaganda." *The Guardian*, June 13. https://www.theguardian.com/technology/2005/jun/14/newmedia.china.
Weber, Max. 2010. "The Distribution of Power within the Community: Classes, Stände, Parties." *Journal of Classical Sociology* 10: 153–172.
Wedeen, Lisa. 1999. *Ambiguities of Domination: Politics, Rhetoric, and Symbols in Contemporary Syria*. Chicago: Chicago University Press.
Werr, Patrick. 2012. "Egypt Pound Hits Record Low under New Currency Regime." Reuters, December 30. http://www.reuters.com/article/us-egypt-currency-idUSBRE8BS09620121230.
Wikan, Unni. 1980. *Life among the Poor in Cairo*. London: Tavistock Publications.
Wolfsfeld, Gadi, Elad Segev, and Tamir Sheafer. 2013. "Social Media and the Arab Spring: Politics Comes First." *International Journal of Press/Politics* 18(2): 115–137.
World Bank. 2014. "Literacy Rate, Adult Total (% of People Ages 15 and Above)." The World Bank Group, June 7. http://data.worldbank.org/indicator/SE.ADT.LITR.ZS.
Wrong, Dennis H. 1997. "Is Rational Choice Humanity's Most Distinctive Trait?" *American Sociologist* 28(2): 73–81.

Yin, Chien-Chung. 1998. "Equilibria of Collective Action in Different Distributions of Protest Thresholds." *Public Choice* 97: 535–567.
Youssef, Abdel Rahman. 2012. "Egypt: Does the Muslim Brotherhood have 'Militias'?" *Al Akhbar*, December 13. http://english.al-akhbar.com/node/14361.
Youssef, Abdel Rahman. 2013. "Egypt: How SCAF Manipulated Its Adversaries." *Al Akhbar English*, July 9.
Zagare, Frank C. 1990. "Rational Choice Models and International Relations Research." *International Interactions* 15(3): 197–201.
Zald, Mayer N. 1996. "Culture, Ideology, and Strategic Framing." In *Comparative Perspectives on Social Movements: Political Opportunities, Mobilizing Structures, and Cultural Framing*, edited by Doug McAdam, John McCarthy, and Mayer N. Zald, 261–281. Cambridge: Cambridge University Press.

INDEX

Page numbers followed by *t* or *f* indicate tables or figures, respectively. Numbers followed by n indicate notes.

Abbasseya, 50
Abdel-Aziz, Mohamed, 181–182, 186, 196
Abdel-Fattah, Alaa, 222–223
Abdullah, Ahmed, 224
Abu Musallim, Egypt, 156–157
activists and activism, 2, 223, 226
   cyberactivism, 57
   hacktivism, 64–65
Adel, Mohammed, 49–50, 97, 209
Affect Control theory, 95–96
affective emotions, 95–96, 117
Afifi, Adel Abdel Maqsoud, 163
Al Ahly, 139
Al Ahram, 194
Ain Shams University, xiii, 40
airline industry, 26
Akayev, Askar, ix
Alexandria, Egypt
   protests, 3, 87–88, 134, 178, 223
   violence against protesters, 90–91
altruism, 85–86
American Islamic Congress, 49–50
American University in Cairo (AUC), 71, 122, 225
Amn al-Dawla (State Security), 34–35, 62–63

Amn al-Dawla Leaks website, 63
Amnesty International, 39, 41
Amr, Mohamed Kamel, 135
Anan, Sami, 126–127, 189–190
ancien regime, 160
anger, 95–96
Anonymous, 64–65
Ansar Bayt al-Maqdis, 209
anti-British nationalism, 105
anti-Christian violence, 136
anti-government protests, 222–223.
   See also protest(s); *specific governments*
AOI. *See* Arab Organization for Industrialization
April 6th Youth Movement, 2–3, 42, 49–50, 58, 167, 182–183
   Facebook page, 2–3, 51, 57–59, 75–78
   A General Protest in Egypt or The Day of Anger in Egypt events, 79
   January 25 Revolution Against Torture, Poverty, Corruption, and Unemployment event, 77–81
Arab nationalism, 105–106
Arab Organization for Industrialization (AOI), 129

Arab Spring protests (2010 and 2011), vii, viii–ix. *See also* protest(s)
   defining events of, 13–15
Arabic Network for Human Rights Information, 61
Armed Forces Land Projects, 130
arrests
   arbitrary, xi, 35–36, 41–43, 49, 224
   mass, 41, 223
art, revolutionary, 122
Ashton, Catherine, 204–205
Aswan, Egypt, 136
Al Aswany, Alaa, 133
authoritarianism, 166, 169
automotive industry, 129–130
Al-Azhar Park, 3, 190–191
Azmy, Emile, 191
Azzam, Maha, 150

Badie, Mohammed, 169
Badr, Mahmoud, 181, 186
Bahrain, vii
Bakiyev, Kurmanbek, ix
"ball scratching incident," 164
Balloon Theater, 134
bandwagoning, 66, 80, 84, 217
al-Banna, Abdelfattah, 135
al-Banna, Hasan, 37–38
El Baradei, Mohamed, 180–181, 183, 196–197, 204–205
El-Baragil, 28
Barany, Zoltan, 125
Battle of the Camel, 93–95, 139–140
BBC Arabic, 90–91
beatings, 3, 88. *See also* violence
el Beblawy, Hazem, 135, 204
Bellin, Eva, 7
al-Beltagy, Mohamed, 179, 201
Ben Ali, Zine El-Abidine, 51, 77–78
Beni Suef, Egypt, 87–88, 91
Al-Bernameg, 151–152
black market, 157
Black Wednesday (May 25, 2005), 2
Blackberry, 61
bloggers, 209

Blue Coat, 226
El-Borai, Ahmed, 128
Boren Fellowship Program, x
Bouazizi, Mohamed, 72
bread subsidies, 45–46
Breda, 129
bribery, 43–46
British colonialism, 104–105
Building and Development Party, 192
Burma, 222
Burns, William, 204–205
bus station attacks, 71

Cairo, Egypt
   anti-government protests, 223. *See also* protest(s); *specific governments*
   bus station attack (April 30, 2005), 71
   January 25, 2011 uprising, 2–3, 14–15, 52, 85–118, 123–126, 139–140, 161
   Mohammed Mahmoud Street, 122, 136–137, 141–142, 149
   Parliament Building protests, 132–133
   street vendors, 42
   Tahrir Square, 41–42. *See also* Tahrir Square
   tourism, 158
Cairo University, 195–196
CALEA. *See* Communications Assistance for Law Enforcement Act
CANVAS. *See* Centre for Applied Nonviolent Action and Strategies
CAPMAS. *See* Central Agency for Public Mobilization and Statistics
CARP. *See* Collective Action Research Program
causal mechanisms, 6–8
CBC, xiii
censorship, 63
Central Agency for Public Mobilization and Statistics (CAPMAS), x
Central Security Forces, 136–137, 180
Centre for Applied Nonviolent Action and Strategies (CANVAS), 49–50, 97
ceremonies, 110–111

chants
  January 25, 2011 mobilization, 50
  January 25, 2011 uprising, 109–110, 118
  July 8, 2011 demonstrations, 134
  July 8 to August 1, 2011 sit-in, 135–136, 150
  November and December 2012 anti-regime protests, 169, 178
  Rabaa al-Adawiya sit-in (June 28th to August 14th, 2013), 200
  June 30, 2013 uprising, 192–193
children, 37
China
  Great Firewall of China, 63–64
  Internet restrictions, 60–64, 64t
Christians, 136, 201
Chrysler, 129–130
class relations
  corruption, 47
  economic grievances, 31–33
  with police, 35–37, 42–43
Cleansing Friday protests (April 8, 2011), 133–134
collective action, 5, 11–12, 109–110. *See also* Facebook; social media
Collective Action Research Program (CARP), 4–5, 12–13, 215–216, 220
collective identity, 103–104, 110, 117–118, 218
colonialism, British, 104
comedy, 151–152
Communications Assistance for Law Enforcement Act of 1994 (CALEA), 61
communications blackout, 89–90, 93
Constitution Party, 182–183
Coptic Orthodox Church, 190–191
corruption, 25, 43–48, 227
  January 25 Revolution Against Torture, Poverty, Corruption, and Unemployment event, 77–81
  SCAF anti-corruption campaign, 131
coups d'état, 173–175, 219
  August 14, 2012, 189–190
  June 30, 2013, 5, 15, 171–214

curfews, xiii, 134
cyberactivism, 57. *See also* hacktivism

Daesh, 210
Damasio, Antonio, 8, 146–147
data sources and collection, 15–18
Day of Anger (2008), 79
Day of Anger (2009), 79
Day of Rage (January 28, 2011), 89–91, 100
death sentences, 225
decision-making, 6–8
deep packet inspection, 226
defining events, 13–15
Deir al-Bahri site (Luxor, Egypt), 70–71
El-Demerdash Hospital (Cairo, Egypt), 99–100
democracy, Islamic, 199
demographics, 17–18
demonstrations, 109–110. *See also* protest(s)
  July 8, 2011, 134–136
  "Legitimacy is a Red Line" (Rabaa al-Adawiya, June 28, 2013), 192
  one-woman, 222–223
  Tagarod, 190–191
detention, arbitrary, xi, 35–36, 41–43, 49, 224
digital divide, 59
disappearances, 224
Dokki Square, 196
Doss, Moheb, 181, 186–187
Douma, Ahmed, 209

economy
  grievances, 25–33, 48
  grievances against Morsi, 157–159
  informal, 27–29, 42
  liberalization of, 44–45, 129
  military interests, 128–132
  prosperity, 113–115
Eddin, Mahmoud Mohie, 131
Egypt
  Air Force, 197
  airline industry, 26

Egypt (*cont.*)
  ancien regime, 160
  annual income, 30–31
  anti-government protests, 223. *See also* protest(s)
  anti-protest laws, 133–134, 209–210, 223
  British occupation of, 104–105
  Central Bank, 157
  Constituent Assembly, 132, 175–177, 181
  Constitution, 106, 140
  corruption, 3, 25, 43–48, 227
  demographics, 17–18
  economy, 25–33, 157–159
  electoral laws, 131–132
  emergency law, 33–34
  export agreements, 45, 160–161
  Facebook Revolution, 52, 86
  foreign exchange reserves, 26, 157
  General Directorate for State Security Investigation (SSI), 33–34, 39, 71
  government violence, viii–ix, 85–118, 127
  High Court, 190, 196–197
  inflation rates, 26, 227
  international representation of, 163–165
  Internet restrictions, 60–64, 64*t*
  Islamic law, 37
  January 25, 2011 uprising, 2–3, 14–15, 52, 85–118, 123–127, 139–140, 161, 215–216
  January 25 Revolution Against Torture, Poverty, Corruption, and Unemployment event, 77–81
  June 30, 2013 uprising, 5, 15, 171–214
  Law 32 of 1964, 55–57
  Law 49 of 1945, 55
  Law 66 of 1951, 55
  Law 153 of 1999, 56
  Law 348 of 1956, 56
  marriage costs, 30–31
  median age, 17–18
  military, 125–134, 141, 219–220
  military coup (June 30, 2013), 5, 15, 171–214
  Ministry of Interior, xi, 33–34, 61, 87–88, 91, 134, 186–187, 193–194, 224
  Ministry of Social Affairs (MOSA), 55–56
  Morsi government, 151–170
  Mubarak regime, 23–50, 70–71
  national anthem, 108, 110–111
  National Day of Love, 3
  national interests, 105
  National Services Projects Organization (NSPO), 128
  nationalization programs, 128
  online communications, 226
  Parliament, 176
  parliamentary elections, 44
  People's Assembly, 38–39, 55
  police brutality, xi, 25, 33–37, 41–43, 49, 87, 115
  political mobilization, 3, 5, 50–84, 183–185, 190–192
  Political Parties Law No. 40 of 1977, 56
  population, 26
  poverty, 27–28
  research in, ix–xiv
  Revolution (1919), 104–105, 107
  Revolution (1952), 105, 128
  Revolutionary Command Council, 33
  shipping industry, 26
  Shura Council, 176–177, 181
  state of emergency, 181
  Supreme Administrative Court, 176
  Supreme Council of the Armed Forces (SCAF), 15, 124–128, 131–150, 176–177, 215–219
  tourism, 26, 158
  unemployment, 26–27
  Universities Law, 55
  U.S. aid to, 126–127, 129–130
  workforce, 26–27
  World Values Survey, x
Egypt Bloc, 176–177
Egypt-Syria Solidarity Conference (June 15, 2013), 156–157

Egyptian-Arabic Union Party, 176–177
Egyptian Citizen Party, 176–177
Egyptian Commission for Rights and Freedoms, 224
Egyptian Conference Party, 182–183
Egyptian flag, 110–111, 197
Egyptian Initiative for Personal Rights (EIPR), 45
Egyptian Movement for Change (Kefaya), 2, 42, 49–50, 75, 108
  protests (2005), 162
Egyptian Museum (Museum of Egyptian Antiquities), 133, 158
Egyptian nationalism, 103–108
Egyptian particularist nationalism, 104
Egyptian pound, 26, 157, 227
Egyptian Social Democratic Party, 162–163
EIPR. *See* Egyptian Initiative for Personal Rights
Elaraby, Nabil, 133
electricity, 160–161
emboldening, post-revolutionary, 145–148, 185, 218
emotions
  affective, 95–96, 117
  post-revolutionary emboldening, 145–148, 185, 218
  in rational decision-making, 6–8
  reactive, 95–96
  in social movements, 95–96
empathy, 102–103, 115–118
employment
  dissatisfaction with, 229n1
  immoral, 29
  January 25 Revolution Against Torture, Poverty, Corruption, and Unemployment event, 77–81
  of men, 29–30
  underemployment, 30
  unemployment, 26–27
  of women, 28–29, 229n1
  youth, 31–32
al-Erian, Essam, 179
espionage charges, 225

el-Essawy, Mansour, 133, 135
Ethiopia, 164
ETI, 129
European Union (EU), 204–205
export agreements, 45
extremism, 71
Ezz, Ahmed, 44–45

Facebook, 6, 205
  April 6th Youth Movement page, 2–3, 51, 57–59, 75–78
  "I Voted" buttons, 81
  istinfar (en garde) postings (December 5, 2012), 179
  January 25 Revolution Against Torture, Poverty, Corruption, and Unemployment event, 77–81
  mobilization through, 11, 51–84, 216–217, 220–221, 226–227
  National Association for Change page, 58–59
  profile pictures, 59, 77, 84
  Tamarod movement on, 182–183
  We are all Khaled Said page, 3, 57–59, 74–75, 108–109
Facebook Revolution, 52, 86
Fahmy, Mohamed Fadel, 209
Fairmont Hotel (Heliopolis, Egypt), 167–168
fajr (morning prayer), 40, 169
falool (supporters and sympathizers of the Mubarak regime), 187
Farouk, Ihab, 136–137
Faruq, 37, 105
fatalities
  Battle of the Camel, 93–95
  foreign researcher, 225–226
  martyrs, 101, 111, 122
  protesters, 87–91, 93, 100–101, 136–138, 180
  Khaled Said, 3
  Shi'ite, 156–157
Fattah, Seif Abdel, 180
fear, 48–49, 70–71, 116–117, 212–213, 226
film editors, 37

"Finish the Job" campaign, 210
FJP. *See* Freedom and Justice Party
flags, 110–111, 197
football, 139
forced disappearances, 224
foreign researchers, 225–226
Free Officers Movement, 105–106, 128
Freedom and Justice Party (FJP), 137, 163, 168, 180, 192, 196, 205
freedom of expression, 178
Freud, Sigmund, 7
Friday protests
    Cleansing Friday (April 8, 2011), 133–134
    Day of Rage (January 28, 2011), 89–91, 100
    The Friday of One Demand (November 18, 2011), 136–137
friendship networks, 11
Frontline, 50
Fry, Christopher, 152
fuel shortages, 160–161, 191

El-Gabry, Abdel Nasser, 94
al-Gama'a al-Islamiyya, 38–39, 70–71, 168, 192
Gamson, William, 64, 150
el-Ganzouri, Kamal, 137, 168
gas, natural, 45, 160–161, 191
Gaventa, John, 69, 72
General Directorate for State Security Investigation (SSI), 33–34, 39, 71
Al Ghar, Mohamed Abu, 162–163
Ghazali, Zainab, 38
Gheit, Ahmed Abul, 127–128
Ghonim, Wael, 3, 58–59, 78, 108–109, 167
Gillard, Julia, 164
Goldstone, Jack, 13–14
graffiti, 122, 159
Grami, Amel, 225
grassroots campaigns, 182–183
Great Firewall of China, 63–64
Green Movement, 52
Greste, Peter, 209

grievances
    against Morsi, 151–170
    against Mubarak, 23–50, 87, 229n1
    over police brutality, 25, 33–37, 115
al-Guindy, Mohamed Abdel Azi, 133, 135

hacktivism, 64–65
Halliday, Fred, 107
harassment, sexual, xii, 34, 161–163
Hawass, Zahi, 135
al-Hefnawi, Reda Saleh, 163
Hizb al-Wasat, 56
homosexuals, 34, 226
Hosni, Ahmed, 191
hospitality, xiv
Howard, Philip, 57
Hudaybi, Guide, 38
human rights abuses, 33, 224–225
Human Rights Watch, xiii, 34, 203–204, 225
Huntington, Samuel, 172–175
Hurriyah Party, 176–177

"I Voted" buttons, 81
identity
    collective, 103–104, 117–118, 218
    national, 104–105, 117–118, 218
Il Manifesto, 225–226
imams (prayer leaders), 167
immoral employment, 29
Impartiality (Tagarod) movement, 190–191
incentives for mobilization, 75–76
inflation, 26, 227
informal economy, 27–29, 42
informants, 48–49, 229n1
information blackout, 89–90
injustice, 97, 116, 118
insider trading, 44
International Monetary Fund (IMF), 158–159
Internet cafes, 61–62
Internet restrictions, 60–64, 64t, 89–90, 226–227
intifada (uprising/rebellion), 78
Iran, 52

ISIS, 212–213
Islam, 39, 106, 167
Islamic democracy, 199
Islamic law, 37, 106
Islamists, 190
  in Constituent Assembly, 175–177
  fear of, 70–71, 212–213, 226
  National Alliance to Support
    Legitimacy, 192
  support for Morsi, 152
  targeting of, 37–40, 70–71, 223
  violent attacks, 163, 201, 209
Ismail, Hazem Salah Abou, 121
Ismail, Salwa, 27
Ismailiya, Egypt, 88–89
Israel: Egyptian exports to, 160–161
Israeli embassy (Cairo, Egypt), 134–136
issue and action formulation, 72
istinfar (en garde) postings (December 5,
    2012), 179
Ittihadiya Presidential Palace, 156,
    178–180, 192
'Izz, Ahmad, 131

January 25, 2011 uprising, 2–3, 14–15,
    85–118, 123–127, 215–216
  Battle of the Camel, 93–95, 139–140
  Day of Rage (January 28), 89–91, 100
  Facebook Revolution, 52, 86
  fifth anniversary of, 223
  mobilization for, 51–84, 183–185
  Revolution Against Torture, Poverty,
    Corruption, and Unemployment
    Facebook event, 77–81
  security and sexual harassment
    during, 161
January 25 Revolution Against
    Torture, Poverty, Corruption, and
    Unemployment event, 77–81
Jasper, James, 147
Al Jazeera, 51, 209
al-Jihad, 38
Joudeh, Safa, 130
journalists, 37, 88, 209
Journalists' Syndicate (Cairo, Egypt), 2

June 30, 2013 uprising (Cairo, Egypt), 5,
    15, 171–214
  funding, 187
  mobilization, 183–185, 190–192
  protest, 184–185, 192–197, 215–216

Kafr El-Sheikh, Egypt, 223
Karagiannopoulos, Vasileios, 226–227
El-Katatni, Saad, 204–205
Kefaya (Egyptian Movement for Change),
    2, 42, 49–50, 75, 108
  protests (2005), 162
Khattab, Youssef, 94
Koslowski, Barbara, 6
Kuran, Timur, 13–14, 54, 65–66, 82,
    184, 217
Kyrgyzstan, ix

land seizures, 45, 47–48, 130
legitimacy, 150, 194–195, 218–219
"Legitimacy is a Red Line" demonstration
    (Rabaa al-Adawiya, June 28,
    2013), 192
al-Leithy, Amr, 180
Leon, Bernardino, 204–205
LGBTQ community, 226
liberalization, economic, 44–45
Libya, vii
Lichbach, Mark, 4–5, 143
looting, 92–93
lower class
  economic grievances, 32–33
  police brutality against, 35–36, 42–43
Ludovici, Derek, 229n2

Madi, Abul Ela, 205
Maged, Assem Abdel, 190–191
Maghrabi, Ahmed, 44
Al-Mahallah al-Kubra, xi
Al-Mahallah al-Kubra strike, 2–3
Maher, Ahmed, 167, 209
Mahmoud, Abdel-Meguid, 190
Mahmoud, Mahmoud Wagdy
    Mohamed, 128
malnutrition, 42

Mansour, Abdul Rahman, 3
Mansour, Adly, 198
Mansura, Egypt, 87–88
Marie, Mamdou Mohyiddin, 127–128
marriage costs, 30–31
martyr murals, 122
martyrs, 101, 111
Masoud, Tarek, 39
Al-Masry, 139
el-Masry, Walid, 181
mass arrests, 41, 223
maximum variation sampling, 17
McAdam, Doug, 5, 124
Mekki, Mahmoud, 180
memory loss, post-revolutionary, xiii
men: employment of, 29–30
Mexico, 43–44
Meyer, David, 64, 150
middle class, 31–32
military (Egyptian)
   curfews, 134
   economic interests, 128–132
   graffiti against, 122
   during January 25, 2011 uprising, 125–127
   June 30, 2013 coup, 5, 15, 171–214
   and Morsi, 173, 188–189, 195–196
   and Mubarak, 129
   and Muslim Brotherhood, 188–189
   protests against, 133–134
   public support for, 207, 211–212
   Rabaa al-Adawiya massacre, 172, 202–206, 213, 219–220
   real estate, 130
   and Sadat, 128–129
   soft coup (August 14, 2012), 189–190
   Tamarod co-optation, 183–188
   violence against protesters, 133–139, 141, 219–220
Military Cooperation Committee, 126–127
military coups d'état, 173–175, 219
mobilization, 50
   causal mechanisms, 6–8
   frames for, 11–12
   through friendship networks, 11
   incentives for, 75–76
   for January 25, 2011 protests, 51–84, 183–185
   for June 30, 2013 protests, 183–185, 190–192
   moral shock, 97–98
   through online networks, 11
   through social media, 51–84, 216–217, 220–221
   stage 1, 68–76
   stage 2, 76–82
   sustaining, 95–102
   Three-Dimensional Approach to, 70
   thresholds for, 67, 72–73
   triggering mechanisms, 67–68, 72
   during uprisings, 65–82, 69f
Mohamed, Baher, 209
Mohamed, Omar, 224
Mohammed Mahmoud Street (Cairo, Egypt)
   graffiti and murals, 122
   violence against protesters, 136–137, 141–142, 149
money laundering, 44
moral outrage, 95–96, 98
moral shock, 95–102, 115–116
morning prayer *(fajr)*, 40, 169
Morsi, Mohamed
   ball scratching incident, 164
   constitutional declarations, 175–178, 181, 190
   death sentence, 225
   election, 140, 152–154
   election campaign, 154–155
   expectations for, 154–155
   Fairmont talks, 167–168
   grievances against, 151–170
   legitimacy, 192, 194–195
   military opposition to, 173, 188–189, 195–196
   overthrow of, 195–196
   political appointments, 167–169
   political rivals, 191
   presidency, 140, 151–170

Index

presidential advisors, 190
promises, 154–155
protests against, 5, 15, 158, 162, 169, 171–214, 215–216
protests in support of, 209
public support for, 152–155, 167–169, 192, 202, 209
religiosity, 169
speeches, 155, 163–165, 191, 194–195
Tagarod petition for, 190–191
Tamarod petition against, 171–172, 182–183
transition and downfall, 121–214
on Twitter, 194
Mostafa Mahmoud Mosque (Cairo, Egypt), 167
Mubarak, Alaa, 114
Mubarak, Gamal, 2, 44–45, 114, 126–127, 131
Mubarak, Hosni, vii
downfall of, 23–118
economic liberalization plans, 129
February 1, 2011 speech, 94–95
graffiti against, 122
grievances against, 23–50, 87, 229n1
legitimacy, 127, 150, 229n1
and military, 129
nationalist ideology, 106–107
patriotism, 113
privatization, 131
protests against, 2–3, 14–15, 52, 77–81, 85–118, 123–127, 139–140, 158, 161–162
resignation of, 123–124, 146–148
support for, xiii, 94, 113–116, 126–127, 187
Mubarak, Suzanne, 101, 114
murals, 122
Museum of Egyptian Antiquities (Egyptian Museum), 133, 158
Muslim Brotherhood, 37–39, 106, 137, 210
Freedom and Justice Party (FJP), 137, 163, 168, 180, 192, 196, 205
Guidance Bureau, 168

istinfar (en garde) postings (December 5, 2012), 179
January 25, 2011 uprising, 89
and Morsi, 152–153, 156, 165–169, 201
opposition to, 181–183, 188–189, 223
in Parliament, 176
public support for, 165–170
at Rabaa al-Adawiya sit-in, 201
Renaissance Project, 154, 159
Shura Council, 176
Supreme Guide, 169
as terrorists, 201–202
violence against protesters, 156, 162–163, 170, 180

Nadeem Center for Rehabilitation for Victims of Violence and Torture, 224–225
Naguib, Mohammad, 105
Al-Nahda Square sit-in, 202–204
Naji, Ahmed, 227
Nasr, Mahmud, 131
Al-Nasr Company for Steam Boilers and Pressure Vessels, 44–45
Nasser, Gamal Abdel, 30, 33, 38, 105–106, 128
National Alliance to Support Legitimacy, 192
national anthem, 108, 110–111
National Association for Change, 58–59, 183
National Council for Human Rights (NCHR), 224
National Day of Love, 3
National Democratic Party (NDP), 131–132
national identity, 104–105, 117–118, 218
National Salvation Front (NSF), 180, 182–183
National Services Projects Organization (NSPO), 128
nationalism, 103–113, 218
nationalization programs, 128
natural gas, 45, 160–161, 191
Nazif, Ahmad, 45, 131

NDP. *See* National Democratic Party
negative cases, 16
New York Times, 45–46, 225–226
NGOs. *See* nongovernmental organizations
Nile River dam project, 164
Nile TV, 91–92
nongovernmental organization (NGOs), 55–56, 225
nonviolence, 49–50, 97
Nour, Ayman, 164
Nour Party, 190–191, 196
NSPO. *See* National Services Projects Organization
al-Nuqrashi, Mahmud Fahmi, 38

Obama, Barack, 52, 126–127
Ohier, Fanny, 225
oil industry, 129–130, 160–161
Olson, Mancur, 5, 53
Omar Makram Mosque, 135–136
One-Dimensional Approach, 70
online communications, 226
online networks, 11, 62–63
online political participation, 51–84
online preferences, 66, 68, 82
online safety, 73, 226
Opp, Karl-Dieter, 149–150
Orascom, 187
Order of the Nile, 189–190
organ theft, 29
organizations, formal, 11
Orientalism, 104
outrage, moral, 95–96, 98

Palestinian Second Intifada, 2
pan-Arabism, 77–78
pan-Islamism, 104
Parliament Building (Cairo, Egypt), 132–133
patriotism, 113
PCP, 162
Pearlman, Wendy, 8
Petersen, Roger, 54, 67
petitions
   El Baradei, 183

"Finish the Job" campaign, 210
   Tagarod, 190–191
   Tamarod, 171–172, 182–183
petroleum industry, 129, 160–161
Pharaonism, 104
police brutality, 33–37, 41–43, 87, 141
   anger over, 3, 25, 33–37, 96–97, 115
   arbitrary arrests, xi, 35–36, 41–43, 49
   Battle of the Camel, 93–95
   beating of Khaled Said, 3, 72
   graffiti against, 122
   against Islamists, 37–40, 70–71, 223
   against protesters, 87–91, 136, 138–139, 181, 205
police corruption, 3, 46–47
Police Day protests, 51
police misconduct, 46–47
political altruism, 86
political appointments, 167–169
political opportunities
   determination of, 60–61
   Synthetic Political Opportunity Theory (SPOT), 4–5, 8–13, 215–216, 220
political opportunity structures, 60–65, 123–125
political participation, 227. *See also* mobilization
   defining events, 13–15
   One-Dimensional Approach to, 70
   online, 51–84
   religion and, 165–167
   in Tamarod movement, 183–184
   Two-Dimensional Approach to, 70
   voter participation, 81
political theater, 143–144
Popovic, Srdja, 49–50, 97–98
popular nationalism, 108–113
popular participatory veto coup, 15, 171–214, 219
Port Said massacre, 139–140, 181
post-revolutionary emboldening effect, 145–148, 185, 218
posters, 200
poverty, 27–28
power
   abuse of, 41–43

Index

One-Dimensional Approach to, 70
Three-Dimensional Approach to, 70
Two-Dimensional Approach to, 70
powerlessness, 72
prayer, morning *(fajr)*, 40, 169
prayer leaders *(imams)*, 167
"The President's Chef" (Hamed 2008), 115
privacy, 65–66
privatization, 44–45, 128–129, 131
Professional Syndicates Union, 192
profile pictures, 59, 77, 84
prostitution, 29
protest(s)
　anti-government, xii–xiii, 222–223. *See also specific governments*
　anti-military, 133–134
　anti-Morsi, 5, 15, 158, 162, 169, 171–214, 215–216
　anti-SCAF, 132–150, 215–216, 218–219
　Arab Spring (2010 and 2011), vii, viii–ix, 13–15
　Balloon Theater (June 28-29, 2011), 134
　Battle of the Camel, 93–95
　Cleansing Friday (April 8, 2011), 133–134
　Day of Rage (January 28, 2011), 89–91, 100
　demands of, 134–135, 227
　deterrences against, 113–118
　The Friday of One Demand (November 18, 2011), 136–137
　graffiti, 122
　Israeli embassy (Cairo, Egypt) (May 15, 2011), 134
　Ittihadiya Presidential Palace (November and December 2012), 156, 178–180, 192
　January 25, 2011 uprising, 2–3, 14–15, 77–81, 85–118, 123–127, 161, 215–216
　January 25 Revolution Against Torture, Poverty, Corruption, and Unemployment event, 77–81
　July 8, 2011, 134–136
　June 30, 2013 (Cairo, Egypt), 184–185, 192–197, 215–216

　Kefaya (2005), 162
　laws against, 133–134, 209–210, 223
　"Legitimacy is a Red Line" (Rabaa al-Adawiya, June 28, 2013), 192
　mobilization, 51–84, 95–102, 141–142, 183, 215–216, 220–221
　Mohammed Mahmoud Street clashes, 136–137, 141–142, 149
　moral shock impetus, 95–102
　against Mubarak, 2–3, 14–15, 52, 77–81, 85–118, 123–127, 139–140, 158, 161–162
　Palestinian Second Intifada (2002), 2
　post-revolutionary emboldening effect, 145–148, 185, 218
　pro-Morsi, 209
　Rabaa al-Adawiya sit-in (June 28 to August 14, 2013), xiii, 192, 198–202, 213
　Rabaa al-Adawiya massacre, 172, 202–206, 213, 219–220
　Ramses Square, 205
　silent stands, 3
　Tahrir Square. *See* Tahrir Square
　Tamarod movement, 171–172
　violence against protesters, viii–ix, 86–96, 99–100, 115–116, 127, 133–139, 141–142, 161–163, 170, 179–181, 195–196, 202–206, 213
pseudonyms, 66
Public Pledge on Self-Discipline for the Chinese Internet Industry, 64
public preferences, 65–66. *See also* grievances
purposive sampling, 17

al-Qaeda, 40
Qandil, Hisham, 168
Queen Boat raid (2001), 62

Rabaa al-Adawiya massacre, 172, 202–206, 213, 219–220
　violence after, 209
Rabaa al-Adawiya sit-in, xiii, 192, 198–202, 213
Radwan, Samir, 127–128

Ramses Square protests, 205
rape, 161–162
Rasler, Karen, 142
rational choice, 5–8, 85–86.
    See also Collective Action
    Research Program (CARP)
reactive emotions, 95–96
Rebel (Tamarod) movement, 181–183
Red Sea, 228
Regeni, Giulio, 225–226
religion, 165–167, 169
religious NGOs, 55
Renaissance Project (Muslim
    Brotherhood), 154, 159
research, 225
    challenges of, ix–xiv
    Collective Action Research
        Program, 4–13
    data sources and collection, 15–18
researchers, 225–226
revolution
    definition of, 13–14
    emboldening effect, 145–148, 185, 218
    thresholds, 67, 72–73
Revolution (Egypt, 1919), 104–105, 107
Revolution (Egypt, 1952), 105, 128
Revolution (Egypt, 2011)
    Facebook Revolution, 52, 86
    January 25, 2011 uprising, 2–3,
        14–15, 77–81, 85–118, 123–127,
        154–155, 161
    mobilization leading up to, 3, 5, 51–84,
        183–185
Revolution (Tunisia, 2011), 52, 72, 222
Revolution 2.0 (Ghonim), 58
Revolution Continues Alliance, 176–177
revolutionary art, 122
revolutionary bandwagoning, 66, 80, 84, 217
Revolutionary Command Council
    (Egypt), 33
Revolutionary Socialists, 2
Roehl, Wolfgang, 149–150
al-Ruweiny, Hassan, 135

Saad, Sohaib, 224
Sabahi, Hamdeen, 211

al-Sadat, Anwar, 33, 38, 106–107,
    128–129, 189
safety, 114
    online, 73, 226
    researcher, xi–xiv
    threshold-based calculations, 78
Sahraoui, Hassiba Hadj, 223
Said, Khaled, 3, 35, 49, 59, 72, 74–75.
    See also We are all Khaled Said
    A Silent Stand of Prayer for the Martyr
        Khaled Said along the Alexandria
        Corniche, 3
Sajwani, Hussain, 44
Salafis, 190–192
el-Salmi Document, 176
sampling, 17
satire, 151–152
Sattar, Noman, 38
Sawey, Assad, 90–91
Sawiris, Naguib, 187
Sayaida Zaineb, Egypt, 90–91
al-Sayyad, Ayman, 180
SCAF. *See* Supreme Council of the
    Armed Forces
Schattschneider, Elmer Eric, 70
Scobey, Margaret, 130
Second Kyrgyz Revolution, ix
sectarianism, 156–157
security, xii, 113, 161–163
See Egypt, 226
Seif, Sanaa, 222–223, 227–228
self-identification, 72
self-immolation, 72
sexual assaults, xii, 34, 161–163
al-sha'b (the people), 109–110
"*Al-sha'b yurid isqaat al-nidham*" (The
    people want the downfall of the
    regime) chant, 109–110
Shafiq, Ahmed, 127–128, 132–133, 140,
    153–154, 167
shaheedas (martyrs), 111
Shahin, Emad, 225
Shahin, Hassan, 181, 186
Sharaf, Essam, 133–135, 137, 143–144
al-Shater, Khairat, 169
Shebin Textile, 44–45

Index

Sheikh Zuweid, Egypt, 89
Sherif, Ghada, 208
Sherry, Virginia, 34
Shi'ites, 156–157
shipping industry, 26
shock, moral, 95–102, 115–116
Shura Council, 176–177, 181
silent stands, 3
Sinai, 188, 201, 209
Sinopec, 129
el-Sisi, Abdel Fattah, 172, 186, 189, 193, 196–197
  protests against, 222–223, 228
  public support for, 207–208, 210–212
#SisiLeaks, 187
sit-ins, 134–137, 179, 192, 199–202
678 (Diab 2010), 161
Skocpol, Theda, 13
Skype, 61, 226
SMOs. *See* social movement organizations
Social Democratic Party, 162–163
social grievances, 49–50
social media
  istinfar (en garde) postings (December 5, 2012), 179
  mobilization through, 51–84, 216–217, 220–221, 226
  Tamarod movement, 182–183
social movement organizations (SMOs), 11, 57
social movements, 95–96
socialism, 128
Socialist Popular Alliance Party, 176–177
sodomy, 37
soft coup (August 14, 2012), 189–190
SPOT. *See* Synthetic Political Opportunity Theory
Springborg, Robert, 131
SSI. *See* General Directorate for State Security Investigation
stability, 113
starvation, 30
State Security. *See* General Directorate for State Security Investigation (SSI)
state subsidies, 45–46
state violence. *See* violence

steel market, 44
street art, 122
street vendors, 42
street violence, 92–93
strikes, 2–3, 133
subsidies, 45–46
Suez, Egypt, 87–91, 134, 178
Suez Canal, 105
Suez Canal Authority, 129
Sulayman, Ibrahim, 131
Supreme Council of the Armed Forces (SCAF), 15
  anti-corruption campaign, 131
  anti-protest laws, 133–134
  concessions to protesters, 148–149
  Constituent Assembly, 176
  constitutional declaration, 140, 177
  cycles of contention, 132–140, 148
  electoral laws, 131–132
  graffiti against, 122
  initial cabinet, 128
  legitimacy, 150
  objectives, 127–128, 148–149
  power grabs, 140
  protests against, 132–150, 215–216, 218–219
  transitional government, 5, 124–128, 132–150, 218–219
  violence against protesters, 136–137, 144
surveillance, 226
symbols, 110–111
sympathy, 102–103
Synthetic Political Opportunity Theory (SPOT), 4–5, 8–13, 215–216, 220
Syria, vii, 1

Tagarod (Impartiality) movement, 190–191
Tahrir Square, 41–42
  anti-Morsi protests (June 30, 2013), 184–185, 192–197, 215–216
  Battle of the Camel, 93–95, 139–140
  Cleansing Friday protests (April 8, 2011), 133–134

Tahrir Square (*cont.*)
  Day of Rage (January 28, 2011), 89–91, 100
  December 4, 2012 protests, 178
  February 25, 2011 protests, 132–133
  January 25, 2011 protests, xii, 2, 14–15, 77–81, 85–118
  July 8 to August 1, 2011 sit-in, 134–136
  July 26th, 2013 protests, 202
  Morsi speech (June 29, 2012), 155
  November 19, 2011 sit-in, 136–137
  November 22, 2011 protests, 137–138
  one-woman demonstrations, 222–223
  sexual assaults, 162–163
  violence against protesters, 87–88, 99–101, 162–163
  violence against women, 162–163
Tamarod (Rebel) movement, 171–172, 181–183, 187
  military co-optation of, 183–188
Tantawi, Mohamed Hussein, 122, 127–128, 134, 136–140, 189–190
Tarrow, Sidney, 5
Tawadros II, 196–197
el-Taweel, Esraa, 224
el-Tayyeb, Ahmed, 196–197
terror attacks, 41
terrorism, 189, 201–202, 209–210, 223
Tharwa Petroleum, 130
theoretical approach, 4–13
Third Square movement, 209
Three-Dimensional Approach, 70
thresholds, revolutionary, 67, 72–73
thugs and thuggery, 93–94, 133–134, 139–140, 191
Tilly, Charles, 5, 123–124
Tilmisani, Guide, 38
torture, xi
  moral shock in response to, 97
  police brutality, 3, 25, 33–37, 49, 72
tourism, 26, 158
Townhouse Gallery, 223
Tulip Revolution (Kyrgyzstan), ix
Tunisia, vii, 51–52, 77–78
Tunisian Revolution, 52, 72, 222

Twitter, 52–53, 90–91, 164, 179, 194–196
  Tamarod movement on, 182–183
Twitter Revolution, 52
Two-Dimensional Approach, 70

Ultras, 139–140
underemployment, 30
UNDP. *See* United Nations Development Program
unemployment, 26–27
  January 25: Revolution Against Torture, Poverty, Corruption, and Unemployment event, 77–81
United Nations Development Program (UNDP), 26
United States
  aid to Egypt, 126–127, 129–130
  Internet restrictions, 60–64, 64t
  national elections, 52, 81
United States dollars, 157
Universities Law, 55
university administrators, 134
university corruption, 47–48
upper class
  complaints about corruption, 47
  economic grievances of, 31–33
  police brutality against, 35–37, 42–43
Urban Communities Authority, 45

Vershbow, Sandy, 126–127
veto coup(s), 173, 197–198
  consolidation of, 206–213
  popular participatory, 15, 171–214
Viber, 226
victimization, 72, 103, 109, 163
violence. *See also* police brutality
  anti-Christian, 136
  Battle of the Camel, 93–95
  fear of, 116–117
  government, viii–ix, 86–95, 127
  military, 133–139, 141, 219–220
  Mohammed Mahmoud Street clashes, 136–137, 141–142, 149
  Al-Nahda Square sit-in dispersal, 202–204

Port Said massacre, 139
by pro-Mubarak demonstrators, 94
against protesters, viii–ix, 86–96,
  99–100, 115–116, 127,
  133–139, 141–142, 161–163,
  170, 179–181, 195–196,
  202–206, 213
Rabaa al-Adawiya massacre, 172,
  202–206, 213, 219–220
after Rabaa al-Adawiya massacre, 209
sectarian, 201
sexual assaults, xii, 34, 161–163
street, 92–93
thugs and thuggery, 93–94, 133–134,
  139–140, 191
against women, xii, 36, 133, 161–163
voter participation, 81

Wafd Party, 176–177
war on terror, 223
al-Wasat Party, 192, 205
wastaa (influence or connections),
  46–48, 114
Watan Party, 192
water, 164–165
We are all Khaled Said (Facebook page), 3,
  57–59, 74–77, 108–109, 167

January 25: Revolution Against
  Torture, Poverty, Corruption, and
  Unemployment event, 77–81
Wedeen, Lisa, vii
WhatsApp, 226
Wolfsfeld, Gadi, 60
women
  employment opportunities,
    28–29, 229n1
  one-woman demonstrations, 222–223
  violence against, xii, 36, 133, 161–163
World Values Survey, x

Yemen, vii, 107
Youssef, Bassem, 151
youth, 37, 191
youth activists, 2, 223. *See also* April 6th
  Youth Movement
youth bulge, 26
youth employment, 26–27, 31–32
YouTube, 63, 72, 203

Zaghlul, Saad, 104
Zahran, Gamal, 45
Zald, Mayer, 185
Ziada, Dalia, 49–50
al-Zomor, Tareq, 189